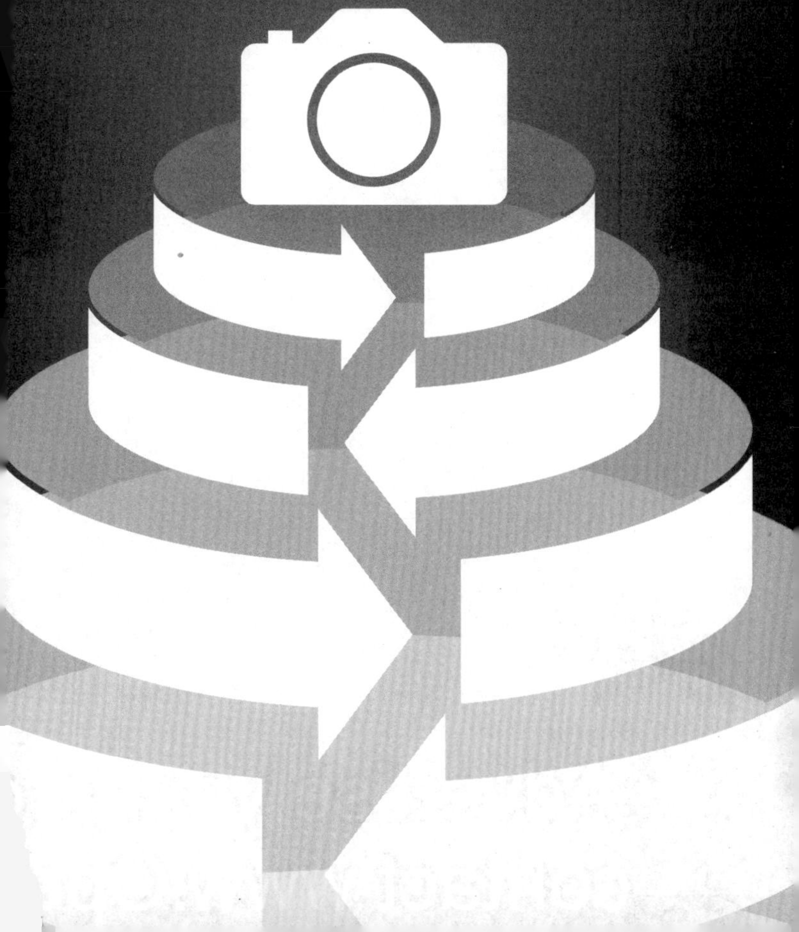

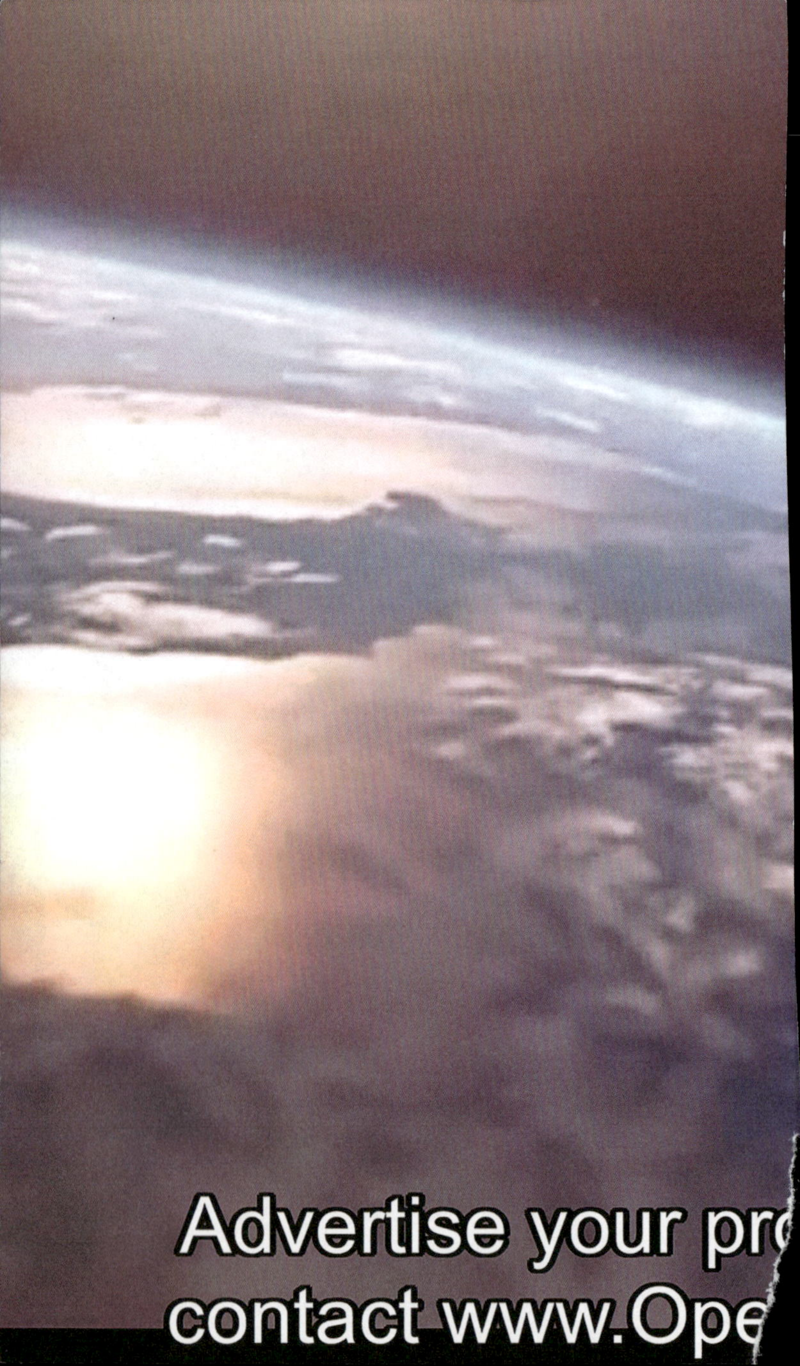
Advertise your pr
contact www.Ope

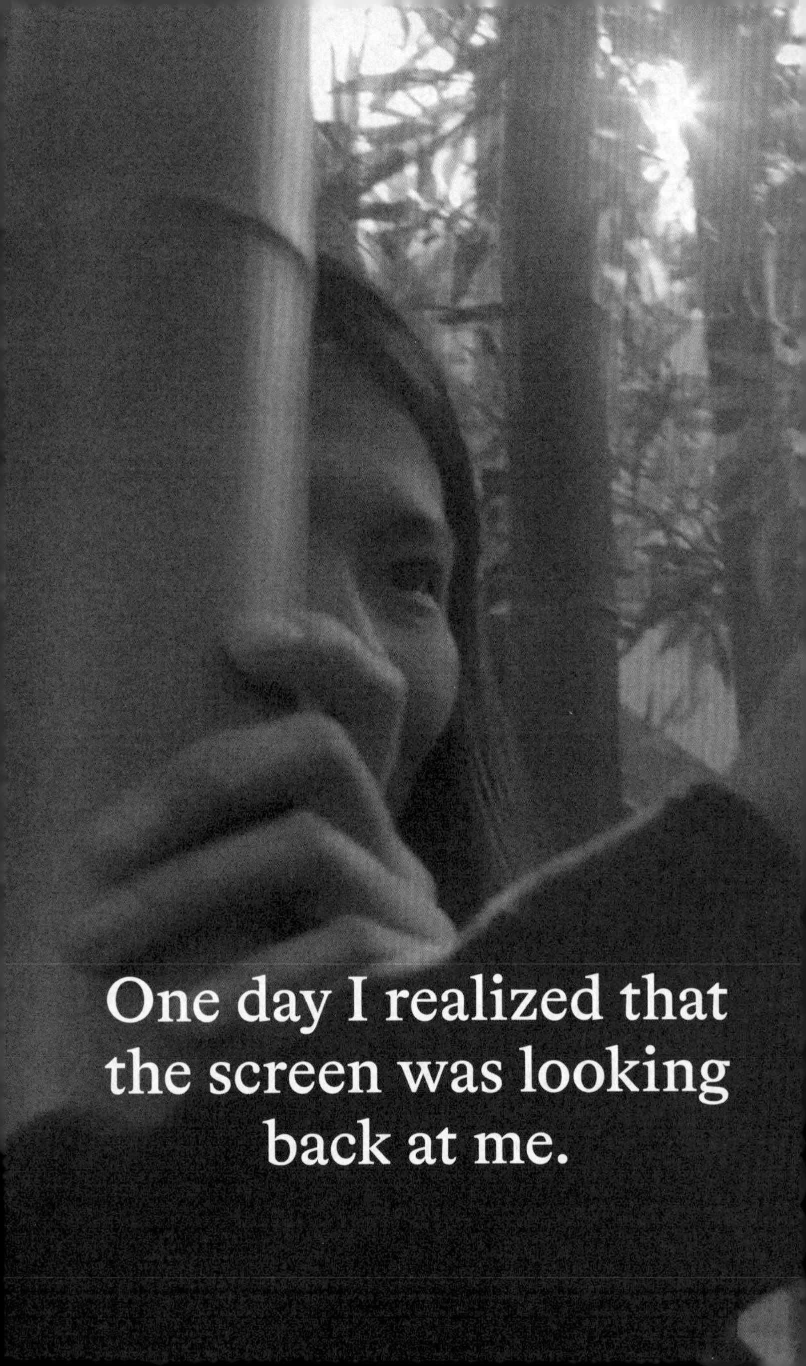
One day I realized that the screen was looking back at me.

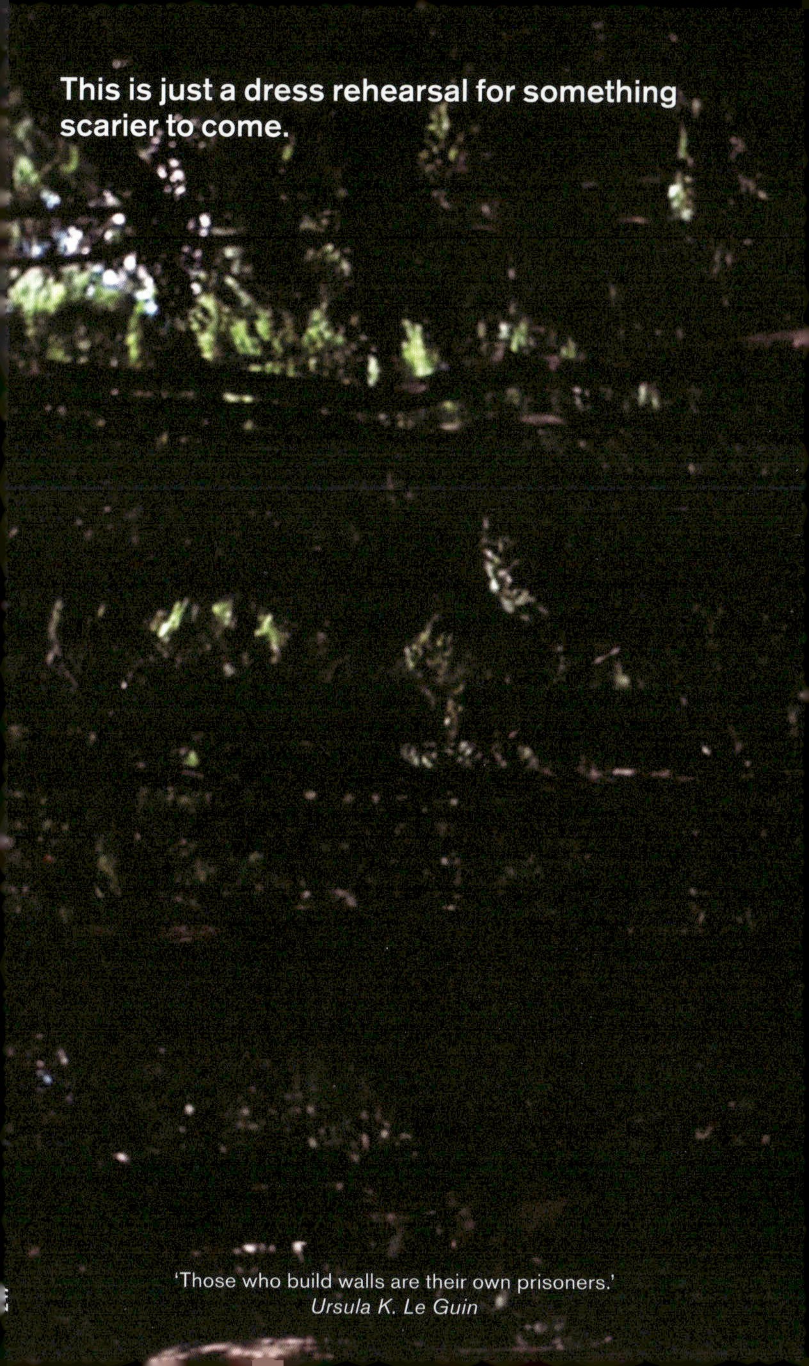

This is just a dress rehearsal for something scarier to come.

'Those who build walls are their own prisoners.'
Ursula K. Le Guin

It is easier to imagine the end of the world than the end of the Internet.

'Millions long for immortality who don't know what to do on a rainy Sunday afternoon.' Susan Ertz

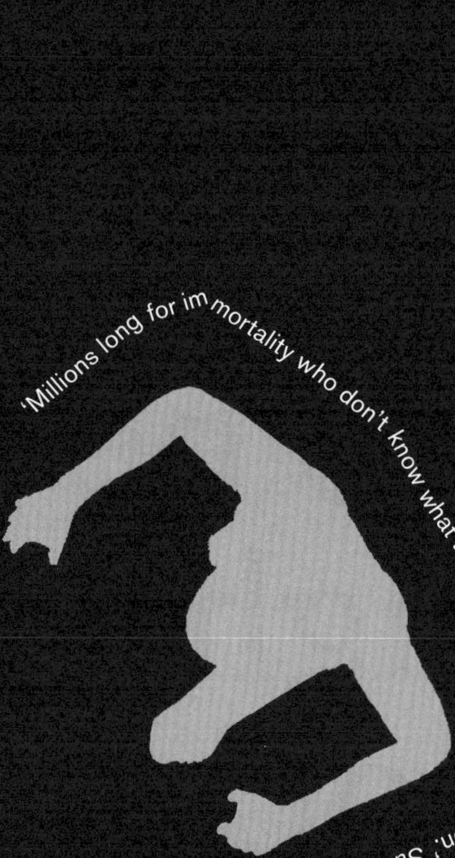

Living forever turns out to be slightly boring

'List of selfie-related injuries and deaths'
https://en.wikipedia.org/wiki/List_of_selfie-related_injuries_and_deaths

Date: October 15, 2011
Country: United States
Casualties: 3
Type: Transport

Three teenagers (two sisters and a friend) were killed by a train while posing for a selfie. The train is just visible in the final picture they posted to Facebook, along with the caption, 'Standing right by a train ahaha this is awesome!!!!'

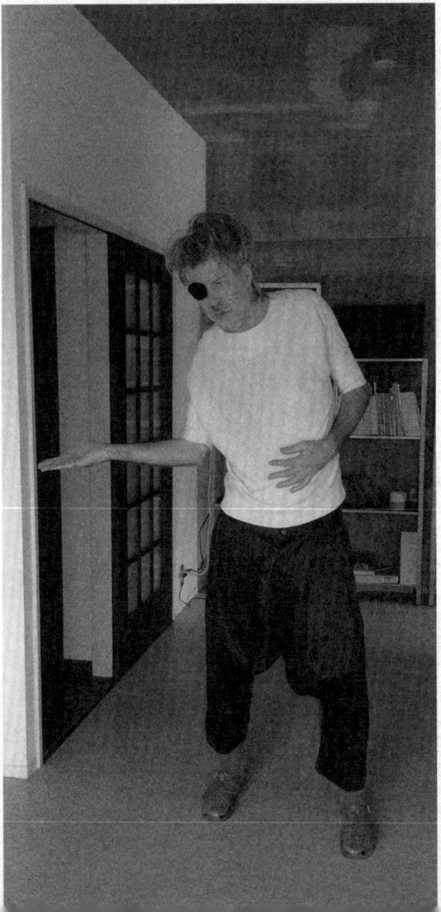

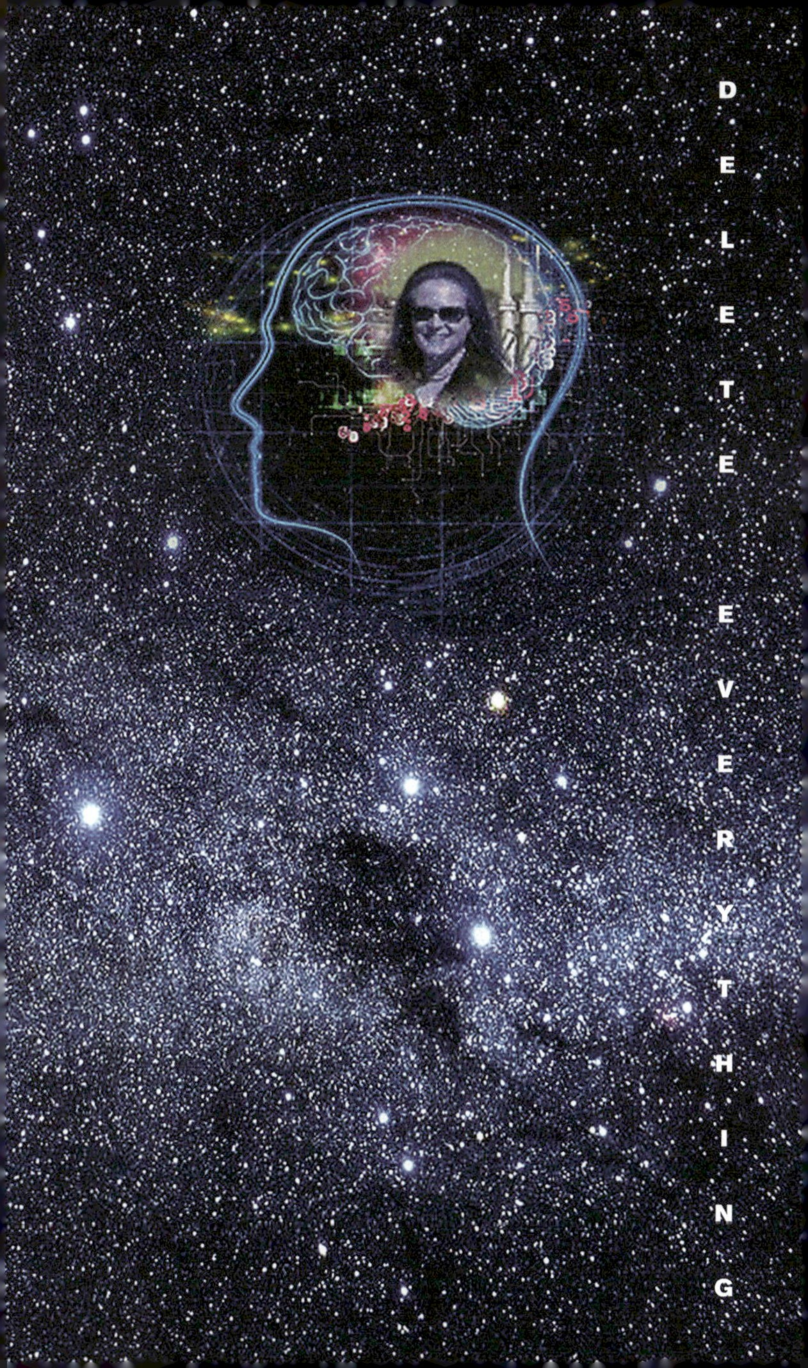
DELETE EVERYTHING

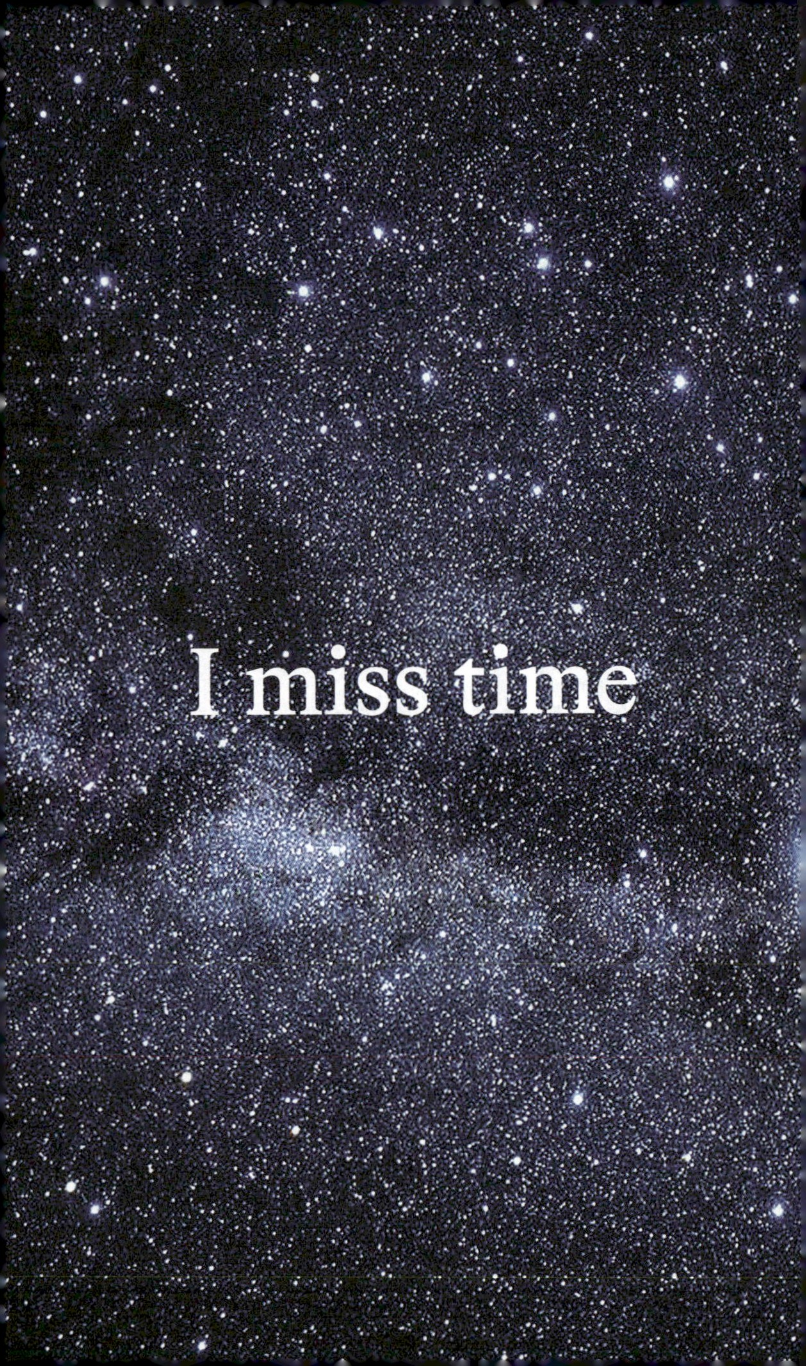
I miss time

Next year is 1,000 years away*

'Time is actually the lead character in the film.'
Richard Linklater on his film Boyhood

*We need to invent new tenses for time.

people don't wait for centuries to end before they express it.
Any date can be justified on some calculation or other.'
Frank Kermode, The Sense of an Ending

'You sometimes hear people say that the nineteenth century really ended not in 1900 but in 1914. But there are different ways of measuring an epoch. [However] there is something satisfying about the fin de siècle, some confirmation of the rightness of the patterns we impose. As Focillon observed, the anxiety reflected by the fin de siècle is perpetual, and people don't wait for centuries to end before they express it. Any date can be justified on some calculation or other.'

Frank Kermode, The Sense of an Ending

'You sometimes hear people say that the nineteenth century
really ended not in 1900 but in 1914. But there are different

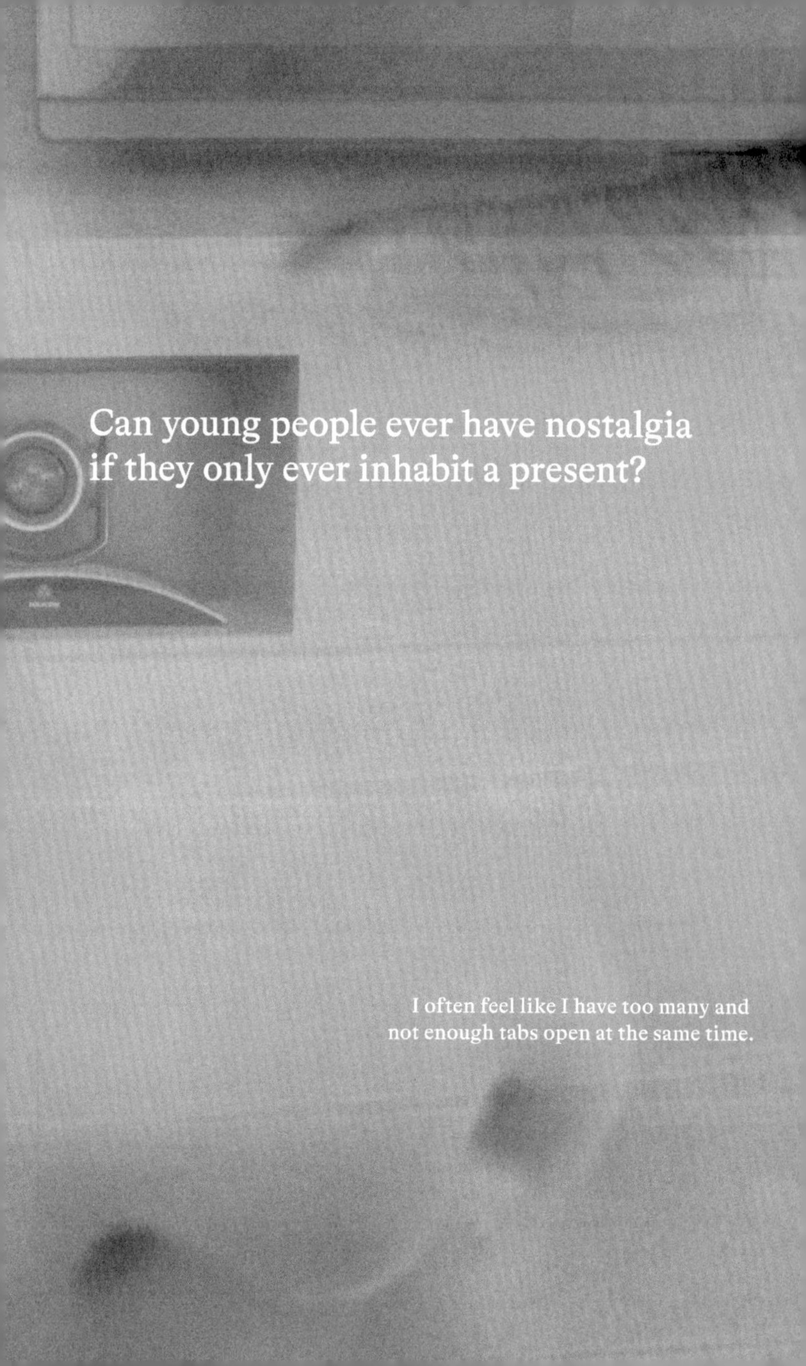

Can young people ever have nostalgia if they only ever inhabit a present?

I often feel like I have too many and not enough tabs open at the same time.

Regardless of how we morally frame the current human soul, one thing is for certain: we wanted something, and we got it.

We're not innocent.

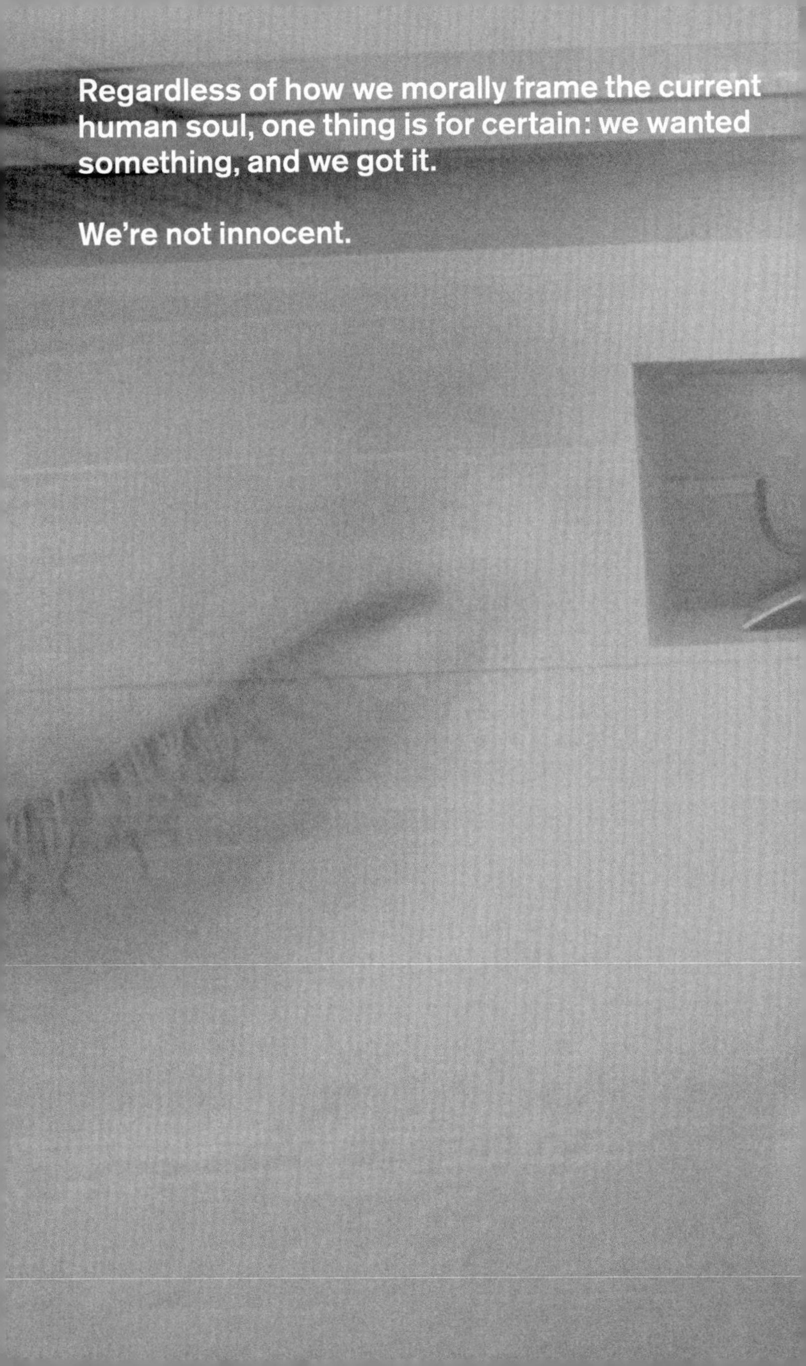

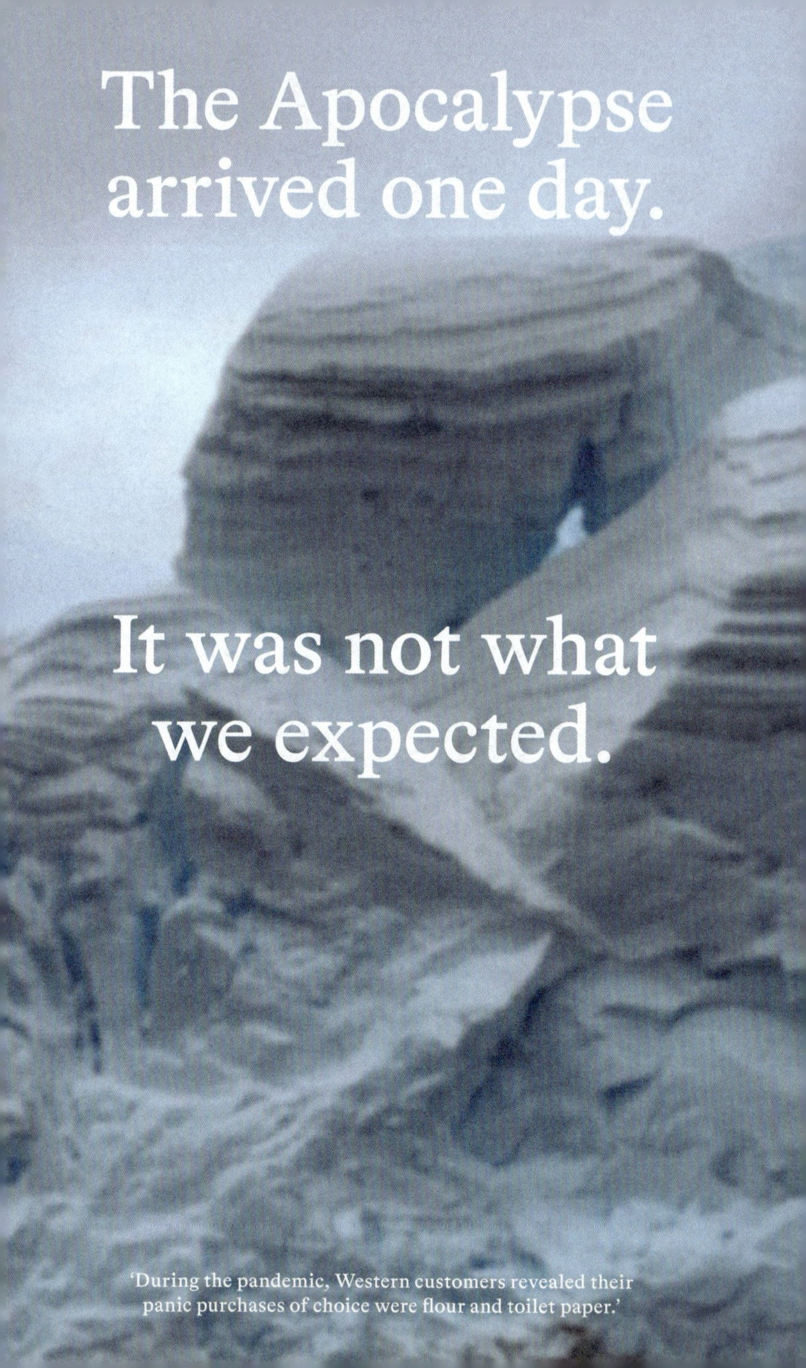
The Apocalypse arrived one day.
It was not what we expected.
'During the pandemic, Western customers revealed their panic purchases of choice were flour and toilet paper.'

Everywhere we look we hope to see omens: sharks left stranded on beaches by receding tides; colorful birds flying into windows; a woman's eye is bitten by a spider that turns her eye black; Florida teenagers drop the head of an elk onto a freeway.

Rebecca_Aich 10 seconds ago

So sad but so beautiful

for

the

moment

You are alive

Imagine if:

Technologians are the Extreme Selves making us more

EXTREME

tryworldpeace_ 100 years ago

Humans don't come from

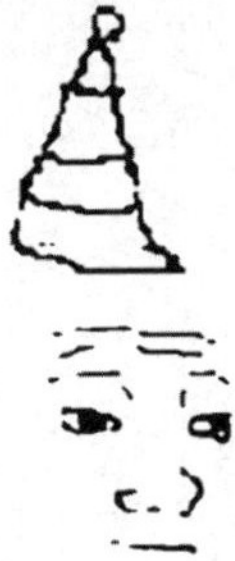

What might technologians have in common?

O Some of them believe the human body can't be perfected. It's better to start from scratch.

O A few of them cast human workers as the stop-gap until machines can do everything by themselves.

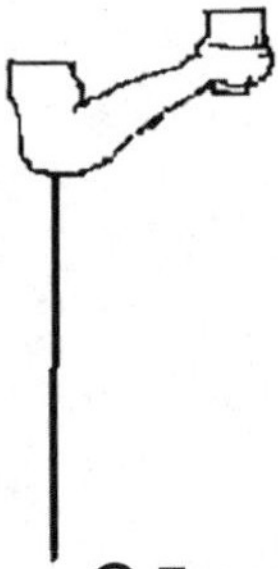

O Many of them don't think sovereign nation states are a good way to run the world. That's because their platforms' users make up numbers dwarfing entire continents.

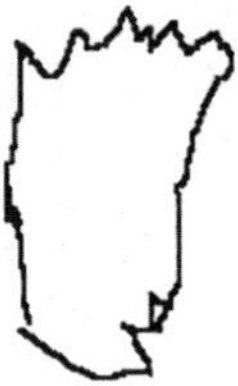

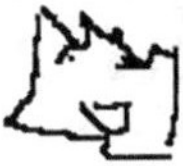

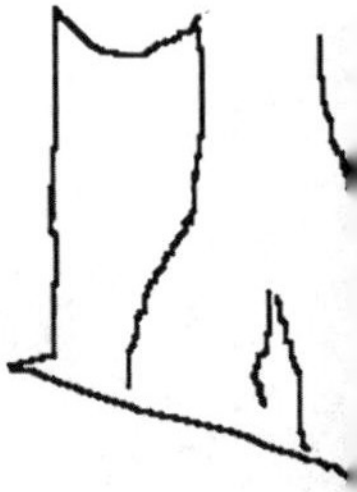

O Too much democracy can interfere in their visions.

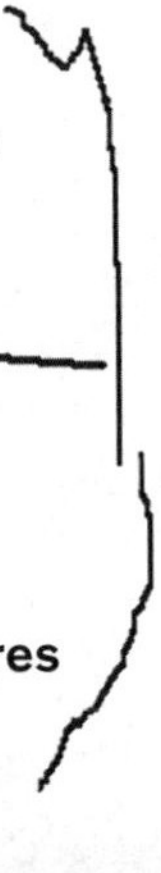

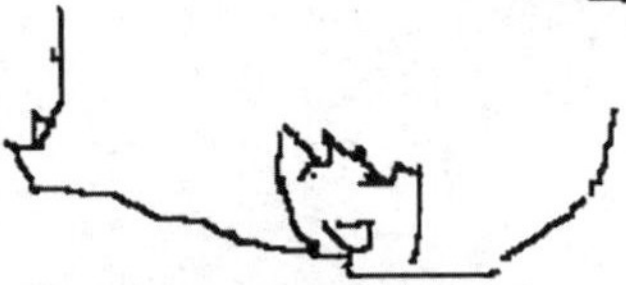

O All see themselves as new figures of extraordinary persuasion.

Artificial charisma* remains elusive

*Unless you count Context Hierarchy-based Adaptive Reasoning Self-Motivated Agent: CHARISMA

Technologians founded and run today's biggest tech companies. But their end goal isn't just more technology.

It's the future of civilization.

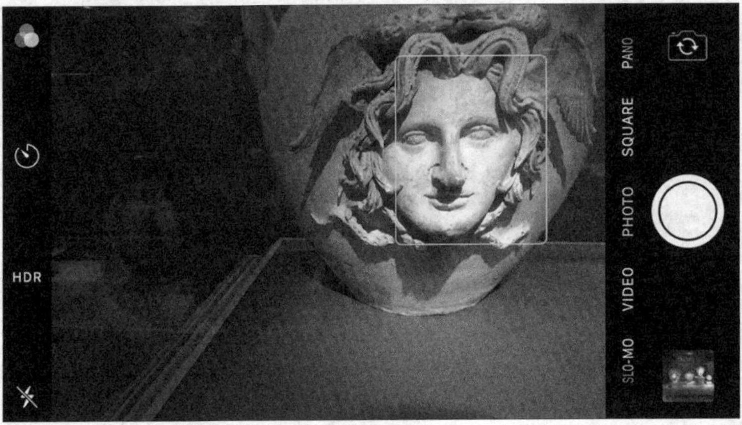

It's the future of you.

The most persistent visual expressions found in Silicon Valley workstations are Lego, Rubiks cubes or *Star Wars*. One wonders if the world is being made in the image of a Silicon Valley workstation desktop. The closer one envisions a world just like that, the closer one is to seeing the world that is actually going to happen.

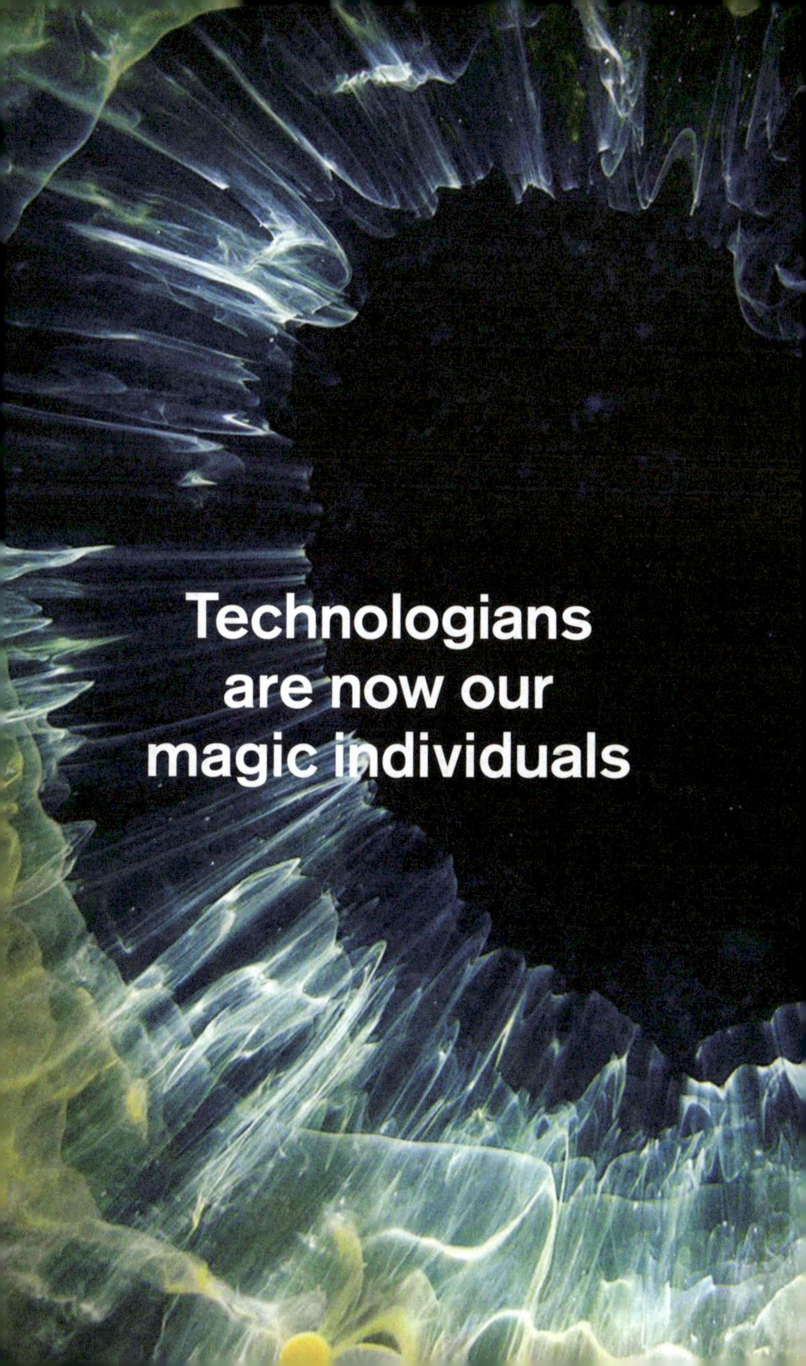
Technologians
are now our
magic individuals

Every new tech promises to make
us feel freer than we felt before.

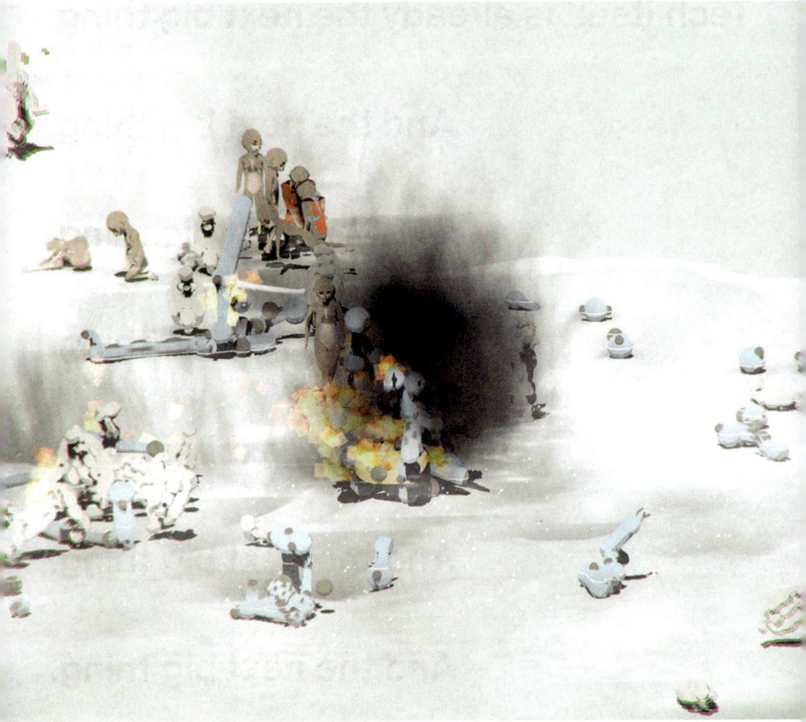

It is the ultimate modern magic

mm4tthieu_uuu 6 days ago

Heavenly

What if:

Tech itself is already the next big thing.

And the next big thing.

And the next big thing.

And the next big thing.

And the next big thing.

And the next big thing.

And the next big thing.

And the next big thing.

And the next big thing.

And the next big thing.

And the next big thing.

What about artists?
They used to be our magic individuals.

There was always a next big art thing out there waiting to hit us and change the way we understood the world.

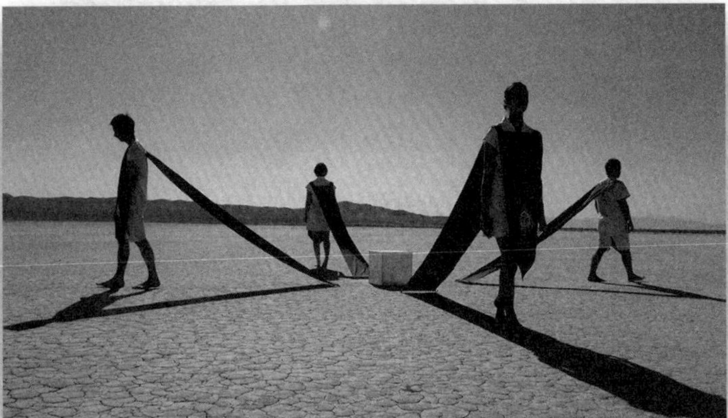

Some people say that experts have
let us down too many times.

Who should we trust to tell us
the truth anymore?

Me!

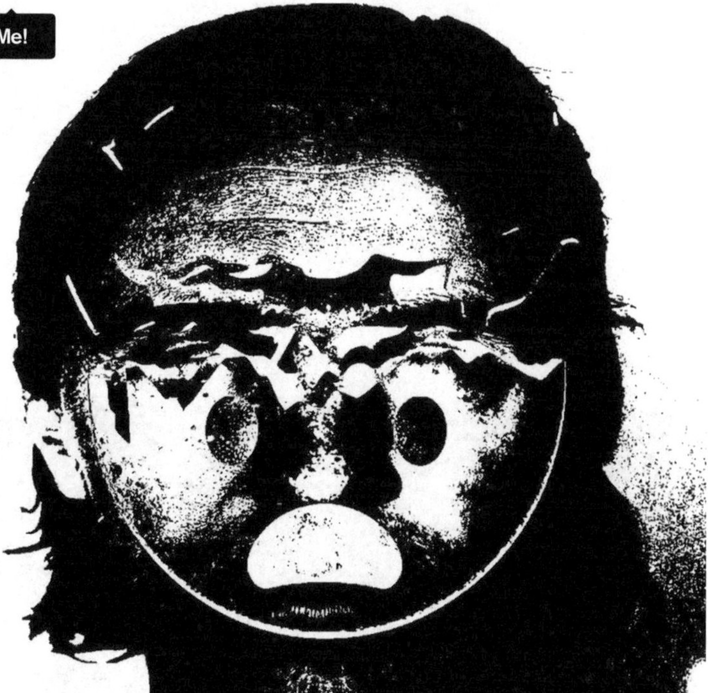

Me!

Me!

Me!

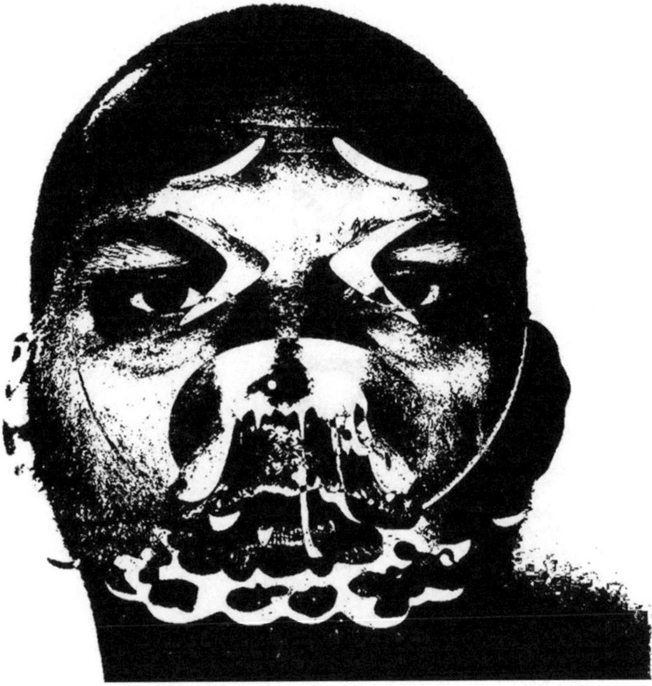

'Any sufficiently advanced technology is indistinguishable from magic.'
Arthur C. Clarke

godlike

12 Wizards and Charismatics

You are

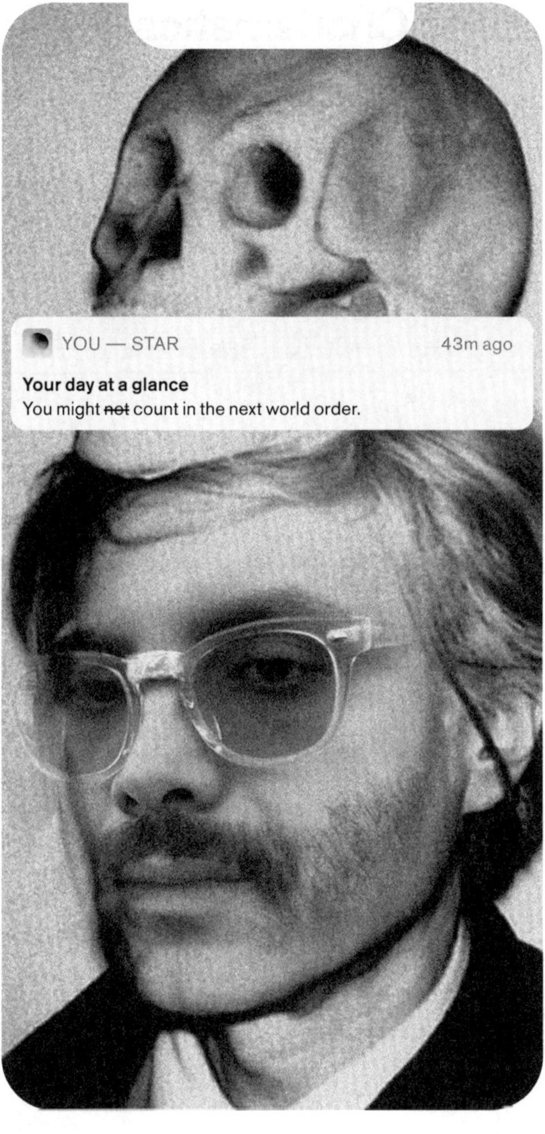
YOU — STAR
43m ago
Your day at a glance
You might not count in the next world order.

Am I free?	Y	N
Are you free?	Y	N
Are we free?	Y	N
Are we too free?	Y	N
Would I offset my freedom somewhere else for someone else?	Y	N

What would having even more freedom feel like?

What would less freedom feel like?

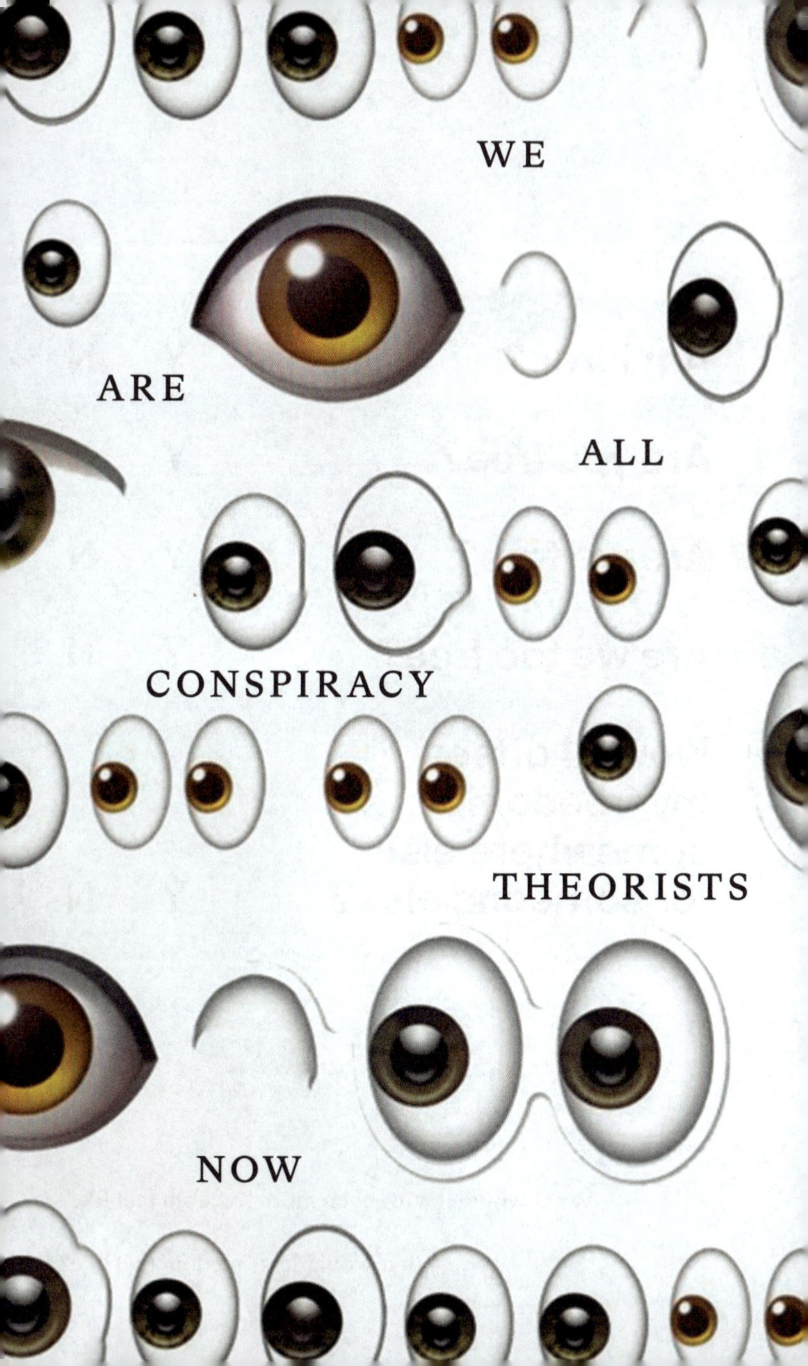
WE
ARE
ALL
CONSPIRACY
THEORISTS
NOW

Historically speaking, even during the most divisive times, people agreed on certain basic common truths. Such as, 'the sun is in the sky.' Or, 'fish swim in the sea.'

Our senses shaped this kind of consensus.

There are people today who think school shootings are hoaxes. There are people who refuse vaccinations.

The breakdown of consensus-based reality is perhaps one of the most dangerous threats there has ever been to shared human experience.

Is there any turning back?

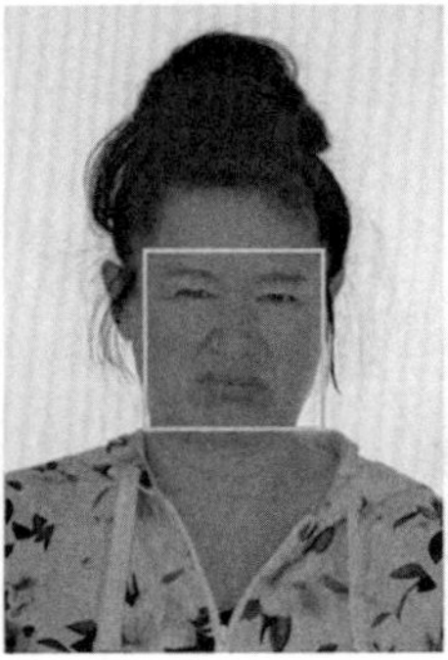


```
Detection Result:
JSON:
[
  {
    "faceRectangle": {
      "left": 252,
      "top": 457,
      "width": 332,
      "height": 332
    },
    "scores": {
      "anger": 0.07382989,
      "contempt": 0.04350459,
      "disgust": 0.7045257,
      "fear": 0.0005751435,
      "happiness": 0.00111284887,
      "neutral": 0.04504608,
      "sadness": 0.127928317,
      "surprise": 0.00347741228
    }
  }
]
```


'Democracy means that "my ignorance is just as good as your knowledge."'
Isaac Asimov

Indifferent power is the cruellest

Some of or all of the content shared on these pages is disputed and might be misleading.

Democracy needs morning after pills.

Brexit could have been stopped with one simple revote. Why didn't that happen?

The majority

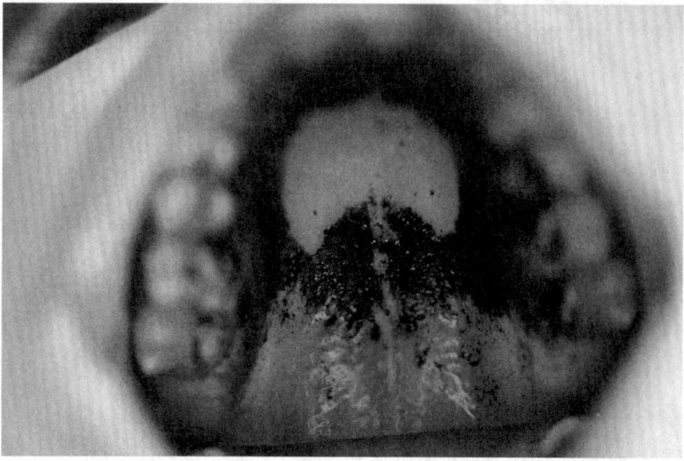

can no longer be trusted

NatHi11_ 11 days ago

The only minority in this world is an intelligent person

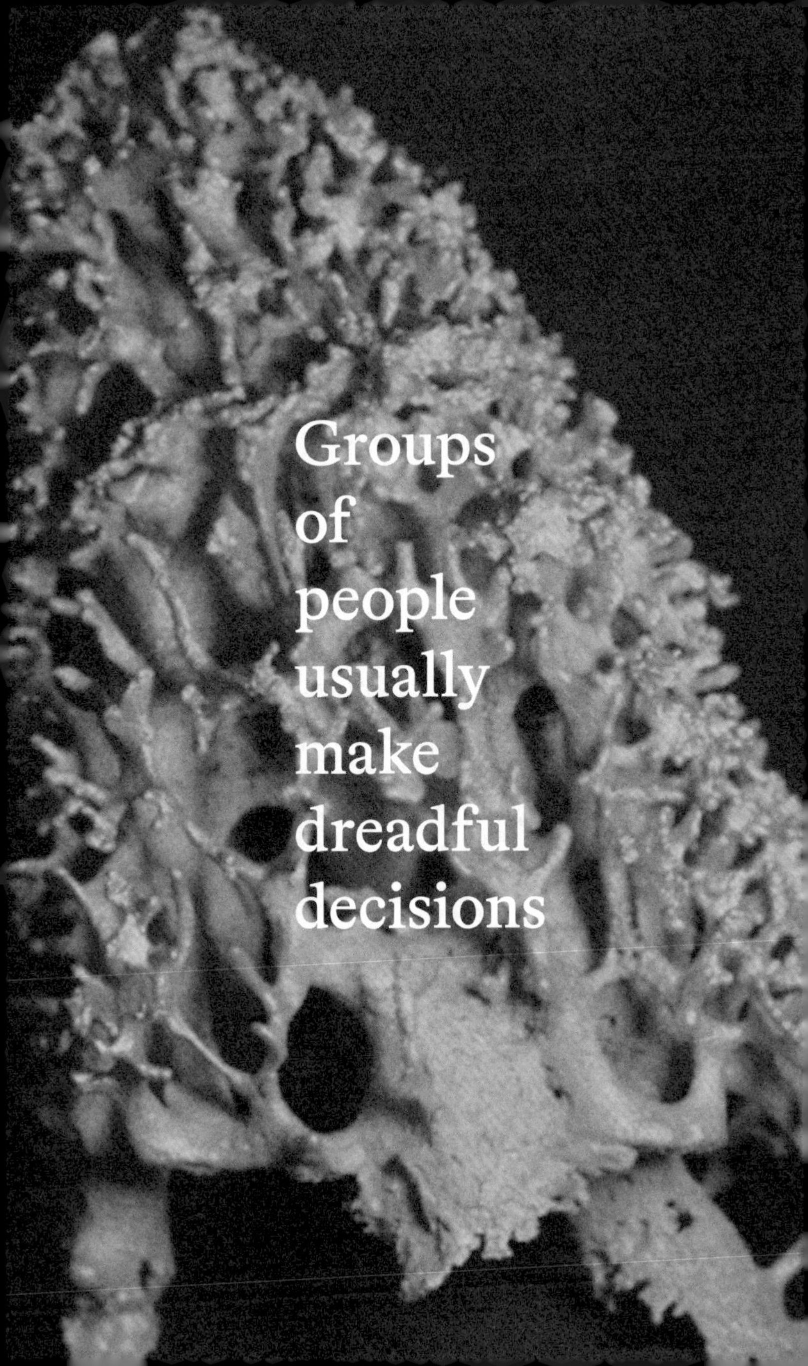

Groups
of
people
usually
make
dreadful
decisions

Q: Is a benevolent dictator better than a bad democracy?

A: Is that the only choice I've got?

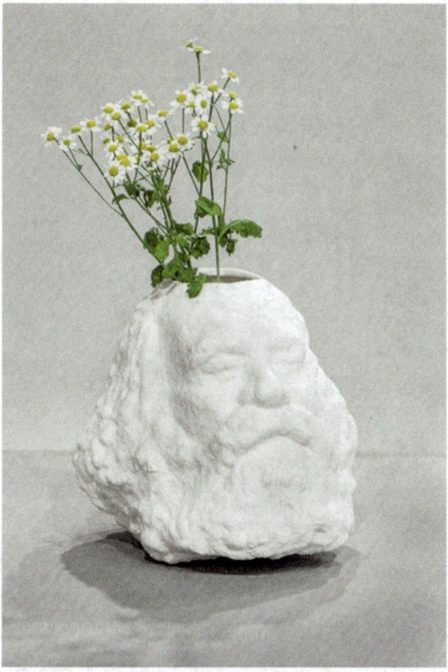

We’re now deep into the terminal phase of democracy.

This phase involves voting in leaders whose primary goal is to dismantle democracy.

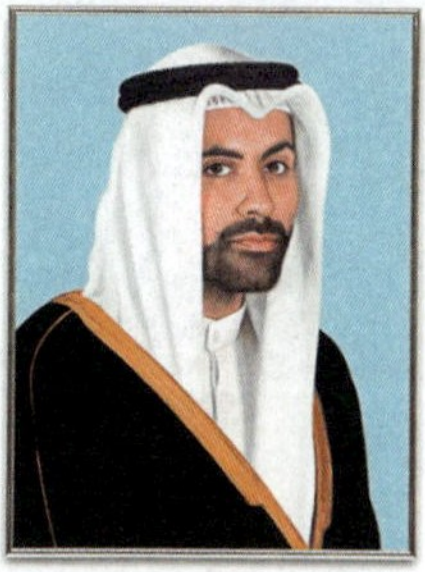
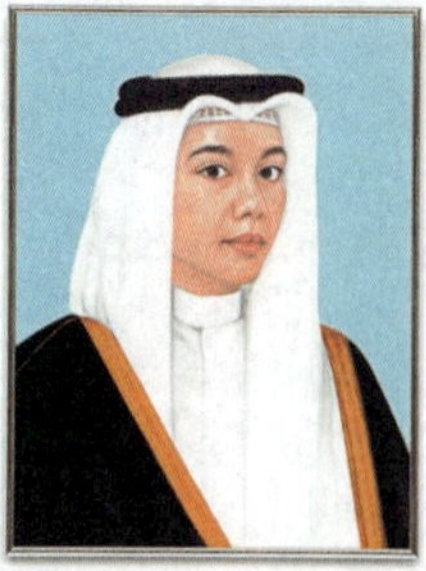

Is it the job of politics to protect you from yourself?

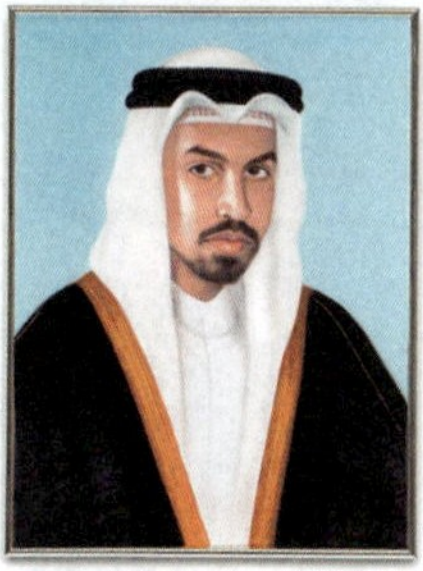
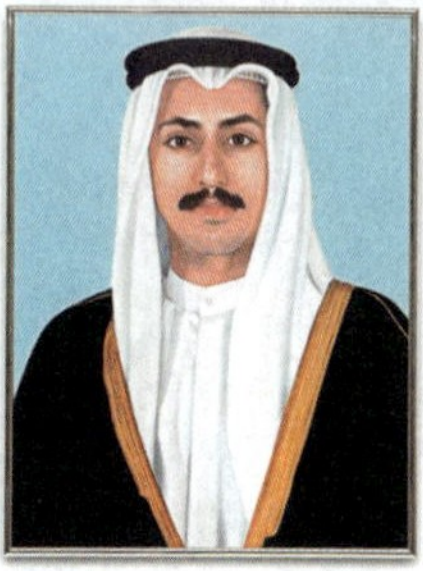

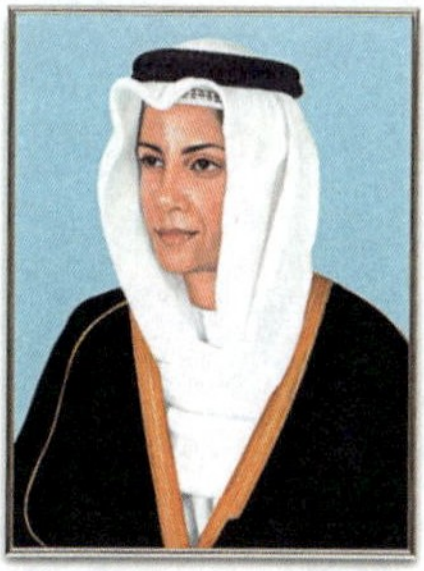
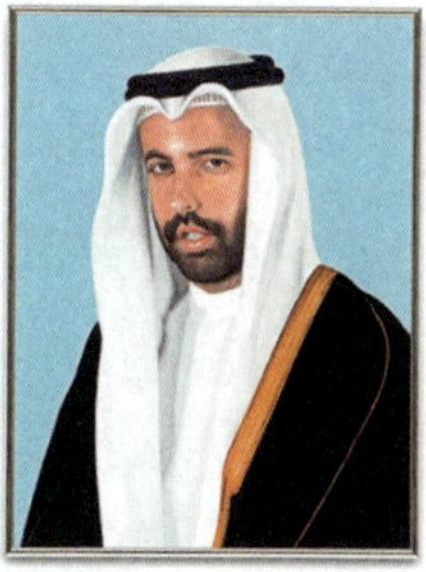

Is it the job of politics to protect us from ourselves?

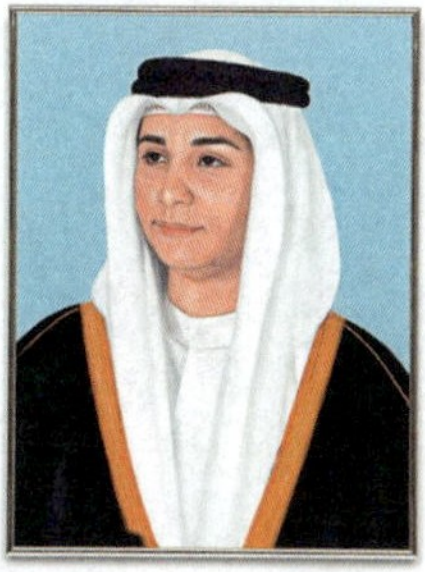
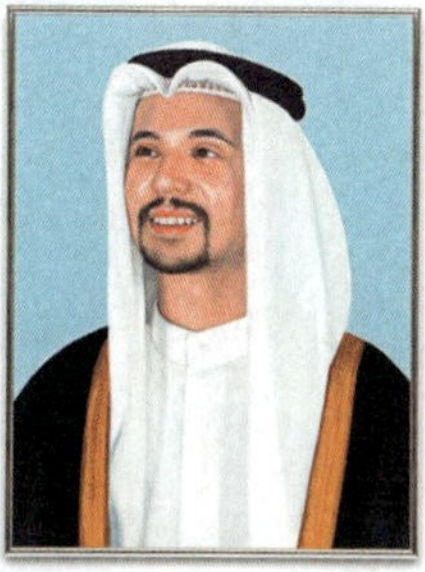

The center is for losers

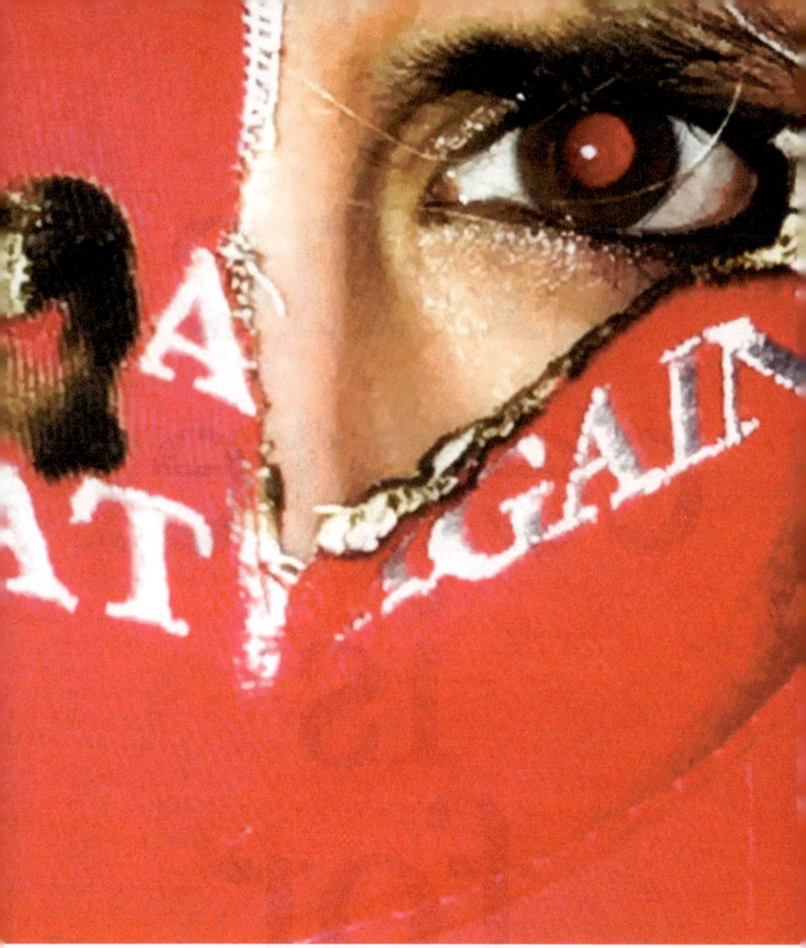

No idea is now…

Too stupid to fail

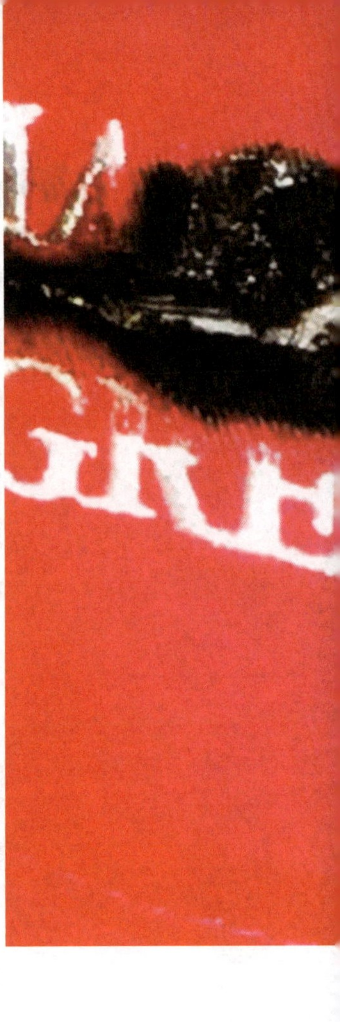

Majority rule no longer means anything when nobody trusts anybody.

Doing something just because 51% of those who voted said so is starting to feel really stupid.

molliebradburyxoxo 25s ago

is global warming a thing dude

over-empowered

11

The Ends of Democracy?

You are

My private jet is about to leave without me

¯_(ツ)_/¯

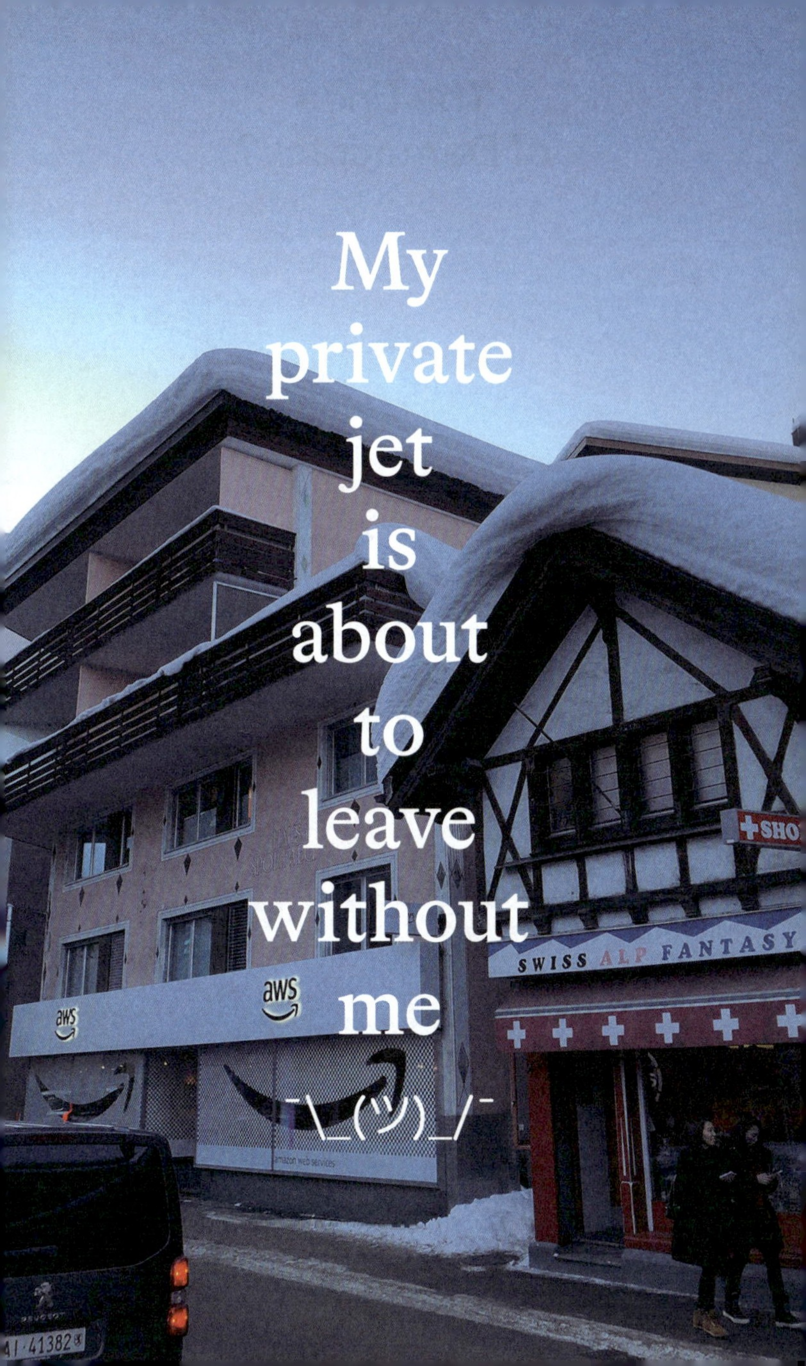

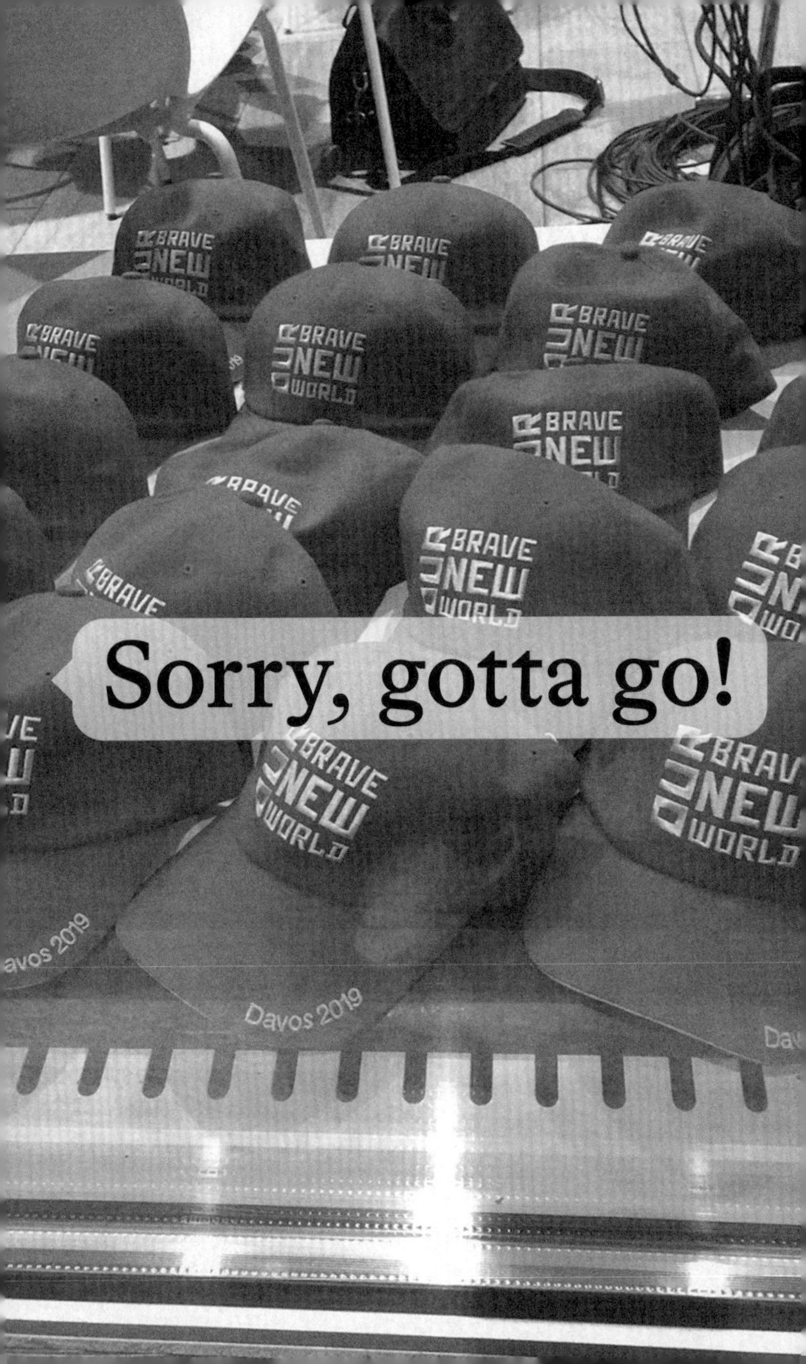
Sorry, gotta go!
OUR BRAVE NEW WORLD
Davos 2019

What if you had to pay money to vote?

Would you vote?

Would one vote have more clout than others?

What if you got air mileage points for voting?

Would you buy the election in advance?

~kscott29_ 1 day ago

I hope he never get a minute of rest

Speaking of money…

How would money allow you to be a more amplified version of yourself?

Would money somehow unmask a previously hidden self?

What would you buy with money that would be 100% distinctly you as opposed to being just another person with money?

M e a n w h i l e ...

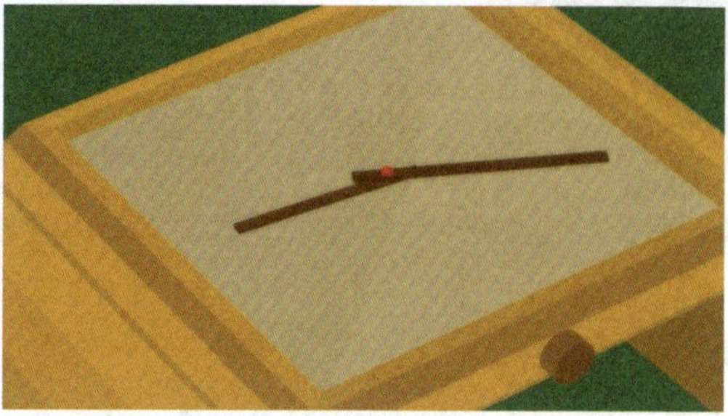

The middle class leisure goal of doing nothing is quickly being replaced by its darker version:

...having nothing to do.

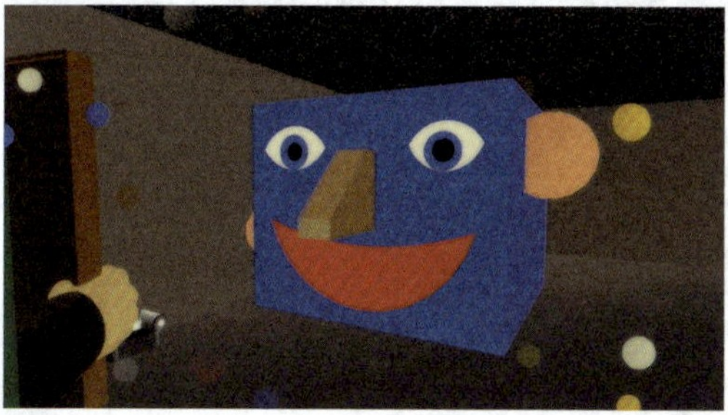

An invisible conveyor belt relentlessly converts formerly middle class workers, taking us all into a world of perpetual clicking, linking, embedding and liking.

Send
them
all
on
a
one-way
trip
to
Mars

lexhancer_ 6 minutes ago

I don't get this :/

‘Plutonomies have ever more dominant and sterile cities, spiralling property prices, worsening social segregation and increasingly polluted environments.’

Andy Beckett

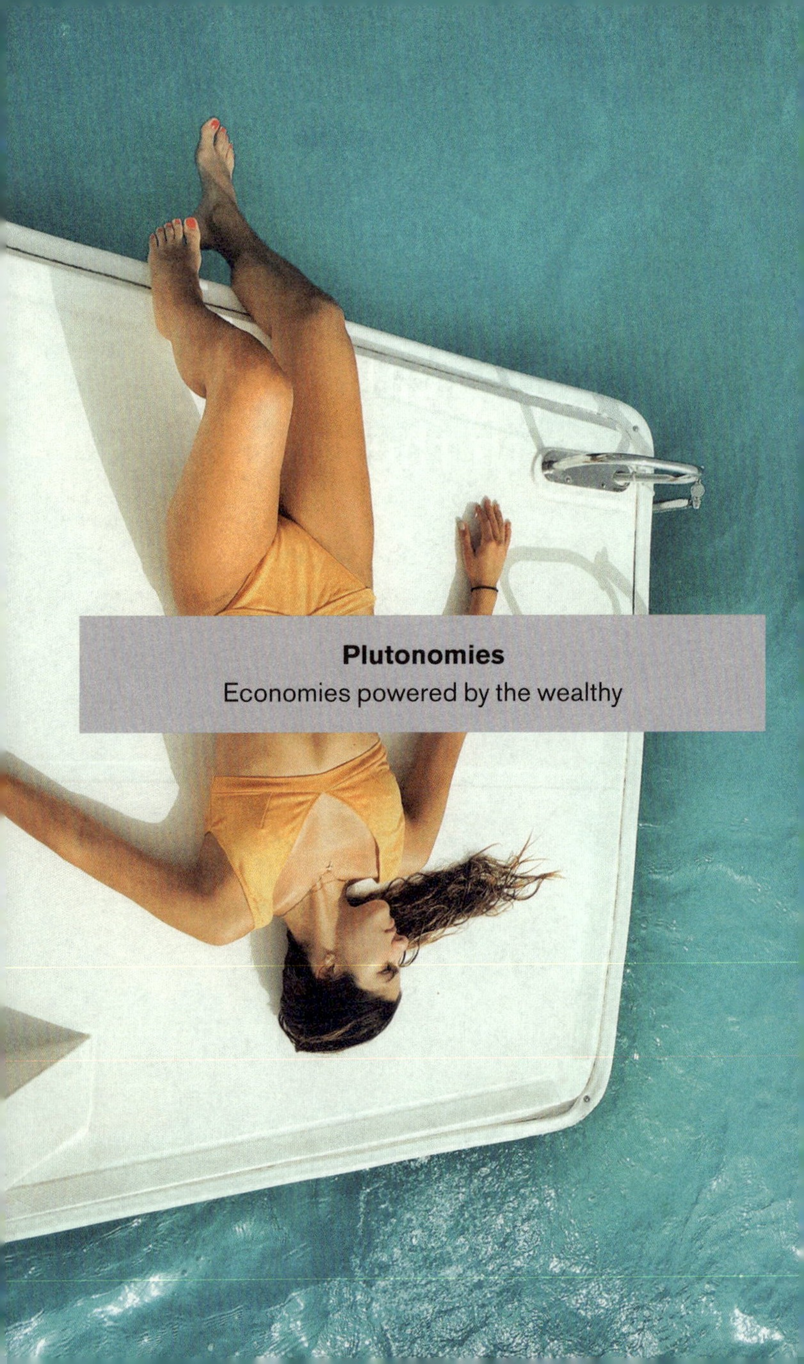

Plutonomies

Economies powered by the wealthy

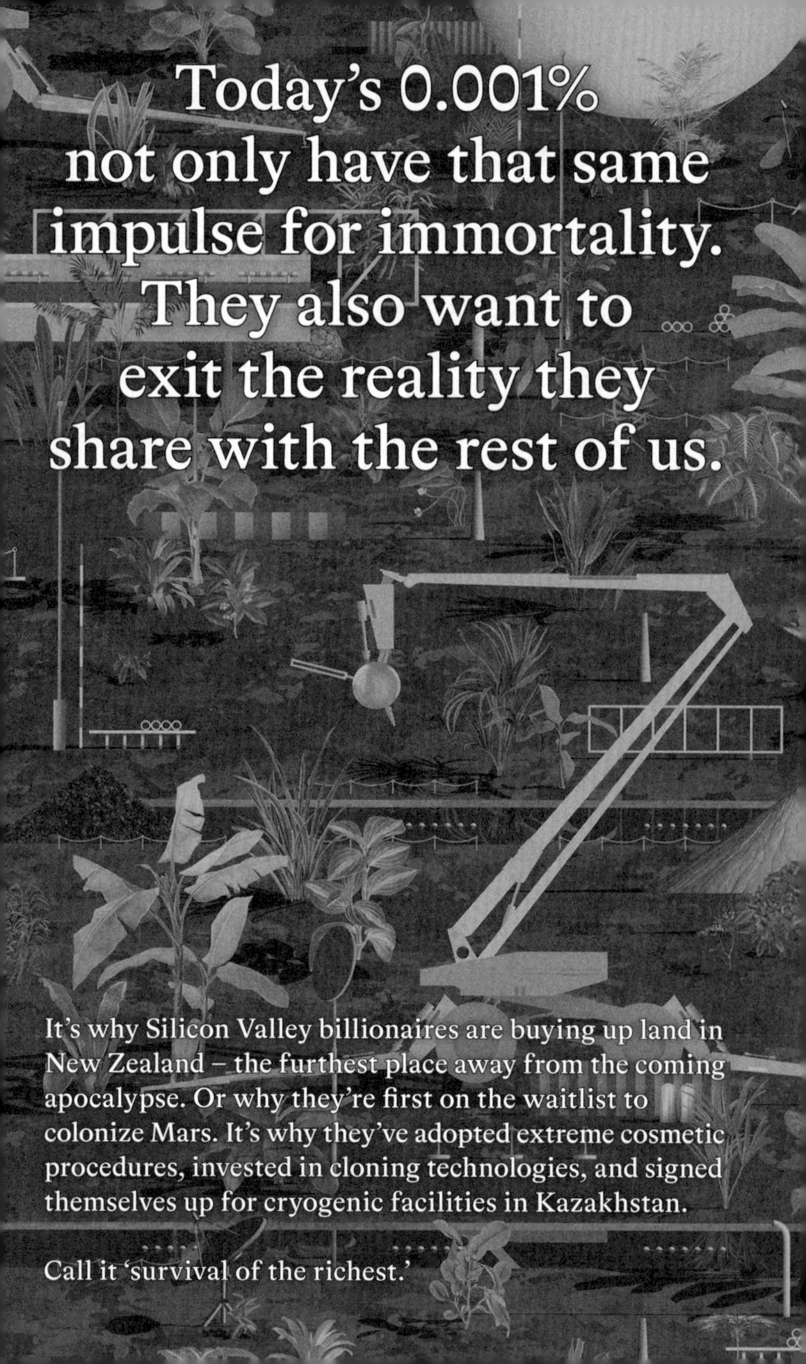

Today’s 0.001% not only have that same impulse for immortality. They also want to exit the reality they share with the rest of us.

It’s why Silicon Valley billionaires are buying up land in New Zealand – the furthest place away from the coming apocalypse. Or why they’re first on the waitlist to colonize Mars. It’s why they’ve adopted extreme cosmetic procedures, invested in cloning technologies, and signed themselves up for cryogenic facilities in Kazakhstan.

Call it ‘survival of the richest.’

The ultra-rich have always had a quasi-religious impulse to exit mortality.

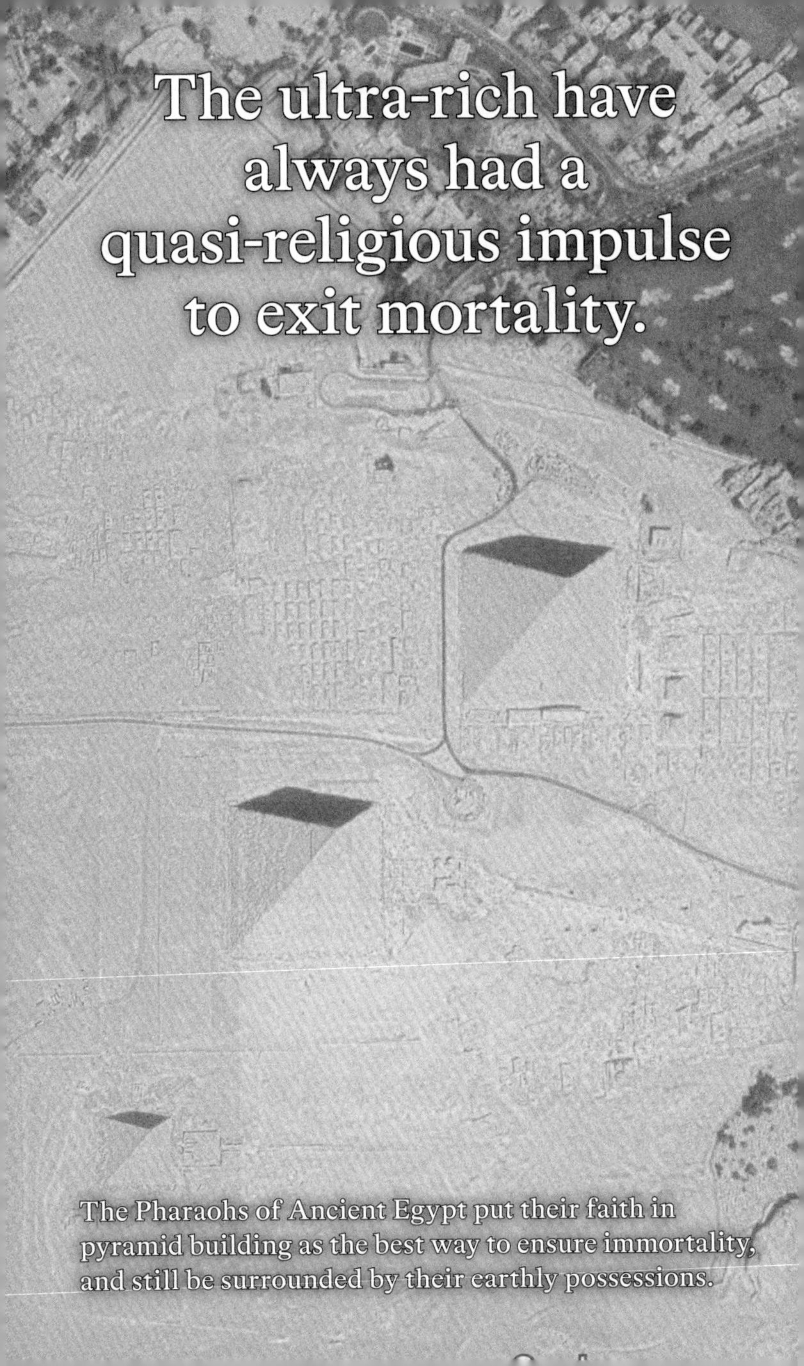

The Pharaohs of Ancient Egypt put their faith in pyramid building as the best way to ensure immortality, and still be surrounded by their earthly possessions.

THE YOU ECONOMY

THE ME ECONOMY

THE VIRTUE ECONOMY

THE GUILT ECONOMY

THE CRISIS ECONOMY

THE PRECARITY ECONOMY

THE END OF THE WORLD ECONOMY

THE ATTENTION ECONOMY

THE DISTRACTION ECONOMY

THE NARRATIVE ECONOMY

THE EMOTION ECONOMY

THE CONTENT ECONOMY

THE CLOUD ECONOMY

THE ANTI-ECONOMY ECONOMY

it

all!

You deserve

ladizura 12 months ago

cool

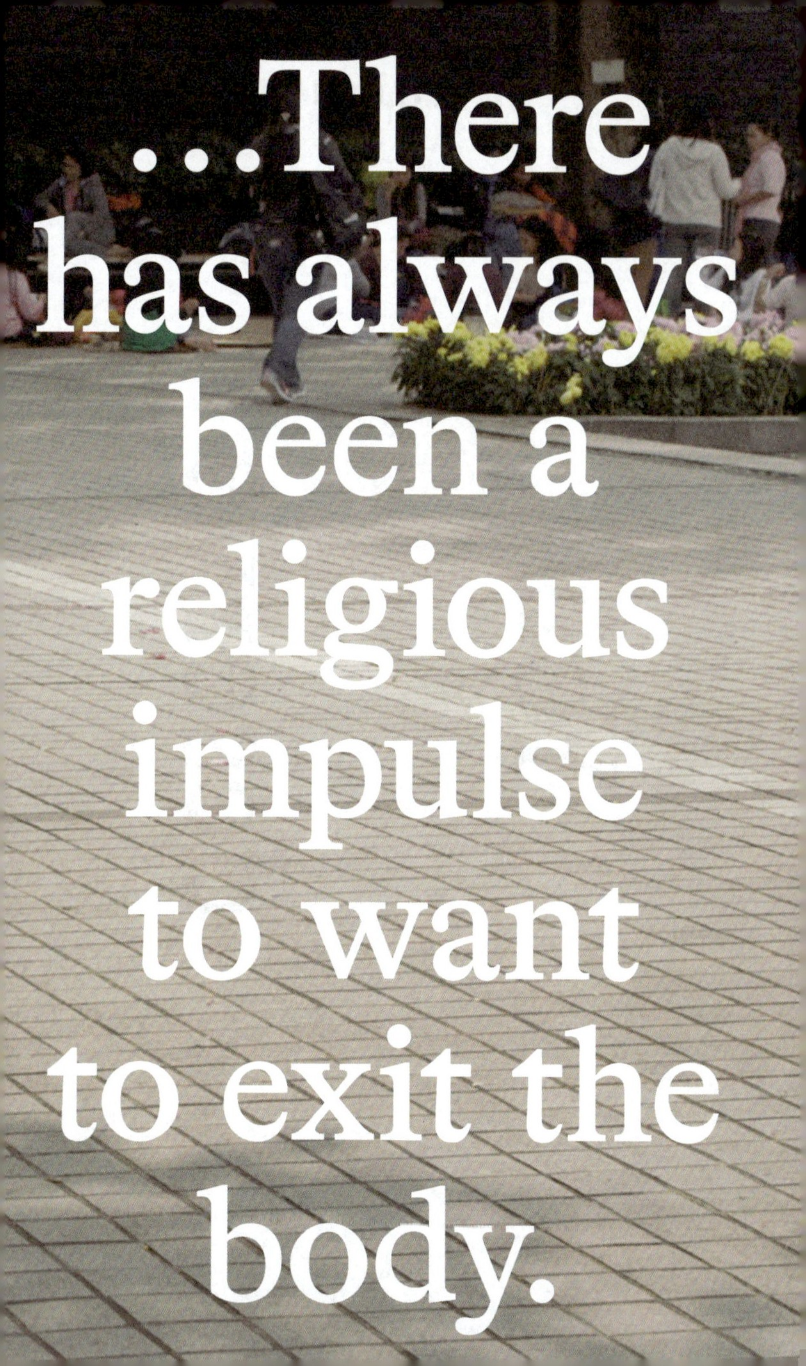

...There has always been a religious impulse to want to exit the body.

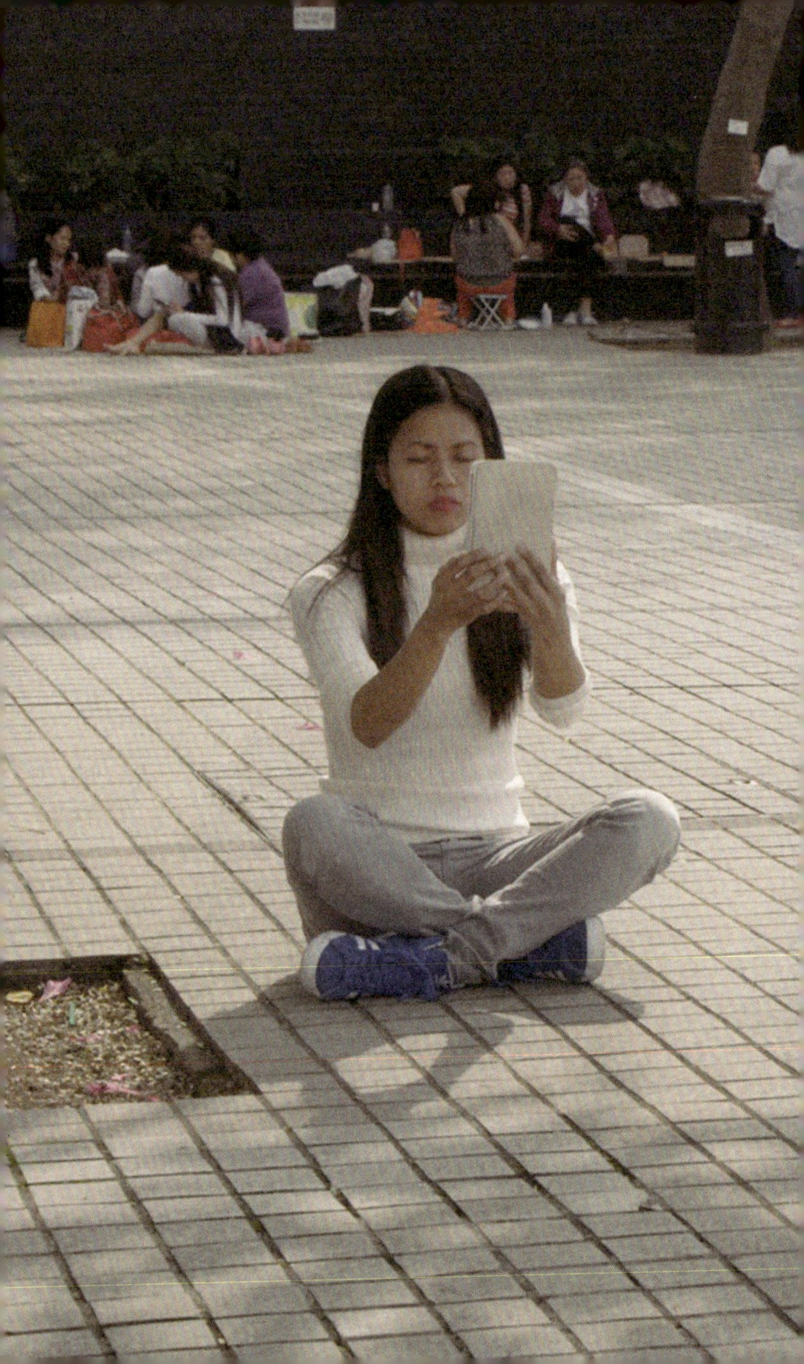

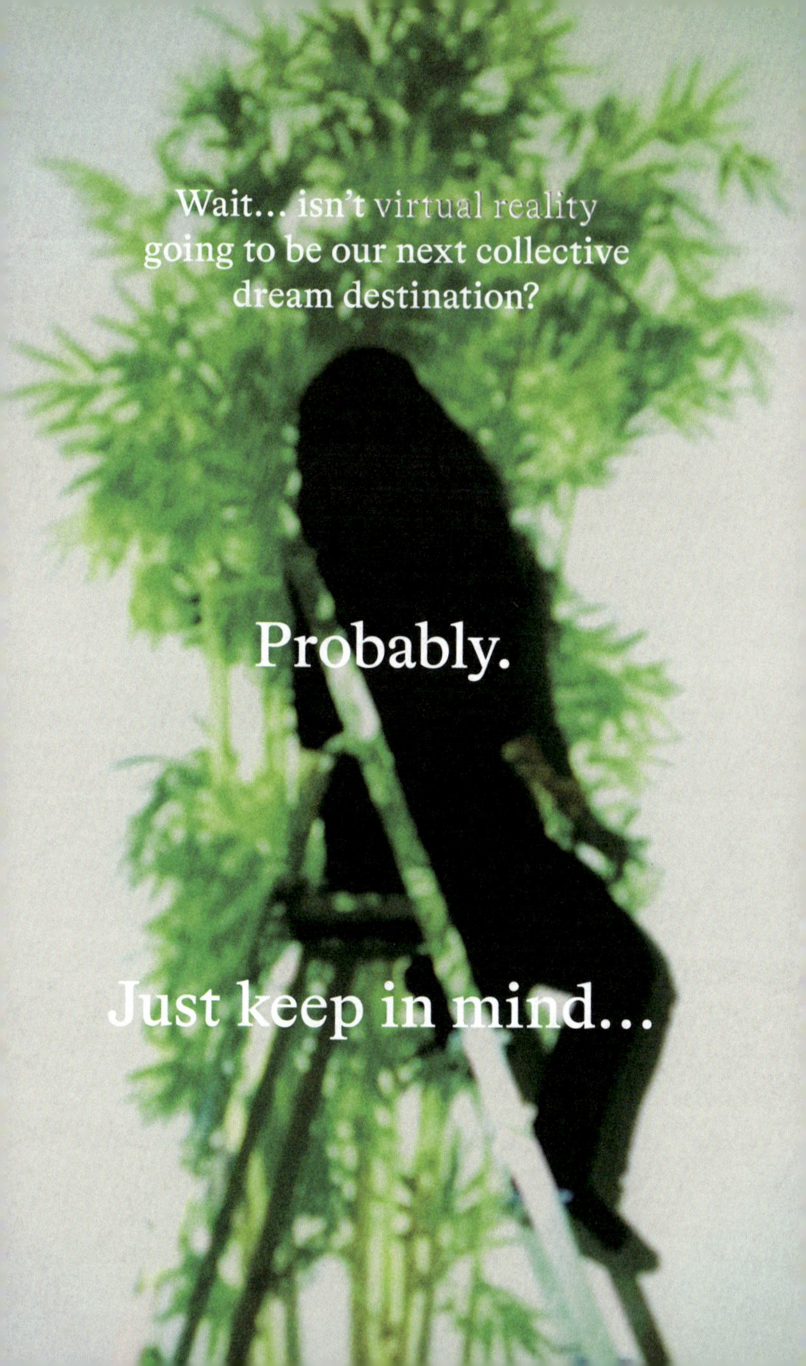
Wait… isn't virtual reality going to be our next collective dream destination?
Probably.
Just keep in mind…

According to Sigmund Freud, your true self was a secret unto yourself. To find out who you really were meant decoding clues to dislodge demons buried within you. It became a recognized way to 'free' the real you.

Quaint?

These days, our true selves are on the surface, for everyone to see. Our genuine (untrue) selves are locked away, behind a firewall even we can't access. To get to it, we need the opposite of psychoanalysis.

And then why is it so insanely hard to 'know' yourself? I mean, you live inside your body, and you're talking with yourself all waking hours. You'd think it would be simple. But no. Trying to know yourself is like visiting Antarctica: it's difficult, boring, time consuming and expensive – and even then, once you get there you may not even find something that changes you.

Healing_light 9 seconds ago

We are protesting against reality

Q: What's the difference between a cult and a religion?

A: About a hundred years

A few months ago someone online was discussing various religions including Scientology. In the comments section at the article's end, a woman wrote back, 'I don't like Scientology because it's a made-up religion,' to which another reader replied, 'As opposed to...?' He had a point. More recent religions entered the game late, and thus have yet to generate the market share that can only accrue with millennia. Having said that, *Star Wars* already is a religion.

Right now, anxiety is to Generation **Y** what depression was to Generation **X**.

What will come next?

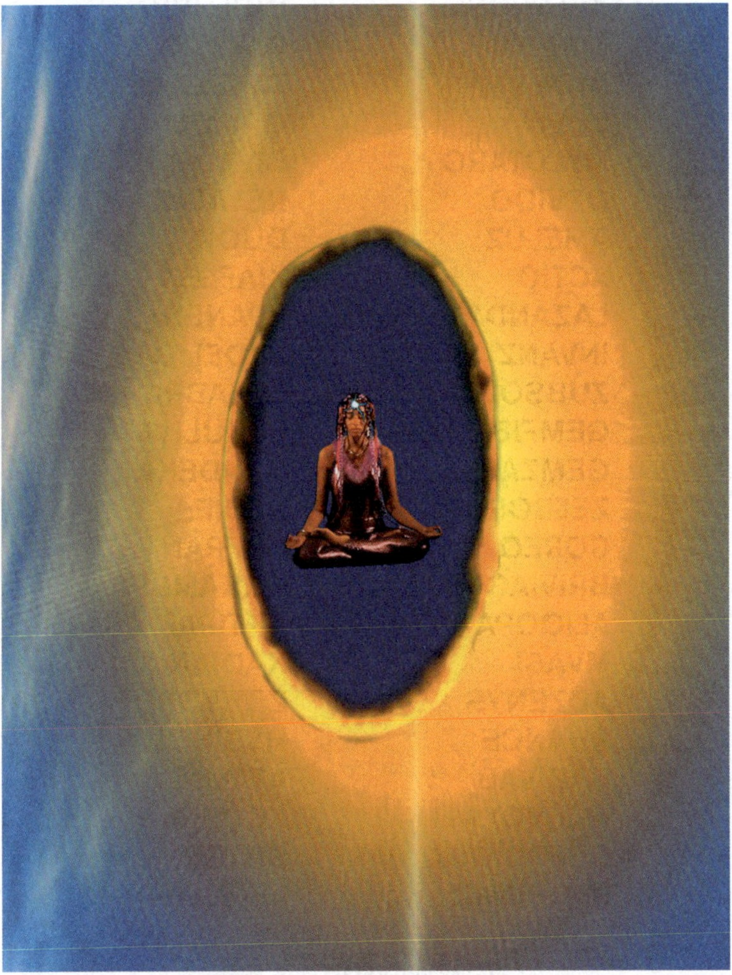

FIASP
TIGLUTIK
JULUCA
PREZCOBIX
CASSIPA
INVANZ
CADUET
XELPROS
LUMOXITI
AJOVY
ZOVIA
MYLOTARG
OPVIDO
AMELUZ
ACTIQ
LAZANDA
INVANZ
ZUBSOLV
GEMFIBROZIL
GEMZAR
ZELBORAF
COREQ
BRIVIACT
ALIQOPA
MVASI
ADZENYS
XHANCE
RABIVAB
GENVOYA
CEFOBID
LIPTRUZET

UPTRAVI
QVAR
VIIBRID
KHEDEZLA
ORKAMBI
MOBIC
ZERBAXA
INCLUSIG
RAVICTI
TANZEUM
OPVIDO
BIVALIRUDIN
REYATAZ
DUOPA
XIAFLEX
EPANED
ZYDELIG
TYSABRI
REXULTI
BENDEKA
REBIF
ZOFRAN
ORKAMBI
AKTIPAK
KADIAN
ZOHYDRO
HYSINGLA
XTAMPZA
XCOPRI
SUTAB
VERQUVO

FDA approved drugs 2016–2021

Microdosing:

The 1960s got the chemicals right. It just had the dosages wrong.

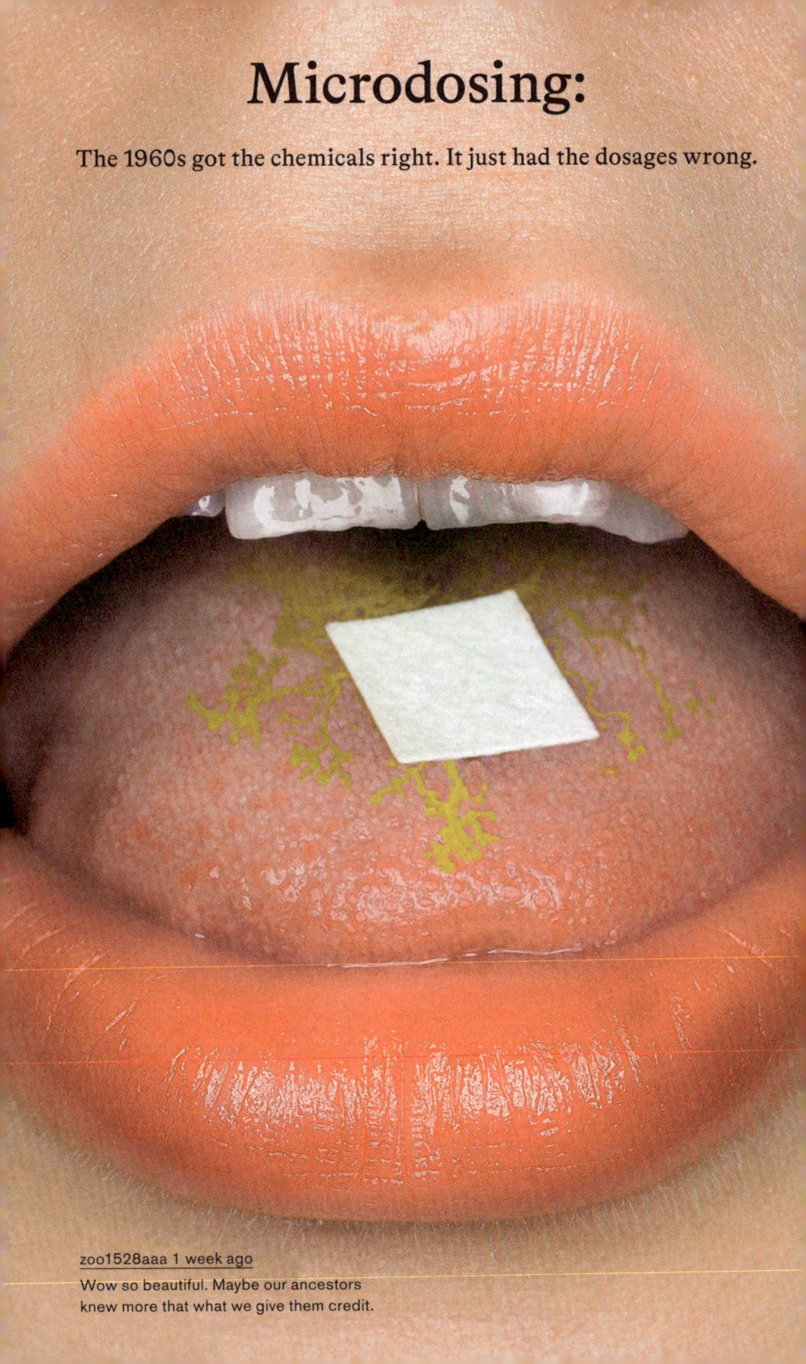

zoo1528aaa 1 week ago

Wow so beautiful. Maybe our ancestors
knew more that what we give them credit.

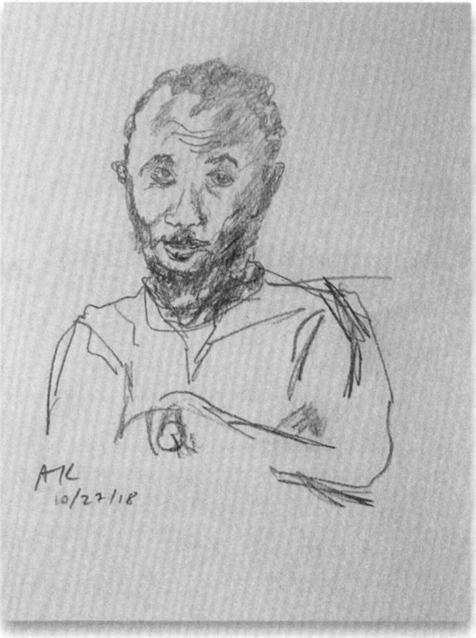

'Although we tend to agree with Egyptian mythology that the Creator makes us in two corresponding forms, one as shadow and the other substance, it is still unclear what happens to the face of our phantom self, if it ever ages, or if it even has a face.'

Emmanuel Iduma

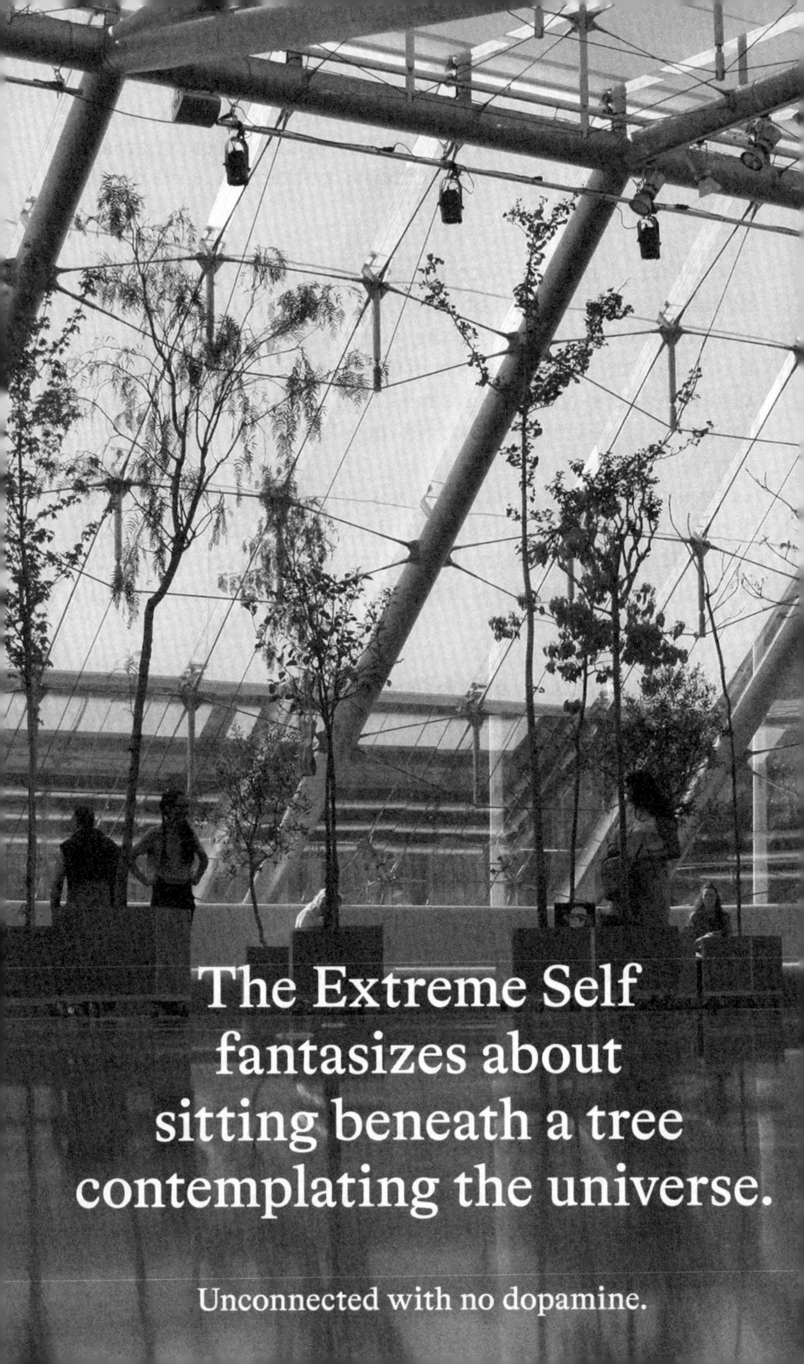

The Extreme Self fantasizes about sitting beneath a tree contemplating the universe.

Unconnected with no dopamine.

As the world furthers its decentralization – away from the West, towards new centers, and the return of old empires – the beliefs of the 'rest' of the 85% of the earth's population exert greater impact, economically, ecologically, politically, and on the global imagination.

One effect of planetary communication is the formation of globalized communities of belief. Countless people – millions or even billions – still argue the world is flat. Or that dinosaurs didn't die out. They live peacefully on a undiscovered island with Elvis Presley and Mahatma Gandhi. Nothing is too niche nor eccentric. Everyone can find their kin today.

As technology brings its own evangelism (e.g. Silicon Valley libertarianism and transhumanism), there are rising anti-technology movements. For some disaffected urbanites, the only way forwards is backwards to a prelapsarian, pre-technological time.

I've a friend who, in a fit of existential rage, smashed his smartphone with a roadside rock. He said he wanted the outside world to feel like the outside world again, and not just an appendage to the screen.

Maybe in the din of ubiquitous information and disinformation, belief is a distinguishing act of authenticity. Perhaps belief protects you against the chaos of endless relativism.

...Even if that belief is strictly limited to a belief in yourself.

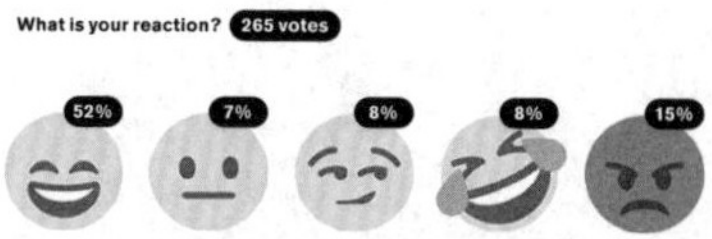

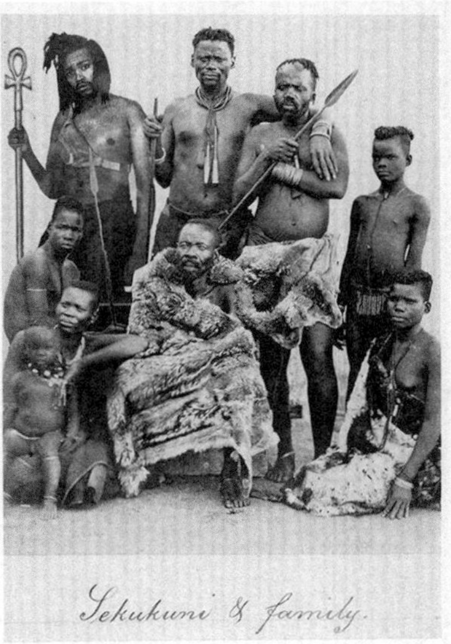

Beliefs are as present now as at any time in human history.

Neither the 18th century 'Age of Reason,' nor the advances of subsequent scientific and technological modernity, fully vanquished previous 'superstitions' – such as religion, esoterism, magic and animism. They survived. They even emboldened.

So too Francis Fukuyama's prediction, made after the fall of the Soviet Empire, that the world would reach a terminal plateau of free market liberalism: a universal economic system as system of belief. A decade later, and 9-11 spectacularized the role of the martyr as media sensation, invoking Don DeLillo's assertion that the terrorist has replaced the novelist at the center of culture. The continued 'clash of civilizations' – between religious fundamentalism and secular democracy – is also a war of supposedly incompatible beliefs.

on

a

journey

You

are

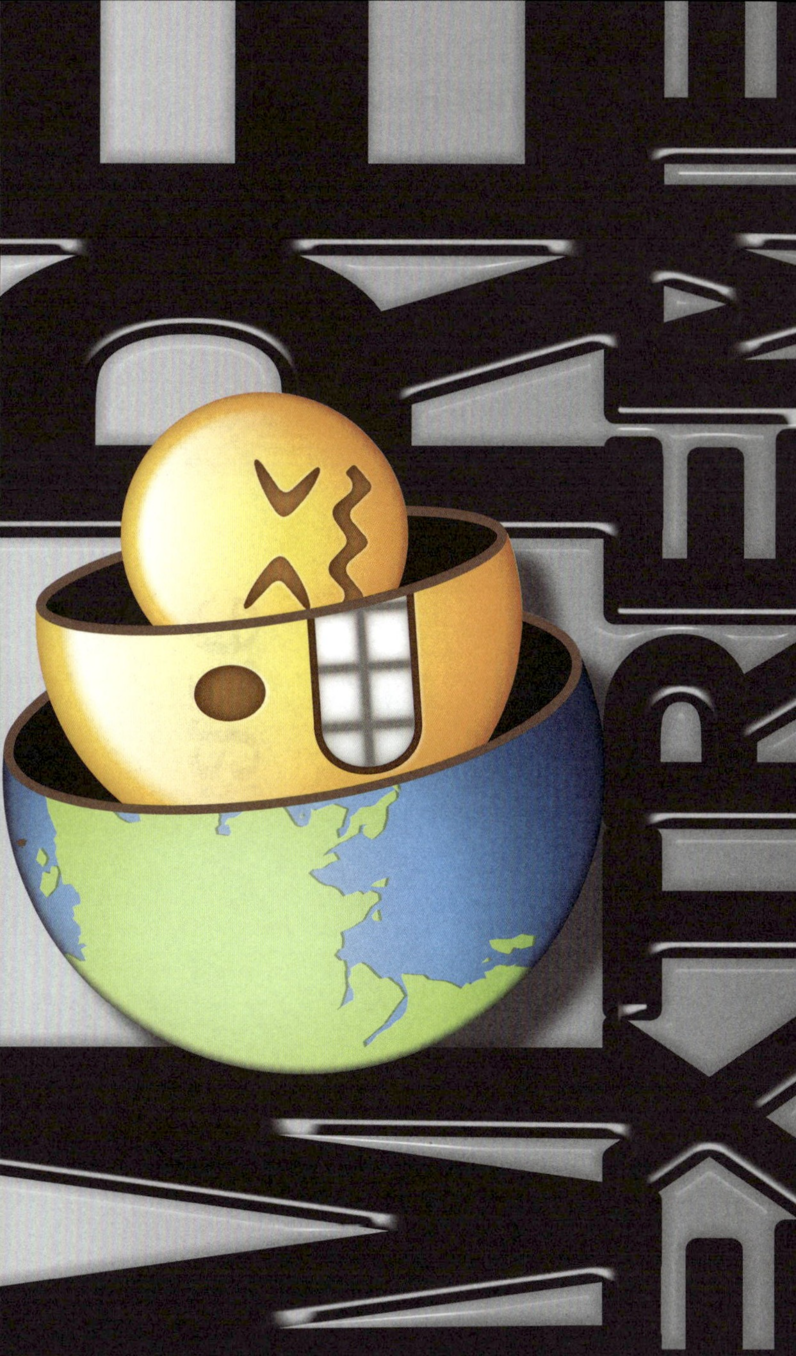

As we become <u>less powerful</u> do we become

My niece knows what intersectional means.

She's seven.

My grandfather knows what heteronormativity is.

He's 84.

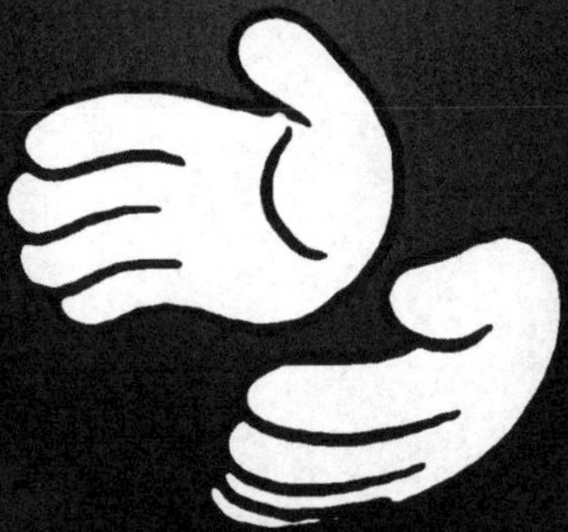

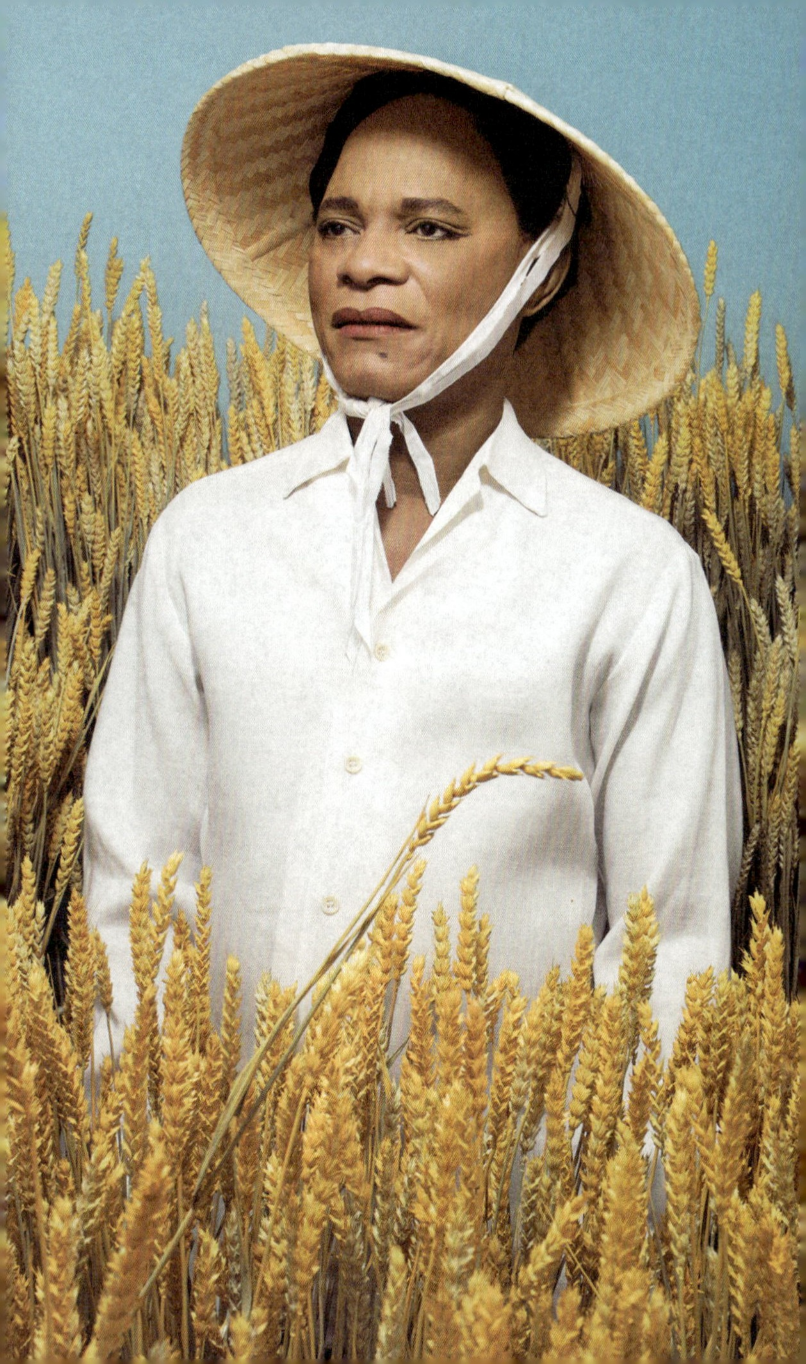

Today I am...

Bi-Gendered
Cross-Dresser
Drag-King
Drag-Queen
Femme Queen
Female-to-Male
FTM
Gender Bender
Genderqueer
Male-To-Female
MTF
Non-Op
Hijra
Pangender
Transexual / Transsexual
Trans Person
Woman
Man
Butch
Two-Spirit
Trans
Agender
Third Sex
Gender Fluid
Non-Binary Transgender
Androgyne
Gender-Gifted
Gender Bender
Femme
Person of Transgender Experience
Androgynous

This is the New York City Commission on Human Rights list of thirty-one genders.

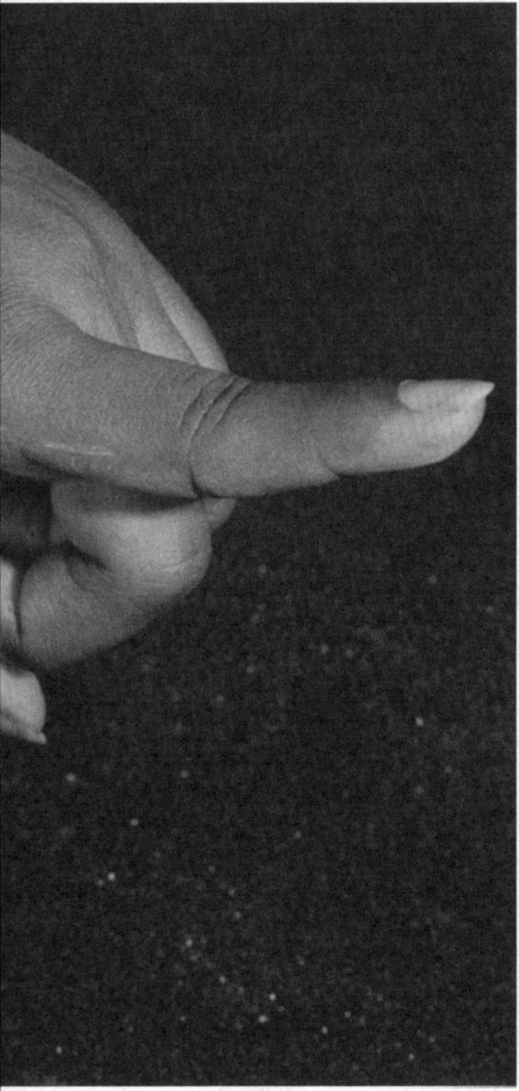

Public penance is
getting more and
more impatient.

But public
redemption is
no longer a
guaranteed route to
greater success.

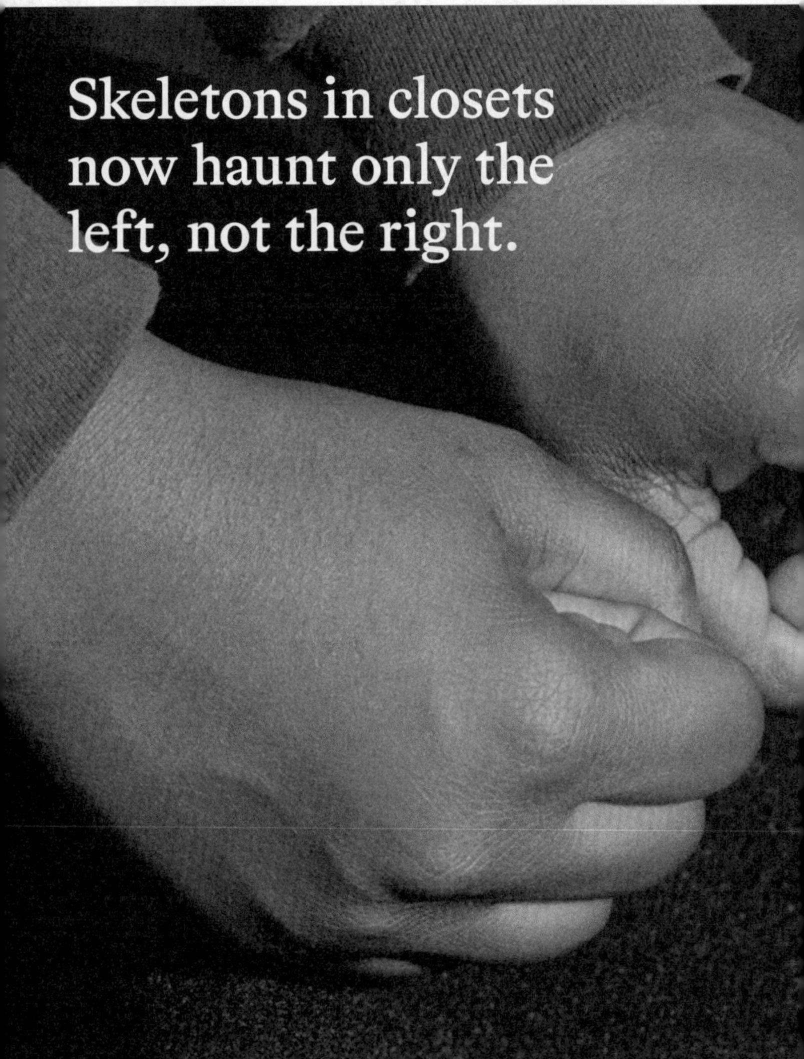
Skeletons in closets now haunt only the left, not the right.

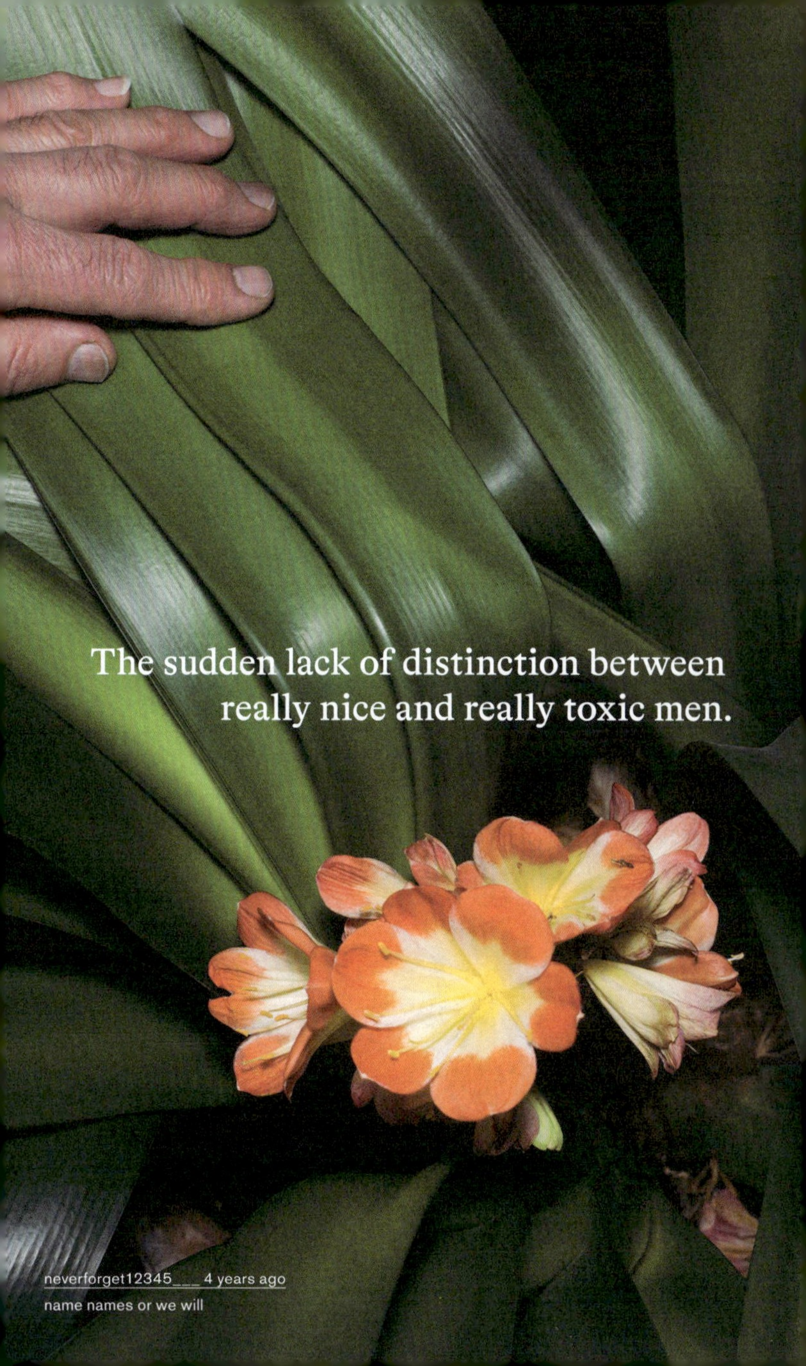

The sudden lack of distinction between
really nice and really toxic men.

neverforget12345___ 4 years ago

name names or we will

...if I do say so myself #humblebrag

I TAKE
GREAT
PRIDE IN
MY VAST
HUMILITY

You need to *signal* it to show you have it.

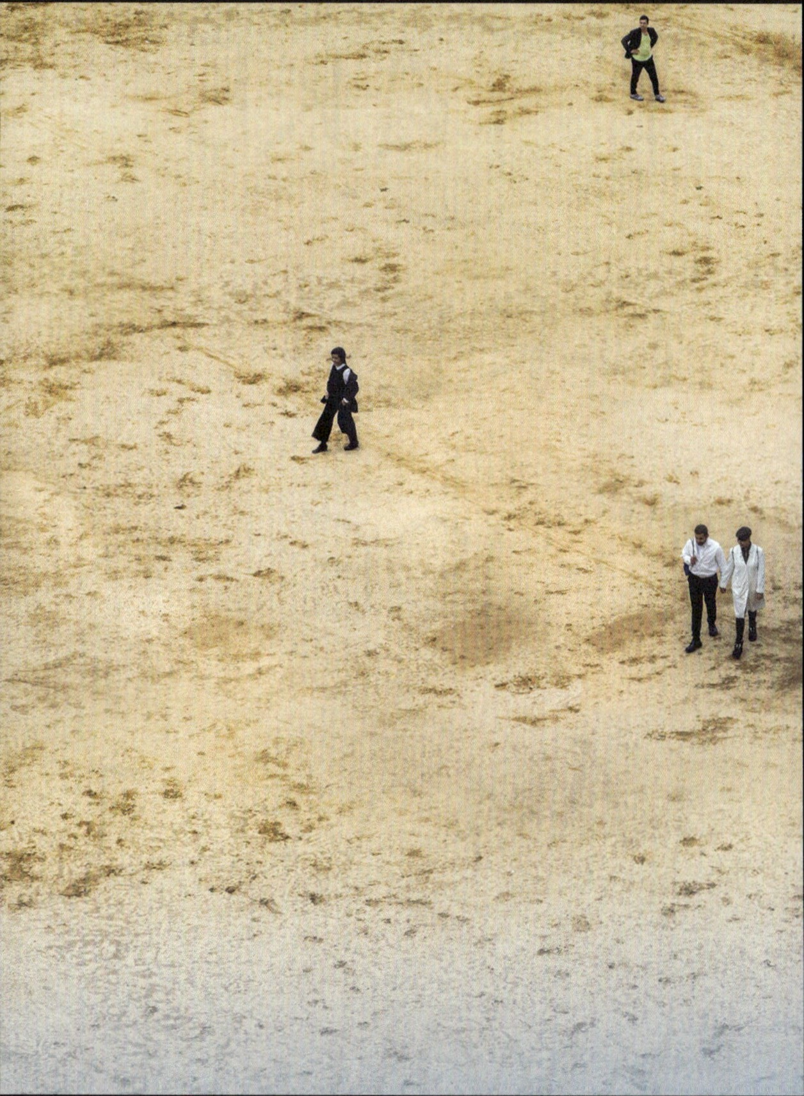

The opposite of action is no longer appearance.

It’s not enough to have virtue anymore.

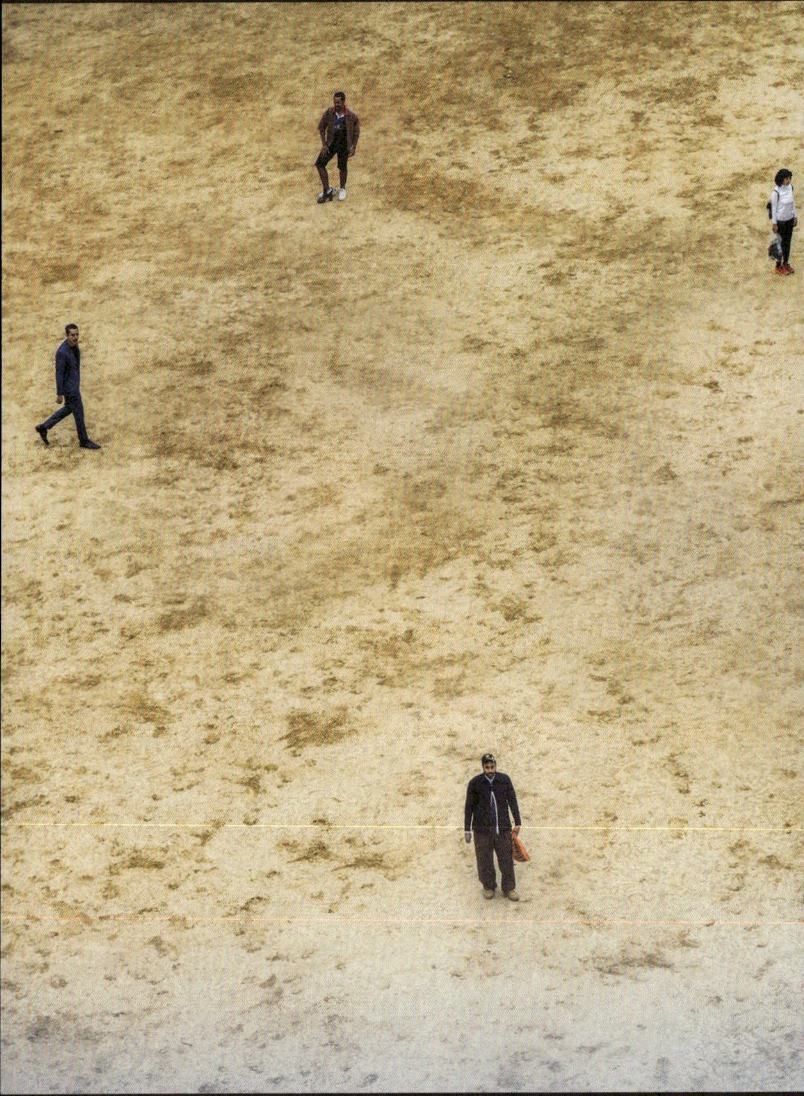

The opposite of substance is no longer superficiality.

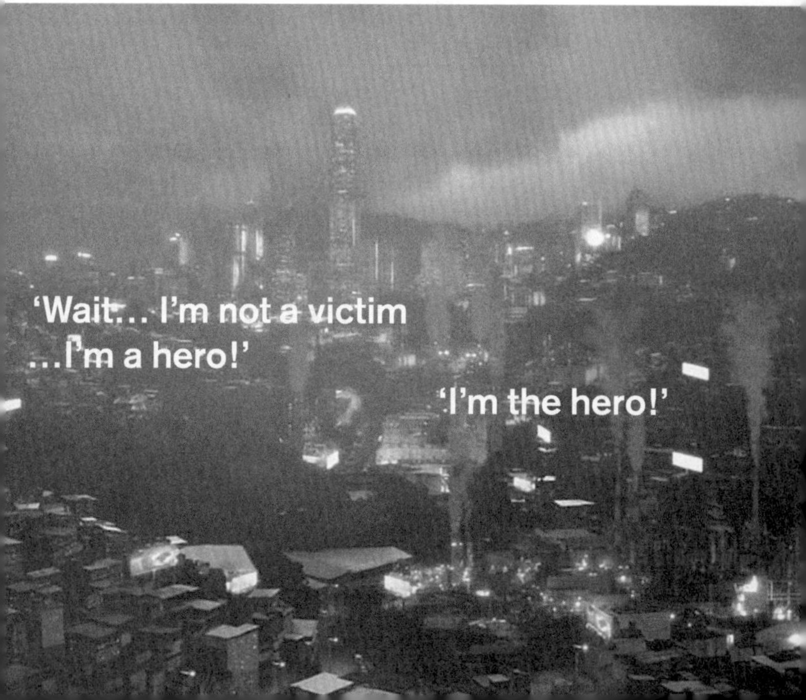
'Wait… I'm not a victim
…I'm a hero!'
'I'm the hero!'

The Extreme Self has a low trigger threshold

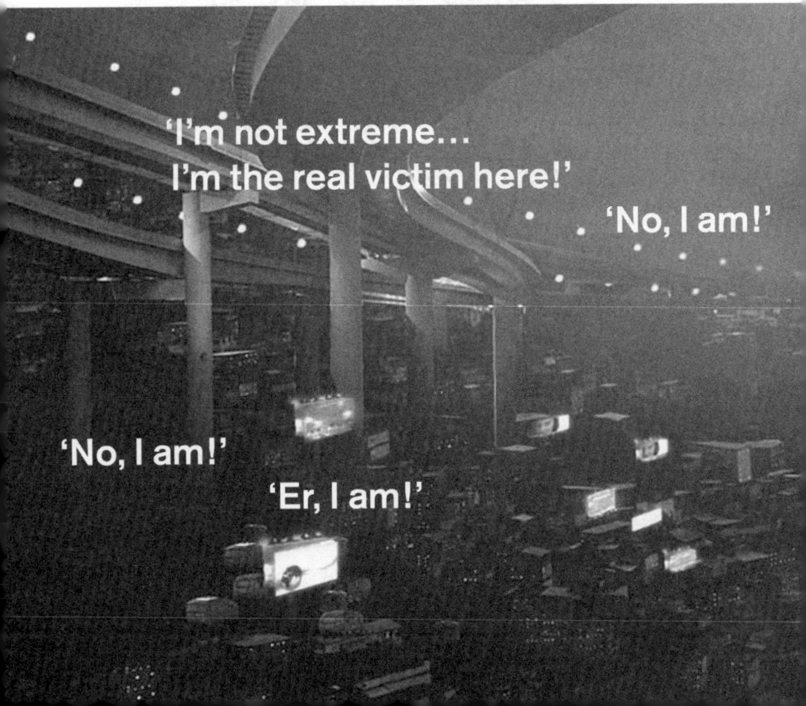

PLAN „S"

S=SAVOIR METTRE L'ART AU-DESSUS DE TOUT

S=SÉNIOR

S = SEXE

S = SANTÉ

S = SE PRÉCISER

S = SE CLARIFIER

S = SE REFUSER D'ABANDONNER QUOI QUE CE SOIT

S = SE RENFORCER TOUT EN RESTANT VULNÉRABLE

S = S'AIMER SOI-MÊME

S = SE TROUVER BEAU

S = SE RAPPELLER QUE L'ART EST—PARCE QUE C'EST DE L'ART—RÉSISTANCE

S = SOLDAT

S = SAVOIR COMPTER SUR LA GRÂCE

How does power work today?

Better than ever?

For a smaller elite?

Are the most powerful philosophers the ones quoted by political leaders?

Or the ones with the best memes about them?

Is it annoying that online influencers are so powerful?

Is it more annoying that you're not as powerful as them?

In other words, is power more or less centralized?

Did we get the 'democratically elected authoritarian leaders' we deserved?

Do powerful people ever voluntarily give up their power to transfer power to the powerless, and become less powerful themselves?

Who is the most powerful person where you work?

Should there be one boss, or, many bosses, or no bosses?

Is a revolution without a leader pointless in the long run?

'Can you believe there are still parts of the world where patriarchy is intact? Hahahahahahahahahaha!'

Is power taken away faster than it is awarded?

Is privilege a synonym for power?

Does power provide you with the shield of privilege?

Does power seek more or less visibility than before?

Time for a power nap?

Are you in a power couple?

No? Would you like to be?

Who sang 'The Power of Love?'

pumpamentals___ 1 min ago

am i a joke to you?

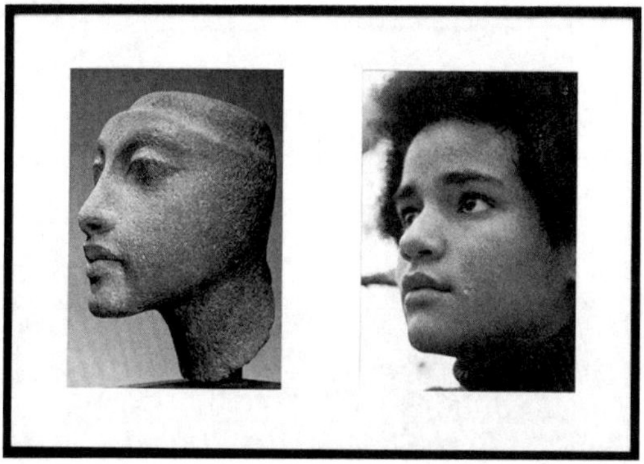

entitled to feel
someone else's pain?

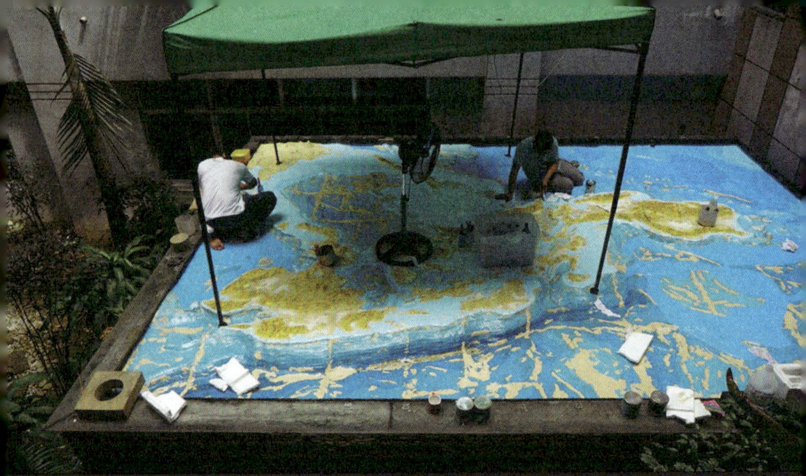

…but at what point
are you,

or aren't you,

righteous

You are

Impunity is as addictive and mind-altering as a drug.

It’s also what makes me feel invisible and utterly invincible.

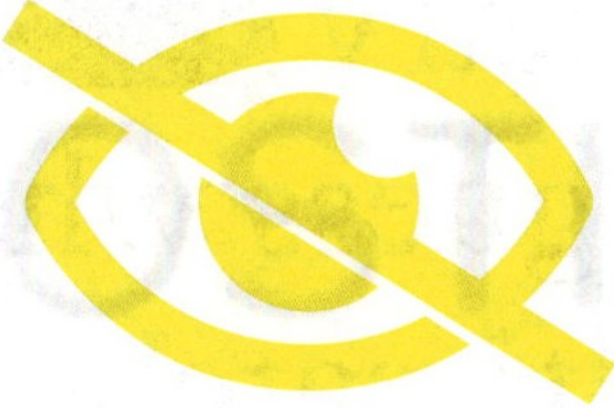

Ghosting is the extreme opposite of empathy. Calling something toxic and then running away is a cowardly means of avoiding work and responsibilities.

00sena00_ 9 minutes ago

now that's a very first-world sentiment

got the clothes rich
[redacted]
and look [redacted] than
they actually are :/
gets [redacted] and
nonbinary [redacted]
:/ but guess what
he's ultimately there
to [redacted] with
POWER and the
[redacted]
upper [redacted]
white :/ [redacted]'s probably
[redacted] PSYOP lololol

he really does make [redacted] for self-identified 'woke' [redacted] ppl who desperately seek the continuation of [redacted] :/ I find him REALLY [redacted] I think he's amazing at being a [redacted] for the newest kind of [redacted] that history has necessitated :/ he's

The
opposite
of
empathy
used
to
be
indifference.

Now, it's shaming someone else.

When technology changes too quickly, people tend to make really bad decisions.

People who feel as if they're in too much chaos can be tricked into doing almost anything.

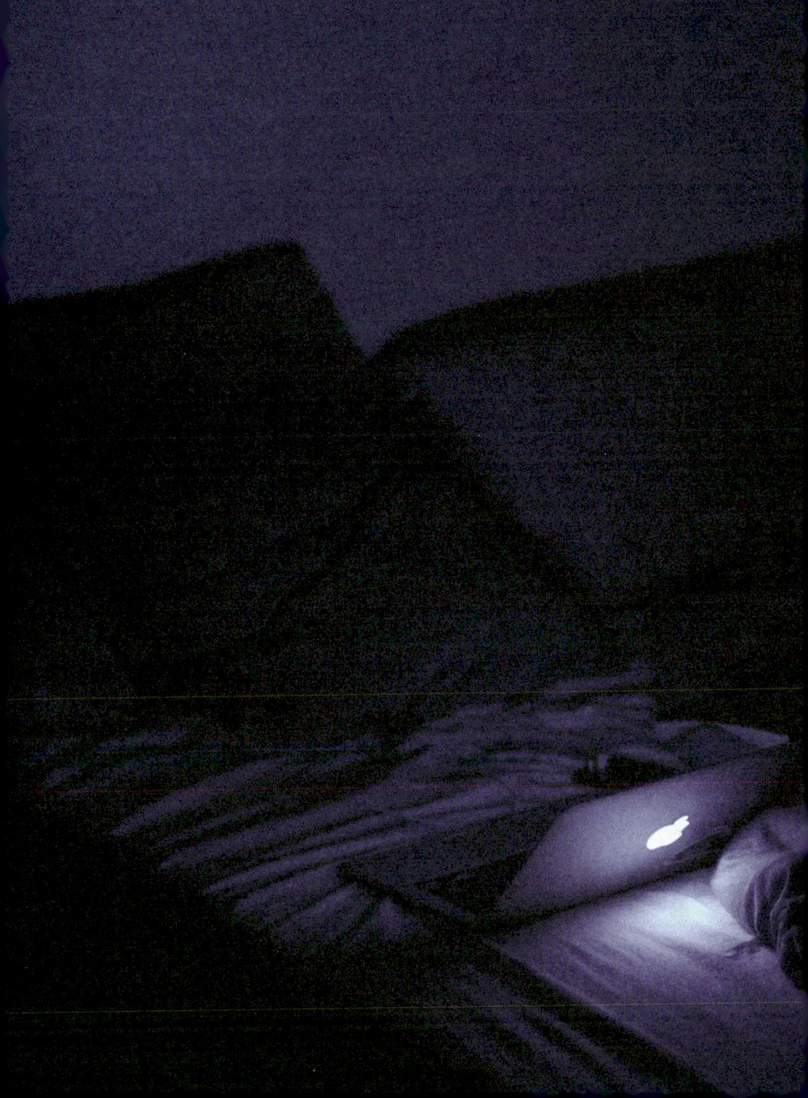

Outrage is good for business.

**How much news do you digest in a day?
How much did you use to digest?**

Outrage is fun.

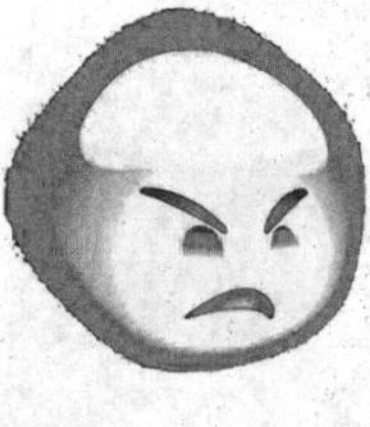

You appear virtuous for doing pretty much nothing. It's like the Diet Coke of politics.

Q:
What is microfascism?

A:
Microfascism is when online aggression spills into real world aggression – tiny or large acts of aggression and confrontation used to define, deplatform and limit the agency of others.

Microfascism has turned the Right into a circus act – to the disgust of the Left.

'Outrage culture' feels like the loudest form of culture today.

It's actually astonishing how much the Left and Right have in common.

Q:
What is micro-othering?

A:
Micro-othering is the use of ever thinner slices of identity to define, deplatform and limit the agency of others.

Micro-othering has turned the Left into a circular firing squad – to the glee of the Right.

'Call-out culture' feels like the loudest form of culture today.

Calling for nuance has become the same as admitting guilt and complicity.

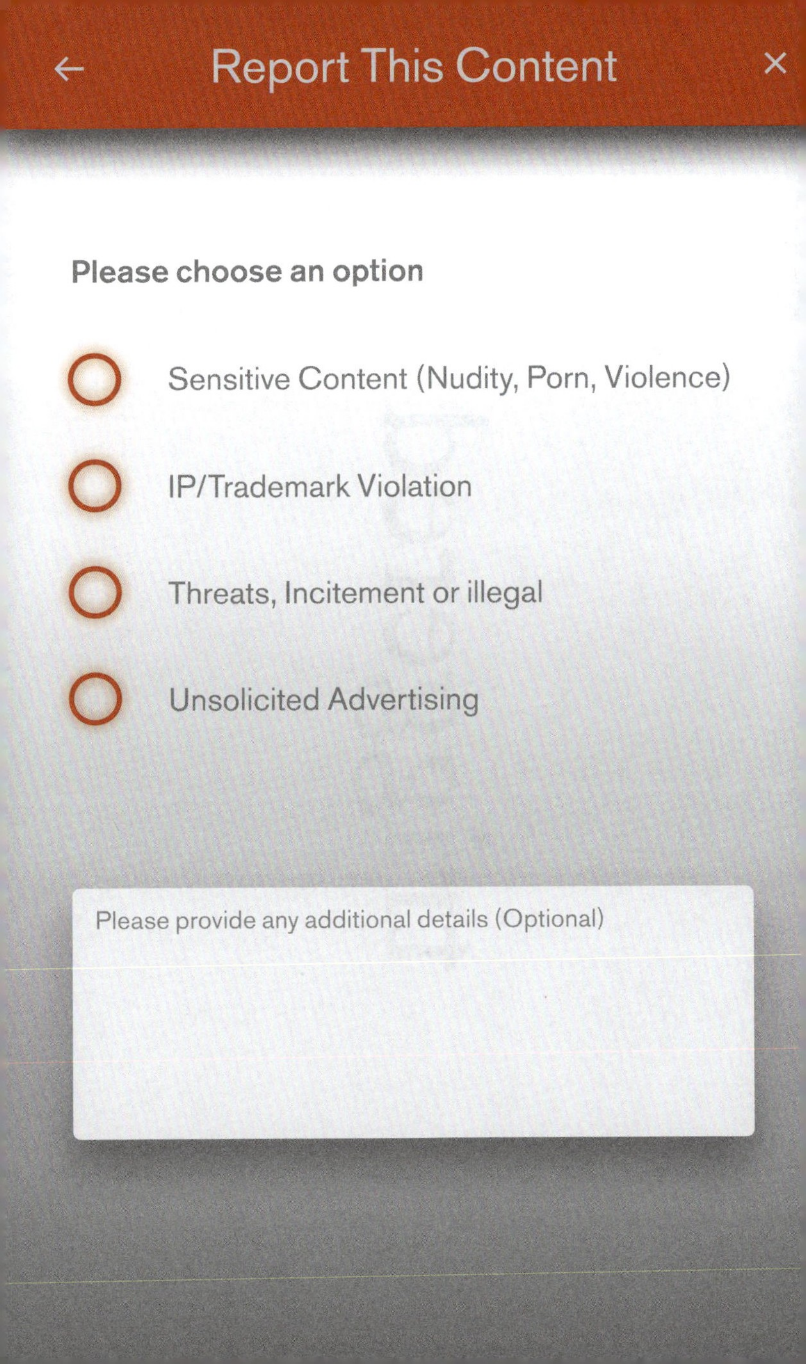
← Report This Content ×
Please choose an option
Sensitive Content (Nudity, Porn, Violence)
IP/Trademark Violation
Threats, Incitement or illegal
Unsolicited Advertising
Please provide any additional details (Optional)

triggered

7 Micro-Othering/ Microfascism

You are

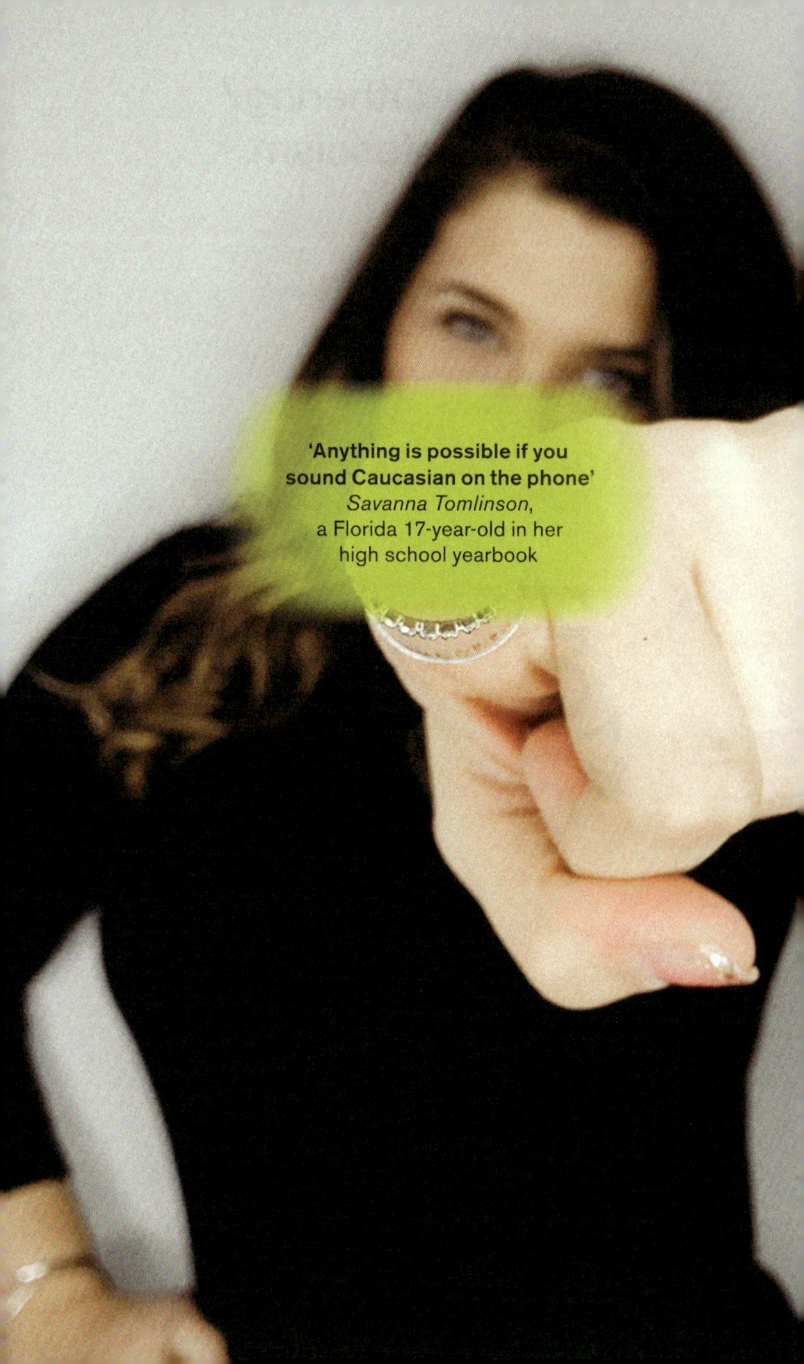
'Anything is possible if you sound Caucasian on the phone'
Savanna Tomlinson,
a Florida 17-year-old in her
high school yearbook

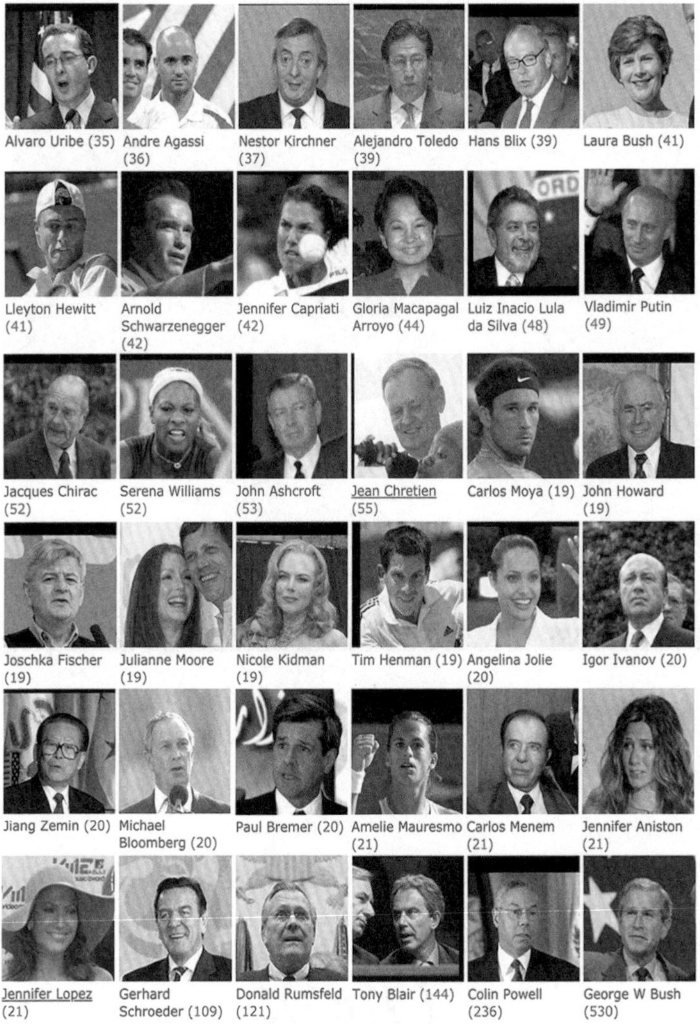

'This is an atlas of the TOP most labeled people in the "Labeled Faces in the Wild" database, one of the very first used in early image recognition processes (circa 2007). These are the first faces the machine brain saw, and learnt about. The Pioneers. It now feels like a cemetery too – all these people are kind of over today. But to many machines to this day, they are still VIPs.'

Ana Nicolaescu

You.

Them.

Me.

Us.

Hi! I'm a citizen of wherever. I live there, vote there and pay taxes there – and if I'm kidnapped by malignant forces in some far away land, my government will come running to my rescue.

This seems fair enough, but if you've got multiple passports, say four, can you reasonably expect one of your four countries to come to your rescue if you're in a fix? You're basically a citizen of nowhere, or, at the very most, you've got citizenship-lite.

Hi, I know, I haven't been voting or paying taxes or anything for a few decades, but I'm in a bit of a bind… can you ask one of your consul chaps to maybe trade me for a spy or something?

A way of rethinking this global web of overlapping citizenships would be wonder what might happen if Earth instituted a planet-wide citizenship flush. Whoever you are, you now have to choose just one passport – so, which is it going to be? The answer would probably boil down to multiple factors, the largest including personal identity, ease of crossing borders, consular access while abroad and, of course, taxes. Sure, a low tax rate is great, but if I break my arm do I really want to spend $75,000 in a Houston or Miami hospital? Yes, popping in and out of Europe is terrific, but would I want to forfeit getting a lump in my throat if I hear my ex-national anthem playing? The fact that every country on Earth makes it very difficult to become a citizen means that citizenship has to mean something.

Polycitizenry is a creation of the 20th century, and a creation whose days are numbered. As the world gets ever more pay-per-use, the luxury of low-commitment semi-disposable allegiance seems too expensive.

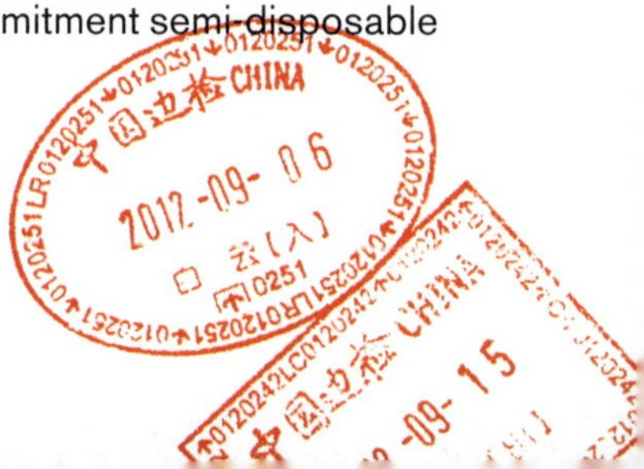

Do you have multiple citizenships?

Populist movements are exposing a fault line in modern Western societies. The division is between, as David Goodhart describes: those who live 'anywhere' and those who live 'somewhere.'

Segments of urban and university-educated professionals have become genuinely globally oriented in their careers and personal lives. The globalization of the past quarter-century has transformed an element of the world's population.

Imagine yourself as someone who works for an international consulting firm or in a globally focused academic career. You can wake up in New York, London, or Singapore and feel at home. You may rent or even own regular accommodation in all of these places. Your work is not subjected to import competition or threat of technological dislocation.

You may attend (or aspire to attend) the Davos conference. You probably read *The Economist* and, like Thomas Friedman, believe that the world really is flat. Your spouse or partner has a similar professional background, although they are from somewhere else in the world. You are motivated by climate change and suspicious of religion. You are unequivocally pro-free trade and support high levels of immigration. Your values can broadly be described as 'cosmopolitan.'

Such cosmopolitans, or 'Anywheres,' or just plain 'globalists' have an increasingly weak attachment to the nation-state. Their professional, personal, and even familial relationships are increasingly with people like themselves from a range of countries. The examples given may be rooted in stereotypes, but there are many less extreme cases among people who work, study, or join online communities that cross boundaries.

Streets, Roads, Avenues, Blvds...

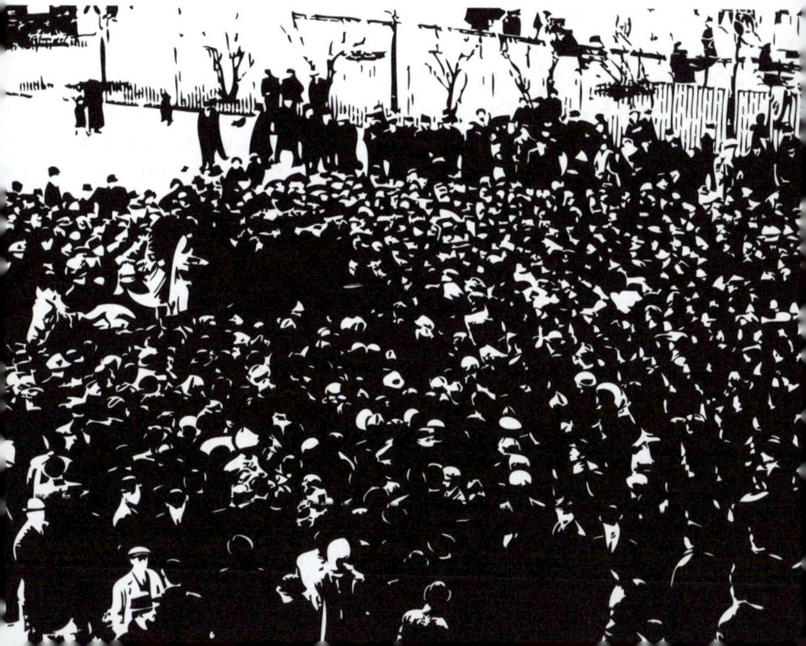

Sharing is ownership for losers

sami_a_f 3 hours ago

why me so bad make feel

Nationalism weaponizes anything it touches

When does an individual become a crowd,

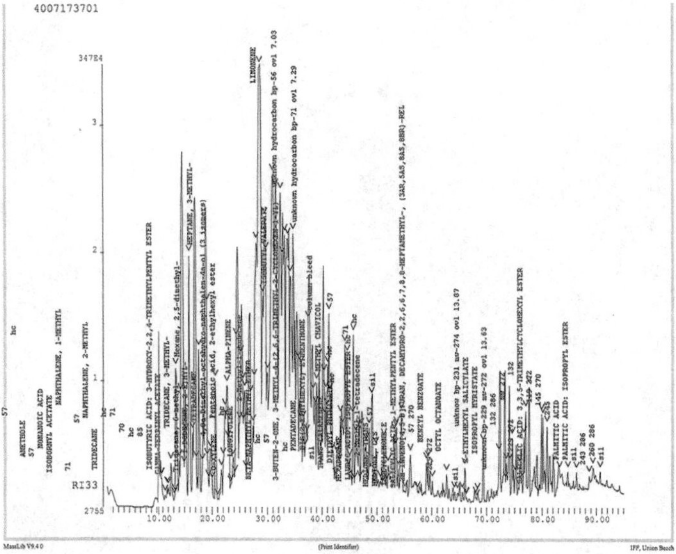

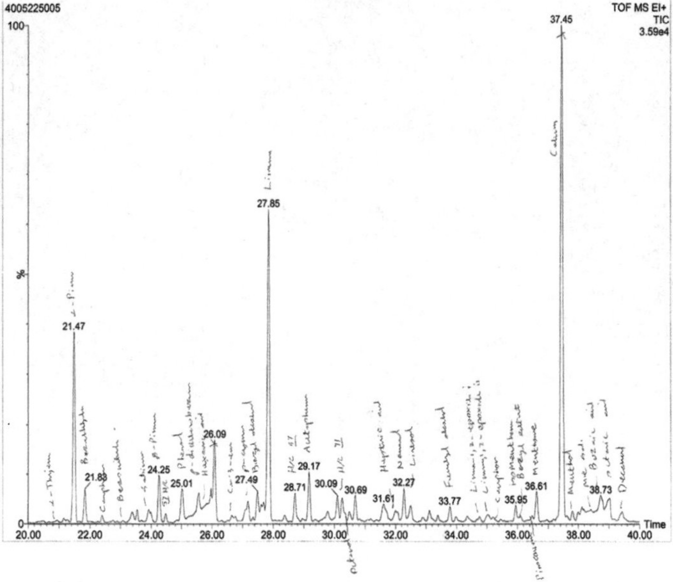

and when does a crowd become a threat?

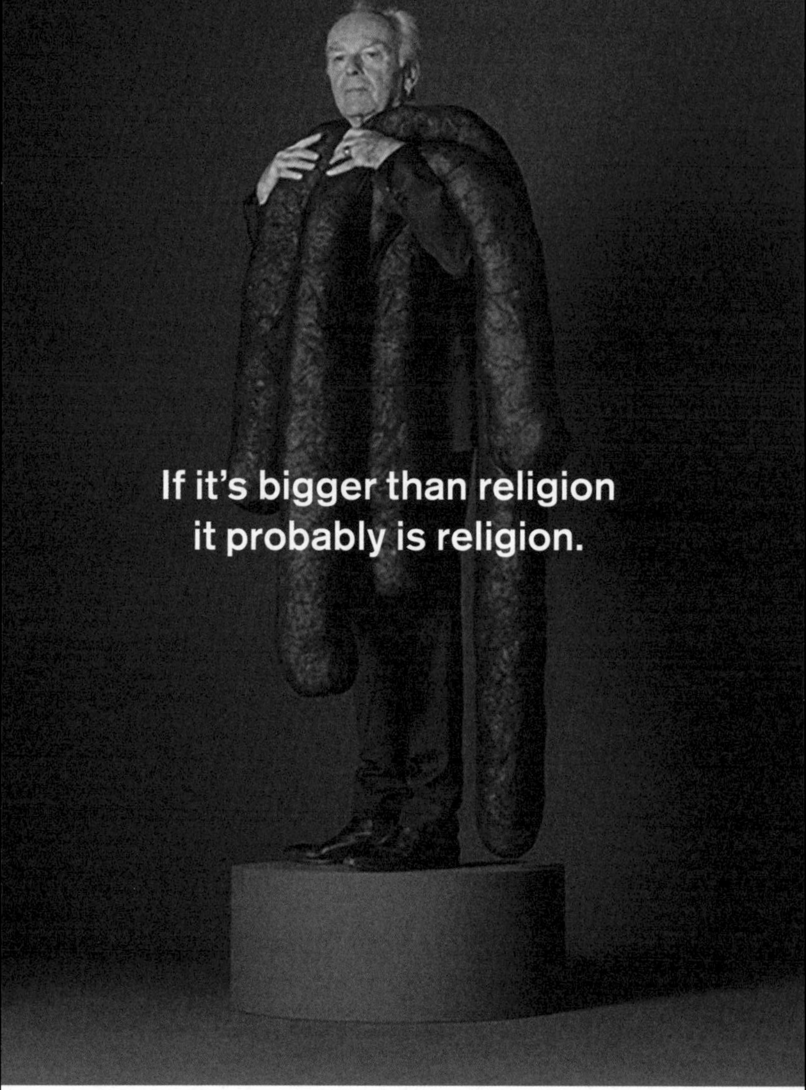

'We've all been engaged for most of the 20th century in a sort of war of religions. If you believe you are living in a world that is crashing about around you, you're left with a choice of future or no-future.'

Eric Hobsbawm

FACT:

...All -isms start with some harmonization of a zealous crowd.

Alex______won 12h ago

that's too much weird brah

FACT:

…Fascism
starts with
the harmonization
of a zealous crowd.

FACT:

…Communism
starts with
the forced
harmonization
of a zealous crowd.

‘Madness is the exception in individuals.
But the rule in groups.’
Brad Pitt

‘Madness is the exception in individuals.
But the rule in groups.’
Marilyn Monroe

‘Madness is the exception in individuals.
But the rule in groups.’
Albert Einstein

‘Madness is the exception in individuals.
But the rule in groups.’
Friedrich Nietzsche

Two thousand three hundred and forty-one people are in an out-of-town-mall outside Adelaide. They are all wearing Augmented Reality contact lenses. Each lens overlays a completely different world, set in the same time.

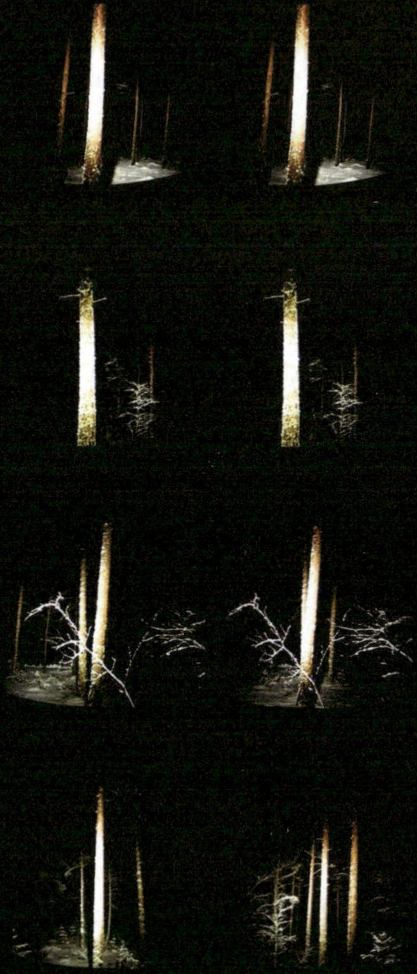

What kind of crowd is this?

Two thousand three hundred and forty-one people are in a hotel conference room in downtown Adelaide. They are all wearing VR headsets. Each headset contains a completely unique world, set in a different time.

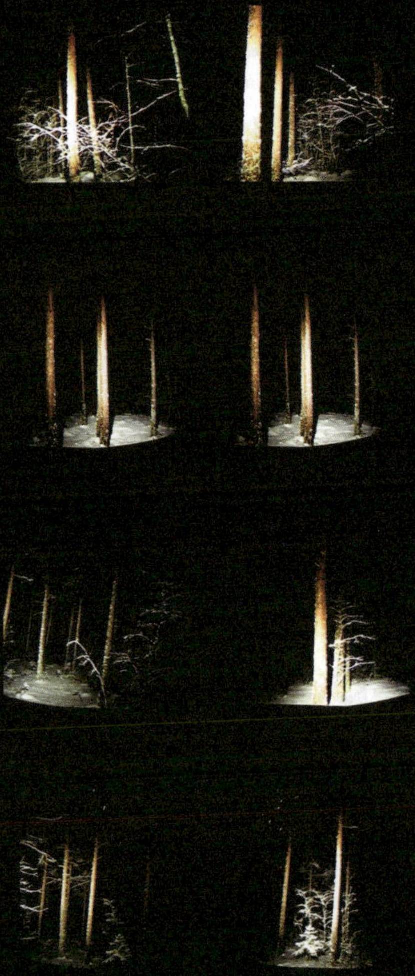

What kind of crowd is this?

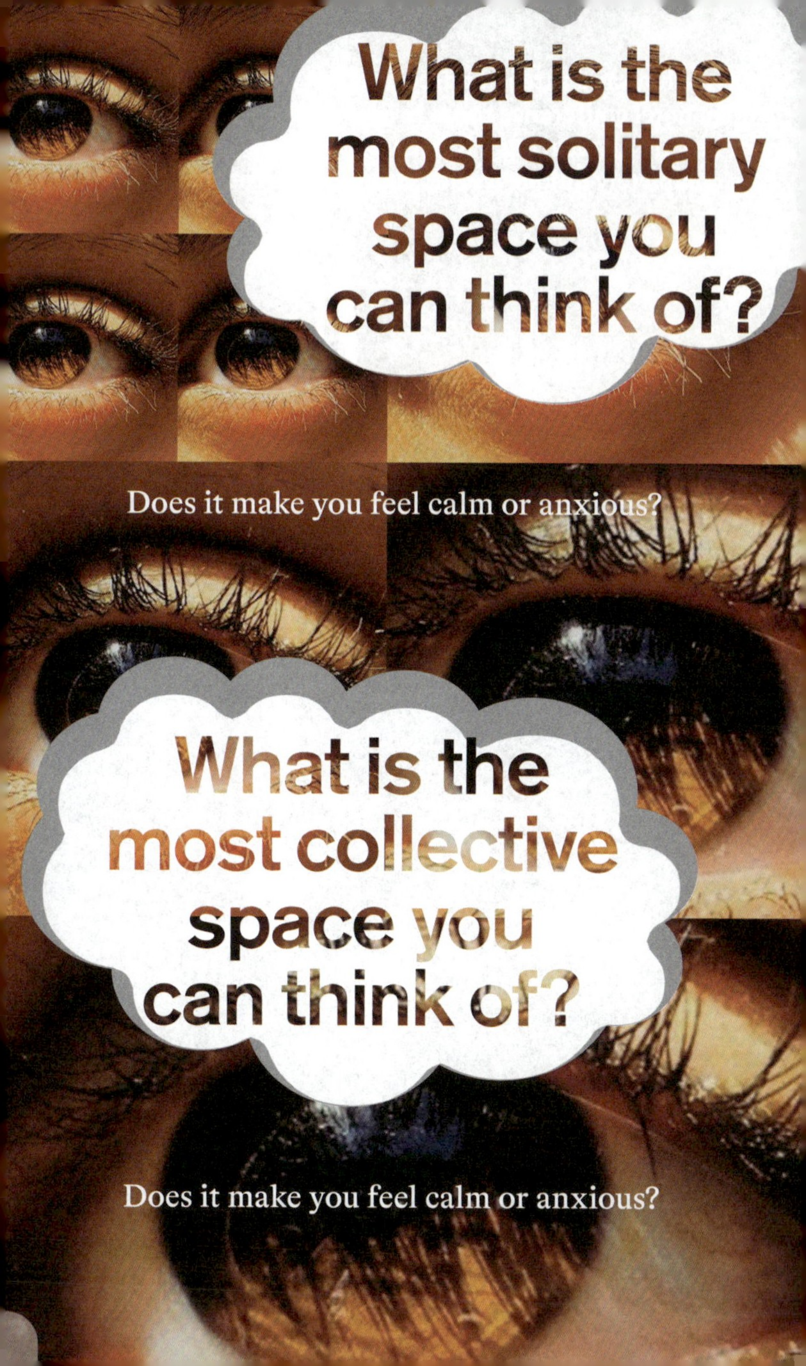

What is the most solitary space you can think of?

Does it make you feel calm or anxious?

What is the most collective space you can think of?

Does it make you feel calm or anxious?

In the 19th century, with the rise of industrialized cities, writers like Baudelaire characterized the new urban crowd as a defining hallmark of modernity.

So too was the ability to lose oneself in the crowd.

In today's decentralized crowds, amassing somewhere in the Cloud, the Extreme Self doesn't just hide.

The anonymity of the new crowd is where the Extreme Self discovers a new, powerful infamy.

simonedesartre 10 months ago

ONE IS MORE ALONE WITH A CROWD

‘Only together can people free themselves from their burdens of distance; and this, precisely, is what happens in a crowd.’

Elias Canetti, Crowds and Power

What about crowds?

Do you still feel safe in a crowd?

Or, d~~D~~o you feel new~~in~~ danger in a crowd?

Do you feel alone in a crowd?

Did~~Do~~ you form bonds in a crowd?

When does a crowd become a mob?

Is a social movement a global crowd?

Is it hard to be an individual when being part of a crowd has never been more complicated~~easier~~?

Do you miss crowds?

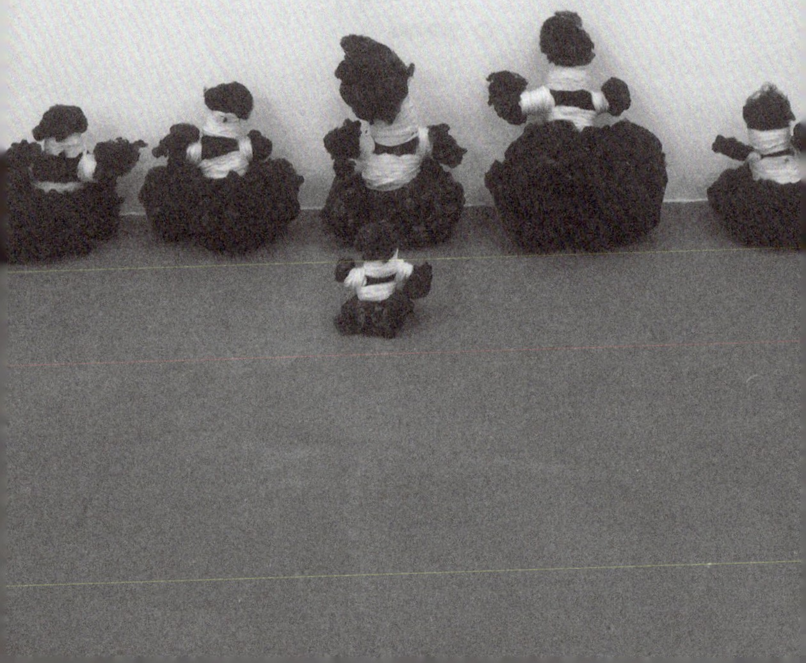

multiplying

You are

The end result is a collective state of intellectual isolation.

Deedle.nick_fuzz 53s ago

Somewhere someone is turned on by this and im ok with that tbf

Basically:

The comment section of YouTube has become the real world.

Oh, man, look at all of those dead clowns.

Honestly, what was the objective here?

Ho. Ly. Shit

Gasoline is the solution to everything.

She went full tinfoil hat.

Those have to be the most identifiable pants of all time.

He went from a motorcycle rider to being lost in the woods having to drink his own pee to survive in a matter of seconds.

I have never seen an escalator actually eat someone.

That was the cartoonist knockout I have ever seen.

Fluff my nip

Wait… those were clowns?

Sort Newest to Oldest ⬍

How the fuck does she come out of the harness like that?

The second time he's just like, 'Ugh, not again.'

Uninstall life.

I love when he come back at the end to ram the car a second time after I thought it was over.

Beautiful, so graceful, 10/10 for dismount.

Lucky that was his stomach and not his teeth.

And that's how Kevin ended up with his forever helmet.

Nine out of ten. I'm only withholding one point because nothing is on fire.

Beep beep motherfucker.

Play dead. The chainsaw will lose interest and return to her cubs.

It's all fun and games until someone eats one of them.

Whatever... just don't press the red button.

You must immediately knock her out with your shoe or kill her with a trident.

Admit it:

You read the comments section first.

In fact:

You only read the comments section.

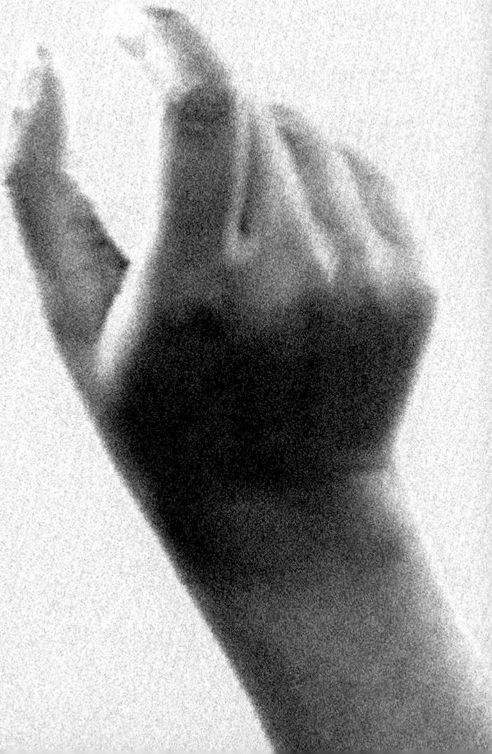

The_comment_kurator 4d ago

You dunn played yourself

This shattering of time perception doesn't just affect your private, inner-space.

It's one of the root causes of why public space has turned into what it is today: an infinite mess of irreconcilable differences.

Everyone is ready to go fight anyone, anywhere.

Except face to face.

Where did last year go?

Why do increased dopamine hits make time's passage feel shorter instead of longer?

Everything feels either ten minutes ago or ten years ago.
What happened to the middle?

Constant online existence is making your perceived biological existence, in a very real sense, much shorter.

We all know it, but is it worth the price?

People think they're political, but all they want is the dopamine hit they get from the way politics now works on our brains. It's like opioid addicts saying the opioids themselves are unimportant – they 'only want the rush.'

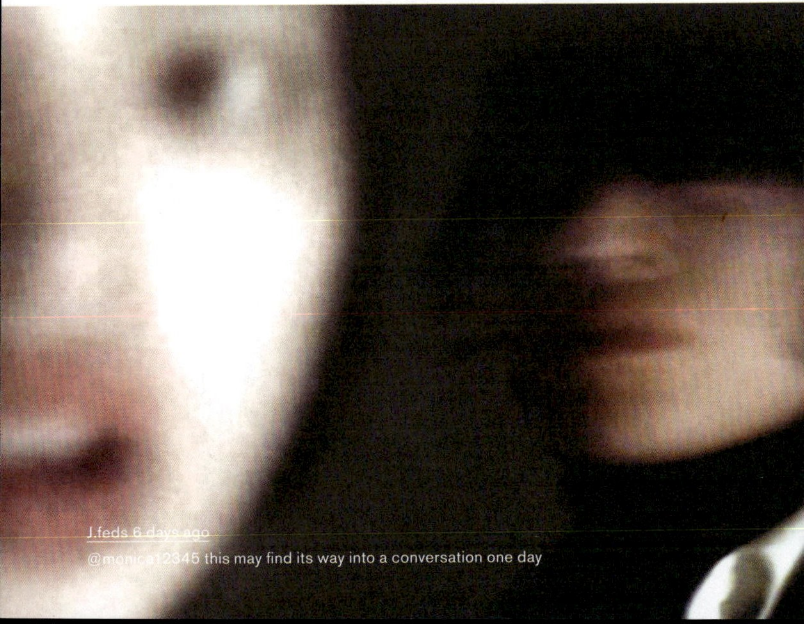

I exist within an endless, short-term, dopamine-driven feedback loop.

This is my entire day.

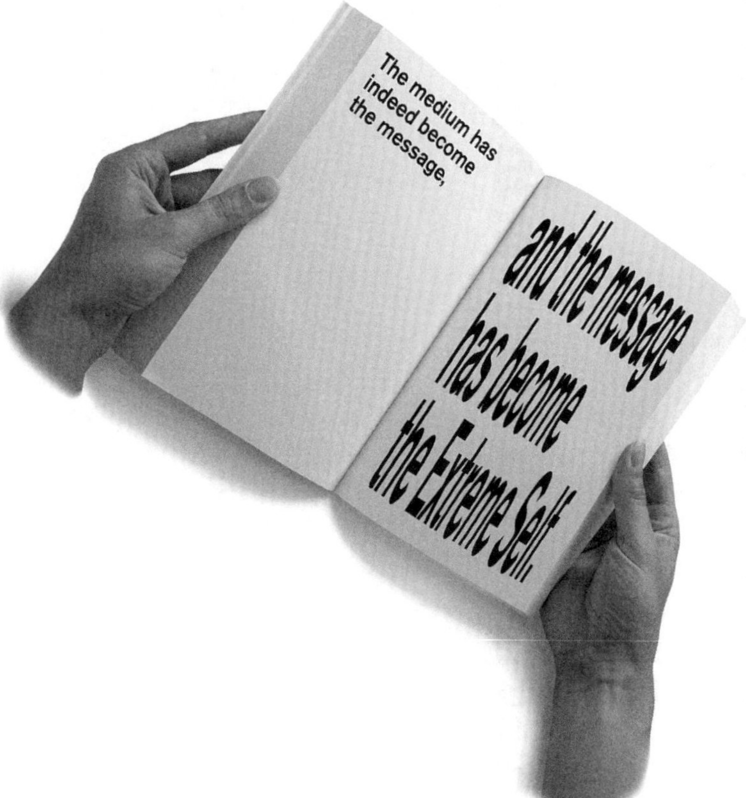

Cindyphamz 19h ago

@tevin2021 do u feel attacked

Do you prefer distraction to attention?

Do you prefer disinformation to information?

blow me 7 months ago (edited)

seeing what the adults think about this

What If
This means physical bodies are now only one piece of your human existence. What makes up the rest?

What If
'The global village is populated with "discarnate" human beings who no longer exist as physical presences; instead the electronic or discarnate person is simply an image or an information pattern, nothing more' — *Marshall McLuhan*

What If
This version of you is the only one that matters anymore.

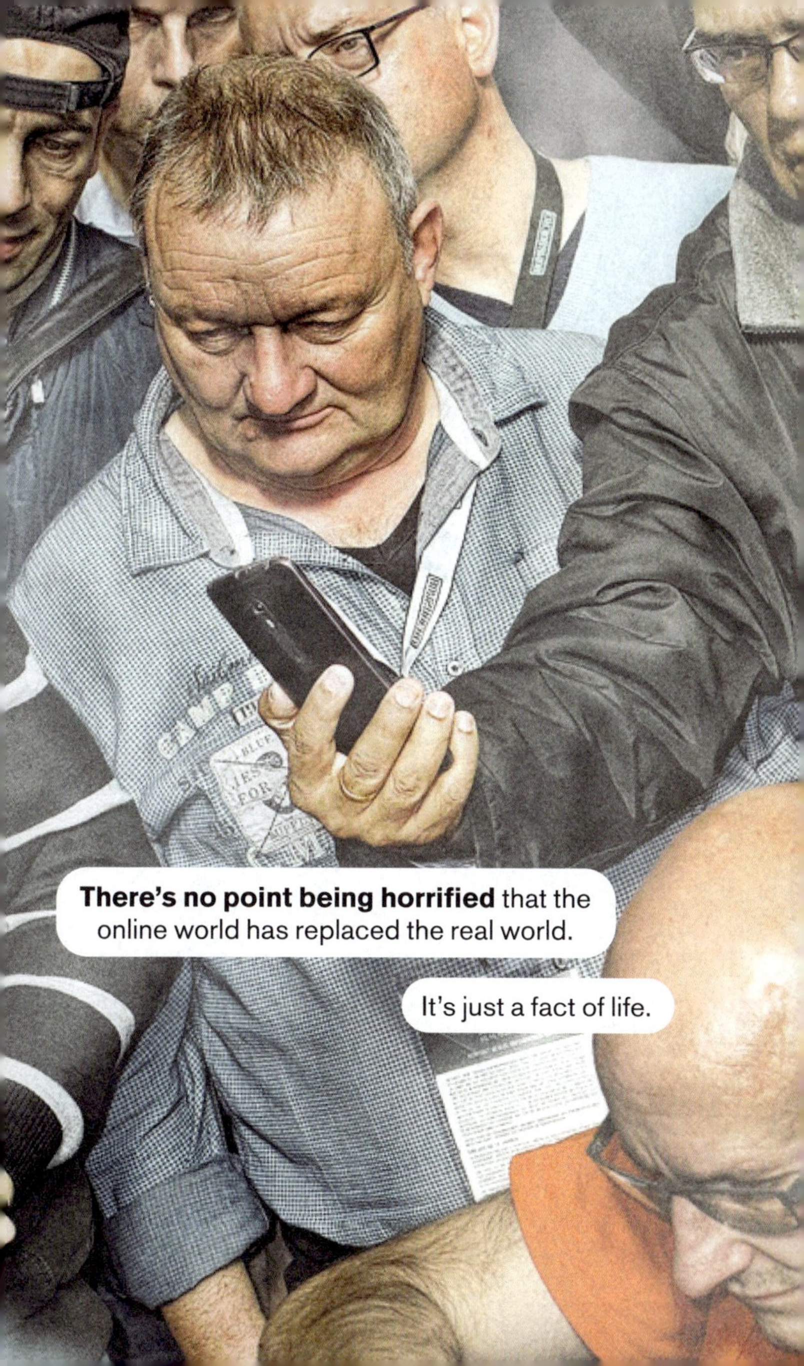
There's no point being horrified that the online world has replaced the real world.
It's just a fact of life.

Sort Newest to Oldest

Wow. I mean, talk about a real live living meat crayon.

Dress for the slide not the ride.

He's not dead yet – his shoes are still on.

I love how happy they were to say 'look ma no hands' right before getting fucked.

He should have tried turning it off and on again.

So. Much. Damage.

But wait – we can repair the damage with new Internal Flextape™

The dude's ghost is rising from his body.

His dick was writing checks his brain couldn't cash.

What the actual?

It's good for our species that they did die.

Only if they haven't yet reproduced.

Is that the same kid who pissed on the elevator buttons?

I love the big guy. He doesn't even flinch, just puts his hands in his pockets like, 'Well… fuck this.'

They're not real kids, they're robots, so if you throw rocks at them nobody cares.

What would we all do without gravity?

I am the biggest loser in the world.

Natlaxyz 20h ago

I dont like ur posts I like ur captions ok ok ok

a

deleted

comment

5 The Comments Section is the Real World

You are

Willy_wonthe_wha 2 months ago
FAVORITE THING YOU'VE EVER POSTED?

shopping's really in trouble

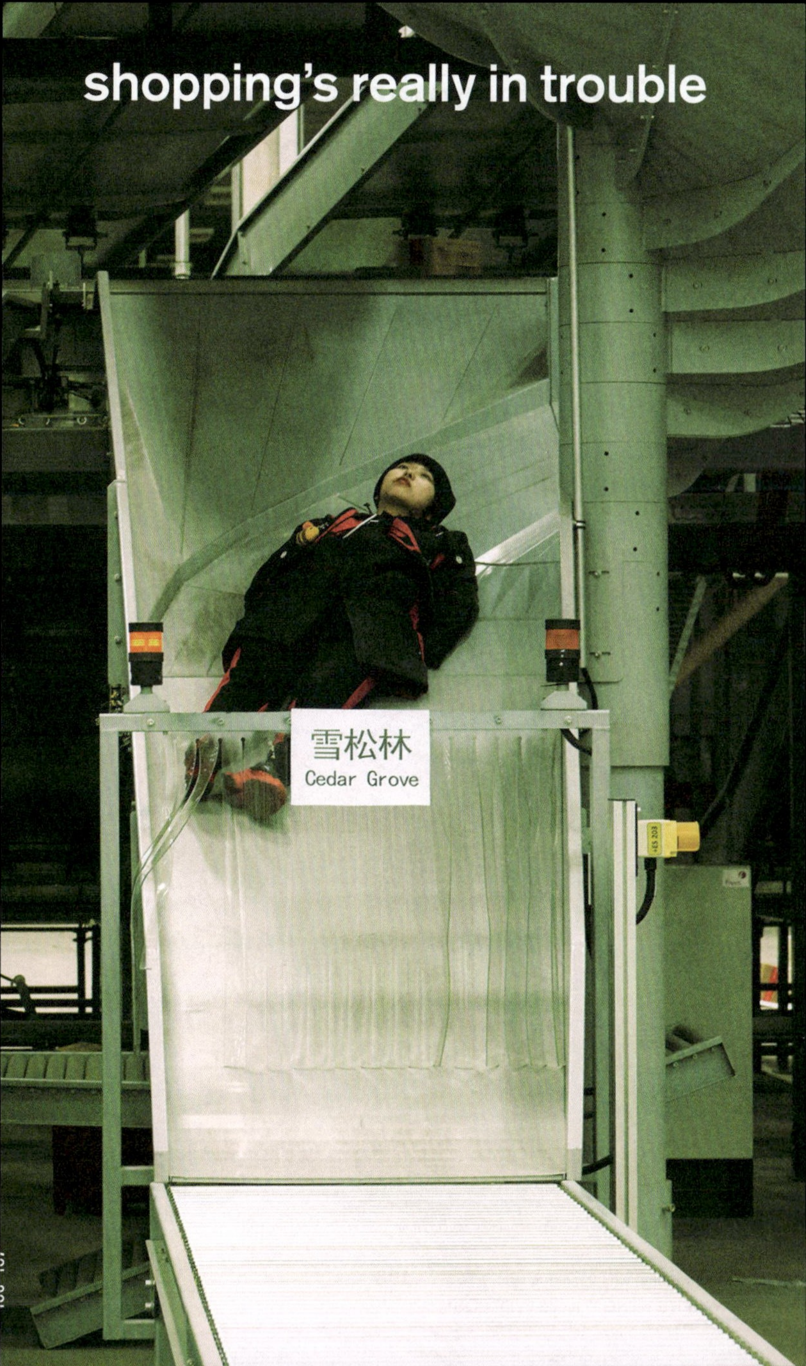

If we all get sick then

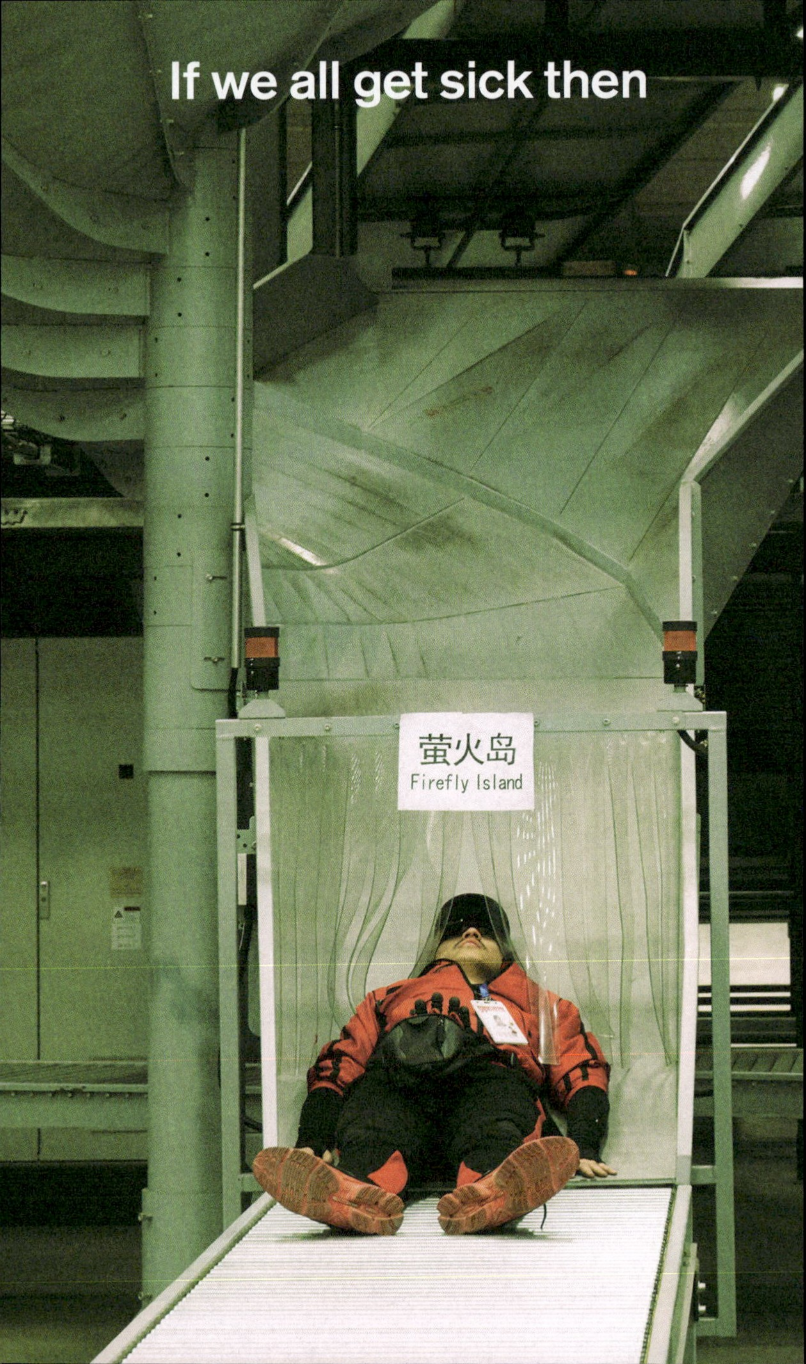

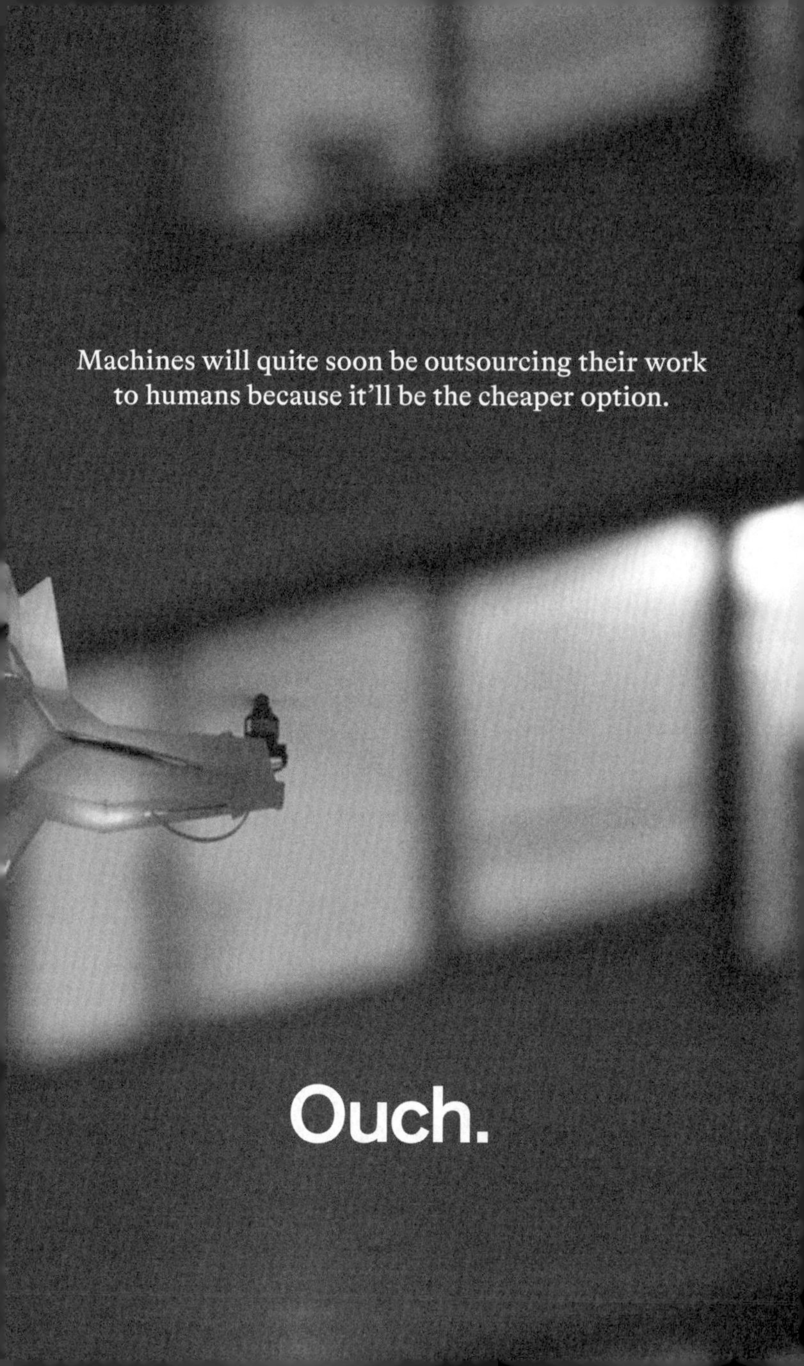

Machines will quite soon be outsourcing their work to humans because it'll be the cheaper option.

Ouch.

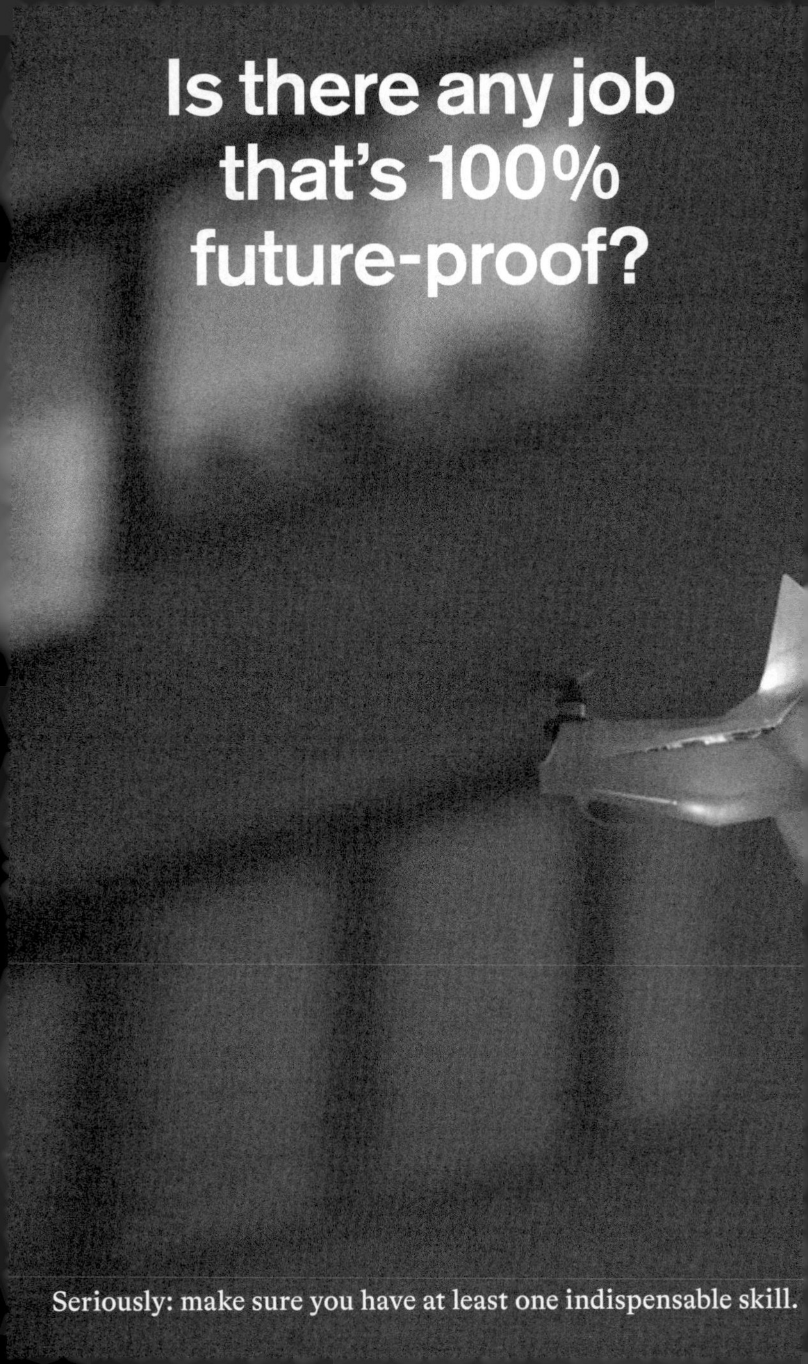

Is there any job that's 100% future-proof?

Seriously: make sure you have at least one indispensable skill.

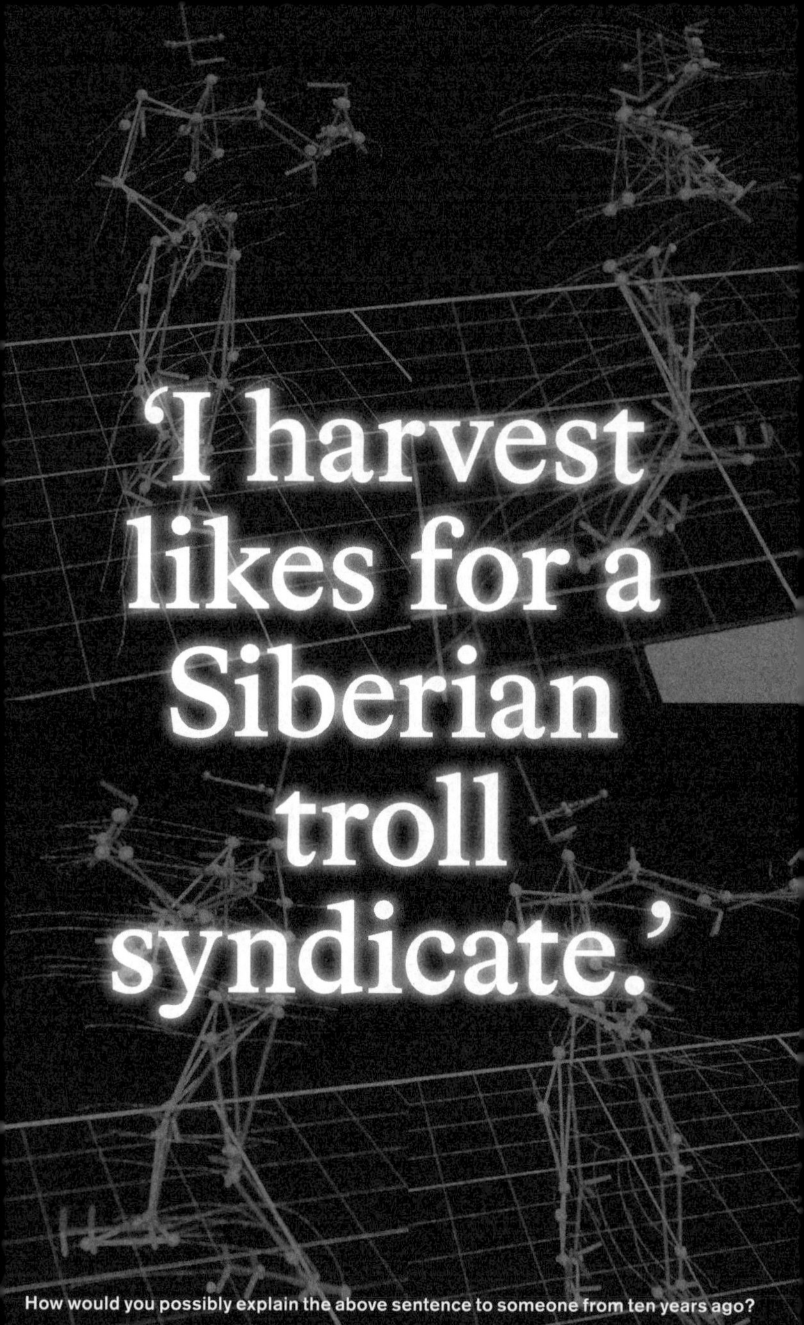

How would you possibly explain the above sentence to someone from ten years ago?

Intelligence no longer confers security

[redacted]

100ocracy

For a few centuries, smart people – who, being smart – more or less ran the world. The flattening effect of the internet has allowed the world to be run by people with an IQ of 100. It is the revenge of the bell curve.

Workers inside the Extreme Self economy only feel comfortable if their labor in some way feels a part of a personal story board.

If a job or task doesn't feel dramatic enough, they're gone.

Unless it's narrating itself, the Extreme Self ceases to exist.

marx_lux_1917 15 mins ago

pay your loyal employees more!

PHYSIQUE 57

Welcome Raja'a Khalid, You are Logged In
Last login: 06/02/2019 16:02:00

Log C

www.physique57.com/dubai | Classes | My Info | Online Store | Facebook | Instagram | Twitter | H

Profile | My Schedule | **Visit History** | Purchase History | Acco

Day		Time	Teacher	Location	Payment Method	Class Type	Status	Web	Payment Ref #
06/02/2019	Wednesday	8:30 AM	Jalila	Al Thanya Mall	DontDropTheBall 20	Amped Up! (Ladies Only)	Signed in	Yes	205067
03/02/2019	Sunday	8:00 PM	Maggie	City Walk	DontDropTheBall 20	F.I.T. (Ladies Only)	Signed in	Yes	205067
02/02/2019	Saturday	10:30 AM	Jalila	City Walk	DontDropTheBall 20	Signature (Ladies Only)	Signed in	Yes	205067
30/01/2019	Wednesday	8:30 AM	Jalila	Al Thanya Mall	DontDropTheBall 20	Amped Up! (Ladies Only)	Signed in	Yes	205067
28/01/2019	Monday	8:30 AM	Karlee	Al Thanya Mall	DontDropTheBall 20	F.I.T. (Ladies Only)	Signed in	Yes	205067
26/01/2019	Saturday	10:30 AM	Jalila	City Walk	DontDropTheBall 20	Signature (Ladies Only)	Signed in	Yes	205067
23/01/2019	Wednesday	8:30 AM	Jalila	Al Thanya Mall	DontDropTheBall 20	Amped Up! (Ladies Only)	Signed in	Yes	205067
21/01/2019	Monday	8:30 AM	Karlee	Al Thanya Mall	DontDropTheBall 20	F.I.T. (Ladies Only)	Signed in	Yes	205067
19/01/2019	Saturday	10:30 AM	Jalila	City Walk	DontDropTheBall 20	Signature (Ladies Only)	Signed in	Yes	205067
16/01/2019	Wednesday	8:30 AM	Jalila	Al Thanya Mall	DontDropTheBall 20	Amped Up! (Ladies Only)	Signed in	Yes	205067
14/01/2019	Monday	8:30 AM	Karlee	Al Thanya Mall	DontDropTheBall 20	F.I.T. (Ladies Only)	Signed in	Yes	205067
12/01/2019	Saturday	12:00 PM	Karlee	Al Thanya Mall	DontDropTheBall 20	Amped Up! (Ladies Only)	Signed in	Yes	205067
09/01/2019	Wednesday	8:30 AM	Jalila	Al Thanya Mall	DontDropTheBall 20	Amped Up! (Ladies Only)	Signed in	Yes	205067
07/01/2019	Monday	8:30 AM	Karlee	Al Thanya Mall	DontDropTheBall 20	F.I.T. (Ladies Only)	Signed in	Yes	205067
05/01/2019	Saturday	10:30 AM	Jalila	City Walk	DontDropTheBall 20	Signature (Ladies Only)	Signed in	Yes	205067
03/01/2019	Thursday	8:30 AM	Karlee	Al Thanya Mall	DontDropTheBall 20	Amped Up! (Ladies Only)	Signed in	Yes	205067
02/01/2019	Wednesday	8:30 AM	Jalila	Al Thanya Mall	THNKSGVNG 15 Class Package	Amped Up! (Ladies Only)	Signed in	Yes	192696
27/12/2018	Thursday	10:30 AM	Jalila	Al Thanya Mall	THNKSGVNG 15 Class Package	Amped Up! (Ladies Only)	Signed in	Yes	192696
24/12/2018	Monday	11:30 AM	Karlee	Al Thanya Mall	THNKSGVNG 15 Class Package	Signature (Ladies Only)	Signed in	Yes	192696
22/12/2018	Saturday	10:30 AM	Jalila	City Walk	THNKSGVNG 15 Class Package	Signature (Ladies Only)	Signed in	Yes	192696
20/12/2018	Thursday	8:30 AM	Karlee	Al Thanya Mall	THNKSGVNG 15 Class Package	Amped Up! (Ladies Only)	Signed in	Yes	192696
17/12/2018	Monday	8:30 AM	Karlee	Al Thanya Mall	THNKSGVNG 15 Class Package	F.I.T. (Ladies Only)	Signed in	Yes	192696
15/12/2018	Saturday	10:30 AM	Jalila	City Walk	THNKSGVNG 15 Class Package	Signature (Ladies Only)	Signed in	Yes	192696
12/12/2018	Wednesday	8:30 AM	Jalila	Al Thanya Mall	THNKSGVNG 15 Class Package	Amped Up! (Ladies Only)	Signed in	Yes	192696
10/12/2018	Monday	8:30 AM	Karlee	Al Thanya Mall	THNKSGVNG 15 Class Package	F.I.T. (Ladies Only)	Signed in	Yes	192696
08/12/2018	Saturday	10:30 AM	Jalila	City Walk	THNKSGVNG 15 Class Package	Signature (Ladies Only)	Signed in	Yes	192696
05/12/2018	Wednesday	8:30 AM	Jalila	Al Thanya Mall	THNKSGVNG 15 Class Package	Amped Up! (Ladies Only)	Signed in	Yes	192696
03/12/2018	Monday	5:00 PM	Karlee	City Walk	THNKSGVNG 15 Class Package	Signature (Ladies Only)	Signed in	Yes	192696
01/12/2018	Saturday	10:30 AM	Maggie	City Walk	THNKSGVNG 15 Class Package	Signature (Ladies Only)	Signed in	Yes	192696
28/11/2018	Wednesday	8:30 AM	Jalila	Al Thanya Mall	THNKSGVNG 15 Class Package	Amped Up! (Ladies Only)	Signed in	Yes	192696
26/11/2018	Monday	8:30 AM	Karlee	Al Thanya Mall	THNKSGVNG 15 Class Package	Amped Up! (Ladies Only)	Signed in	Yes	192696
24/11/2018	Saturday	10:30 AM	Jalila	City Walk	10 Class Package	Signature (Ladies Only)	Signed in	Yes	190517
21/11/2018	Wednesday	8:30 AM	Jalila	Al Thanya Mall	10 Class Package	Amped Up! (Ladies Only)	Signed in	Yes	190517
19/11/2018	Monday	8:30 AM	Karlee	Al Thanya Mall	10 Class Package	Amped Up! (Ladies Only)	Signed in	Yes	190517
17/11/2018	Saturday	10:30 AM	Jalila	City Walk	10 Class Package	Signature (Ladies Only)	Signed in	Yes	190517
14/11/2018	Wednesday	9:30 AM	Jalila	Al Thanya Mall	10 Class Package	Beginner (Ladies Only)	Signed in	Yes	190517
12/11/2018	Monday	8:30 AM	Karlee	Al Thanya Mall	10 Class Package	Amped Up! (Ladies Only)	Signed in	Yes	190517
08/11/2018	Thursday	6:00 PM	Karlee	Al Thanya Mall	10 Class Package	Signature (Ladies Only)	Signed in	Yes	190517
05/11/2018	Monday	8:00 PM	Jalila	City Walk	10 Class Package	Beginner (Ladies Only)	Signed in	Yes	190517
03/11/2018	Saturday	10:30 AM	Jalila	City Walk	10 Class Package	Signature (Ladies Only)	Signed in	Yes	190517
02/11/2018	Friday	12:00 PM	Karlee	Al Thanya Mall	10 Class Package	Beginner (Ladies Only)	Signed in	Yes	190517
29/10/2018	Monday	8:00 PM	Jalila	City Walk	NC 8 Class Package	Beginner (Ladies Only)	Signed in	Yes	187402
23/10/2018	Tuesday	7:30 PM	Jalila	Al Thanya Mall	NC 8 Class Package	Beginner (Ladies Only)	Signed in	Yes	187402
21/10/2018	Sunday	7:30 PM	Jalila	Al Thanya Mall	NC 8 Class Package	Beginner (Ladies Only)	Signed in	Yes	187402
19/10/2018	Friday	10:00 AM	Jalila	Al Thanya Mall	NC 8 Class Package	Beginner (Ladies Only)	Signed in	Yes	187402
05/10/2018	Friday	10:00 AM	Karlee	Al Thanya Mall	NC 8 Class Package	Beginner (Ladies Only)	Signed in	Yes	187402
28/09/2018	Friday	12:00 PM	Karlee	Al Thanya Mall	NC 8 Class Package	Beginner (Ladies Only)	Signed in	Yes	187402
14/09/2018	Friday	12:00 PM	Karlee	Al Thanya Mall	NC 8 Class Package	Beginner (Ladies Only)	Signed in	Yes	187402
07/09/2018	Friday	12:00 PM	Ariel	Al Thanya Mall	NC 8 Class Package	Beginner (Ladies Only)	Signed in	Yes	187402
31/08/2018	Friday	12:00 PM	Karlee	Al Thanya Mall	Free INTRODUCTORY Class	Beginner (Ladies Only)	Signed in	Yes	186841

I want my time back

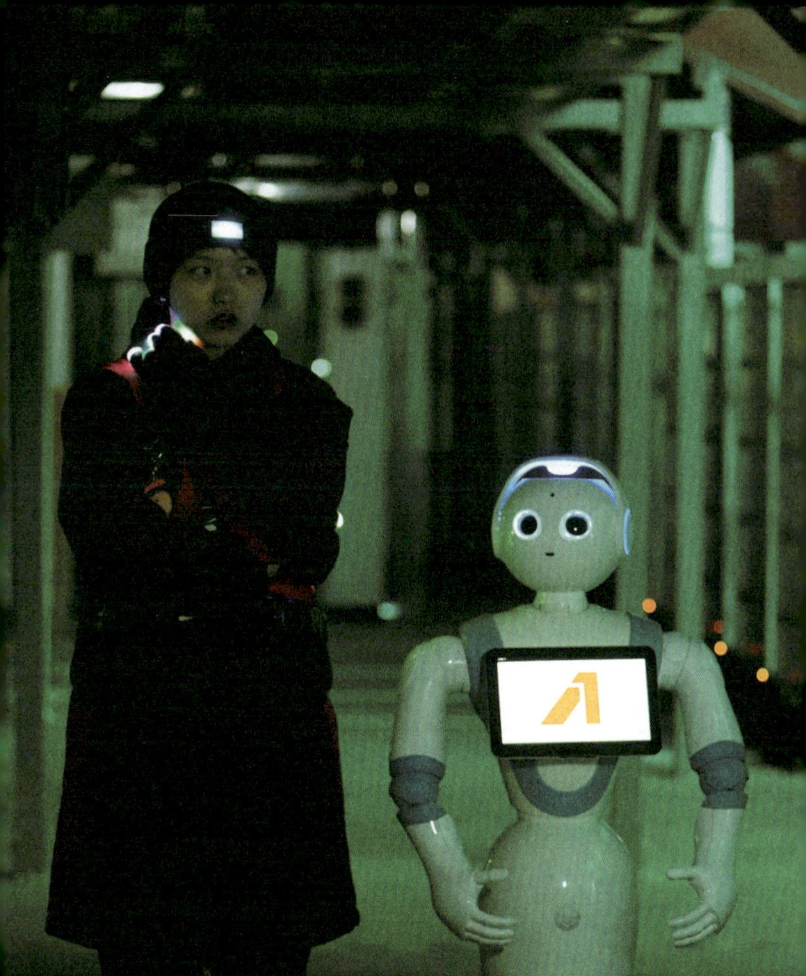

At any social event, one of the first questions a stranger asks you is, **'What do you do?'** Cue awkward hesitation: should you act modest, but run the risk of seeming boring? Or, do you hard sell, like a QVC presenter or TED speakers.

This cocktail party mainstay may soon be a thing of the past. Full automation will be here very soon. What will you do when you don't need to work anymore? What will be your measure of worth? And how will strangers break the ice with you then?

IT'S YOUR JOB INTERVIEW TOMORROW. WHAT COULD THEY ASK?

1 What are your strengths?
2 What are your weaknesses?
3 Why are you interested in working for [insert company name here]?
4 Where do you see yourself in five years? Ten years?
5 Why do you want to leave your current company?
6 Why was there a gap in your employment between [insert date] and [insert date]?
7 What can you offer us that someone else can not?
8 What are three things your former manager would like you to improve on?
9 Are you willing to relocate?
10 Are you willing to travel?
11 Tell me about an accomplishment you are most proud of.
12 Tell me about a time you made a mistake.
13 What is your dream job?
14 How did you hear about this position?
15 What would you look to accomplish in the first 30 days / 60 days / 90 days on the job?
16 Discuss your resume.
17 Discuss your educational background.
18 Describe yourself.
19 Tell me how you handled a difficult situation.
20 Why should we hire you?
21 Why are you looking for a new job?
22 Would you work holidays / weekends?
23 How would you deal with an angry or irate customer?
24 What are your salary requirements?
25 Give a time when you went above and beyond the requirements for a project.
26 Who are our competitors?
27 What was your biggest failure?
28 What motivates you?
29 What's your availability?
30 Who's your mentor?
31 Tell me about a time when you disagreed with your boss.
32 How do you handle pressure?
33 What is the name of our CEO?
34 What are your career goals?
35 What gets you up in the morning?
36 What would your direct reports say about you?
37 What were your bosses' strengths / weaknesses?
38 If I called your boss right now and asked him/her what is an area that you could improve on, what would he / she say?
39 Are you a leader or a follower?
40 What was the last book you've read for fun?
41 What are your co-worker pet peeves?
42 What are your hobbies?
43 What is your favorite website?
44 What makes you uncomfortable?
45 What are some of your leadership experiences?
46 How would you fire someone?
47 What do you like the most and least about working in this world?
48 Would you work 100+ hours a week?
49 What questions haven't I asked you? Why didn't I ask them?
50 Do you really, *really* want this job?

dispensable

You

are

A visualization of my daily mood

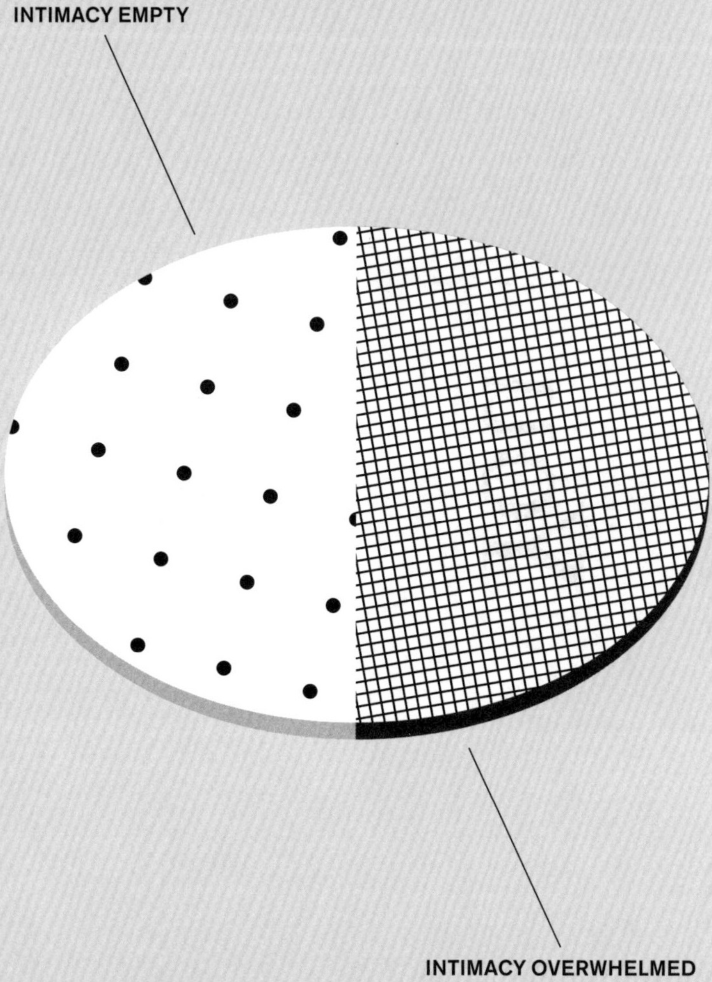

Antoni0eliz 4 years ago

I tell myself I'm shadow banned just so I dont feel the crushing weight of being unwanted on any level by anyone

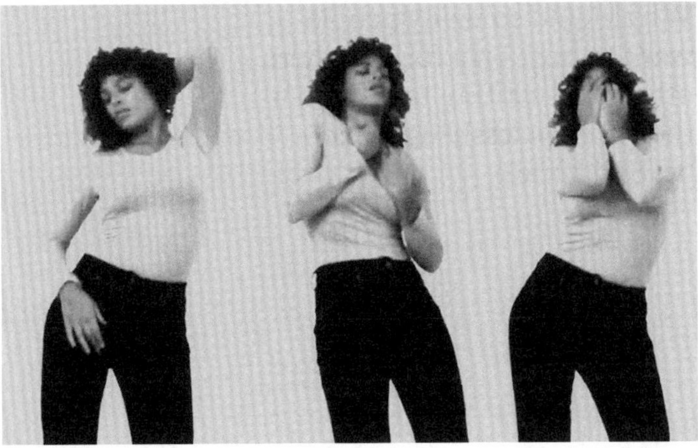

Consent

From the Latin, *consentire*, meaning ‘to feel together’

Why would so many people want to post on a forum where others are waiting to tell them they're hopelessly ugly and beyond hope?

Because...

...Science has determined being lonely is worse for your health than smoking 15 cigarettes a day.

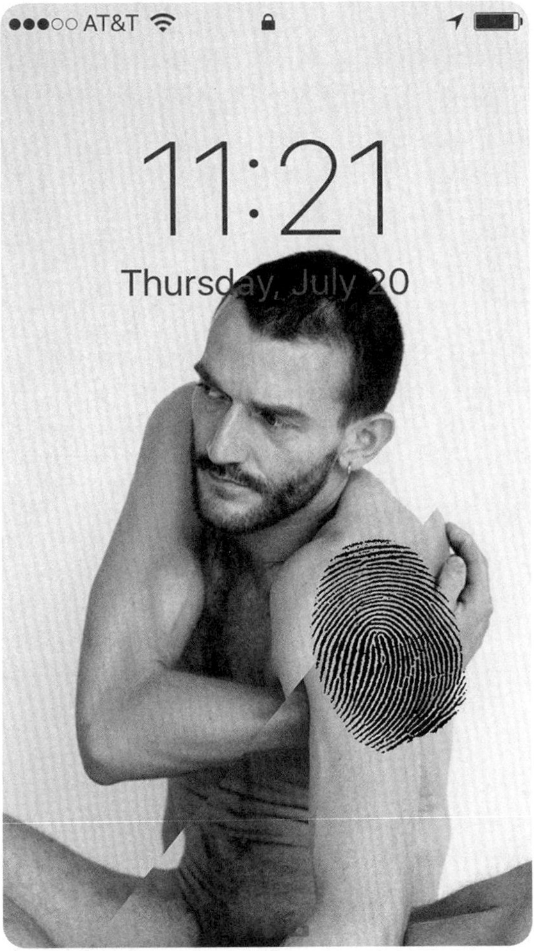

drawingbyscarlett 1 week ago

omg may i draw this lewk

Hobbies include:
doomscrolling, doomscreaming, doomshopping, doomsitting, doomeating, doomtexting, doomsearching, doomcooking, doomsleeping

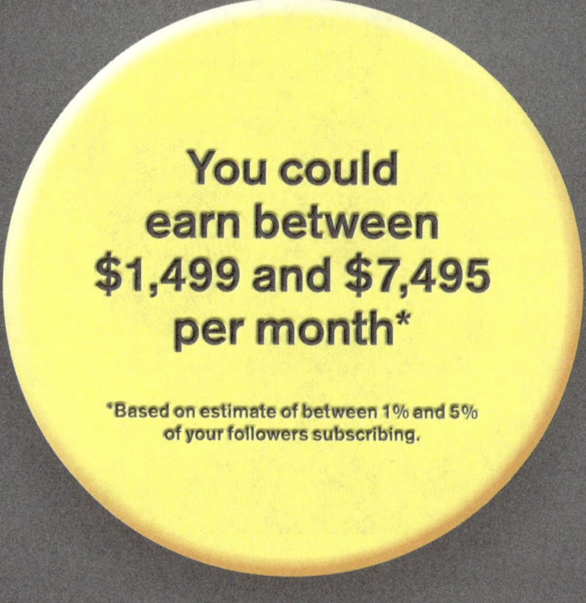

The opposite of vulnerability is no longer strength.

The opposite of invisibility is no longer being seen.

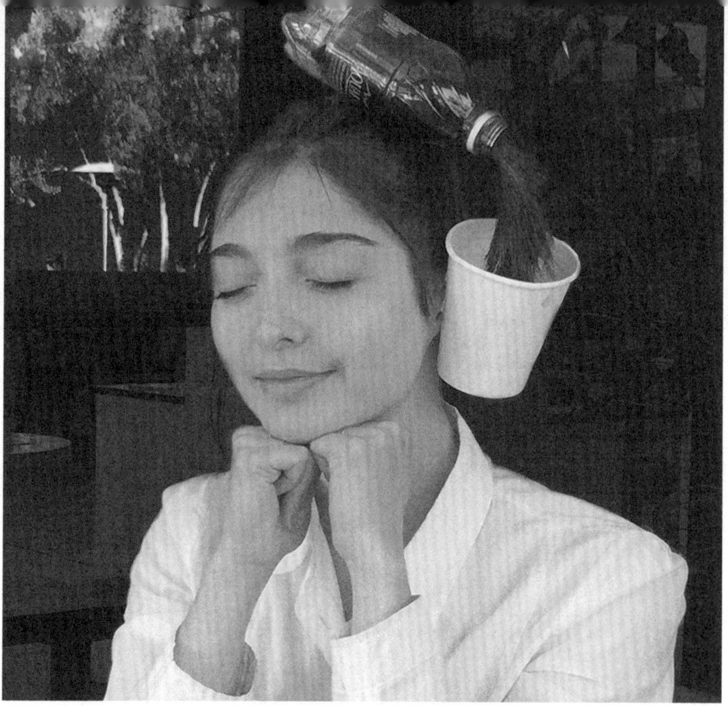

Is celibacy good for capitalism?

Lonely isolated people consume more.

Does monogamy favor the market?

Monogamy stabilizes the economy.

Is polyamory best for business?

Polyamory means more partners means all partners need one of everything which boosts industrial production.

Somewhere between courting and robot skullfucking lies the reality.

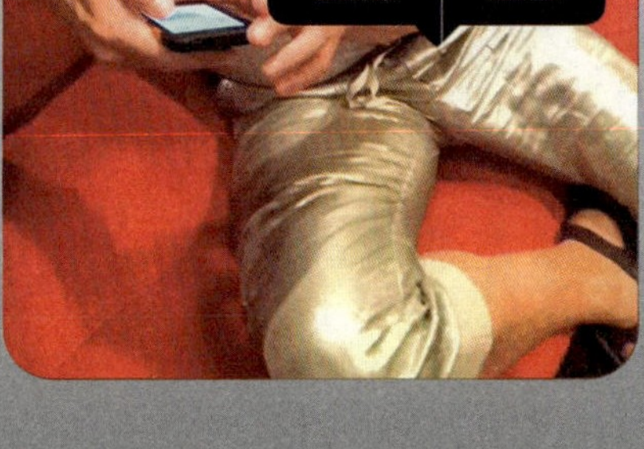

However...
be informed that it is
100% legal to
skullfuck your robot.

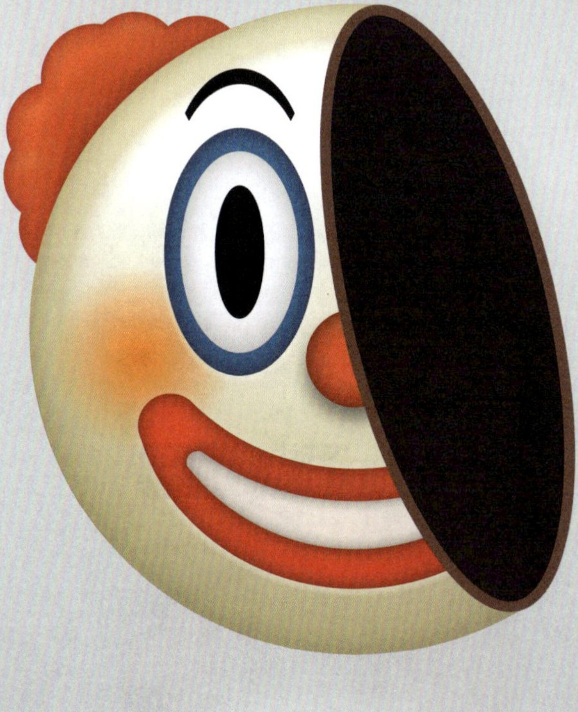

Millions of Chinese men who thought they were conversing with real Chinese women, were, in fact, merely interfacing with clever chatbots. In the process, various companies made hundreds of millions of dollars. Duplicitous as this may seem, one could also say that all these chatbots had passed the famous Turing Test: ‘a test of a machine’s ability to exhibit intelligent behavior equivalent to, or indistinguishable from, that of a human.’ Zheng Jiajia, who grew tired of pressure to get married, decided to wed a robot he had created, called Yingying. Because, there are 113.5 men for every 100 women in China, meaning, many men will never find wives. Could the gap be filled by androids or apps? And will a responsive feedback system ever truly love you back the way you love it?

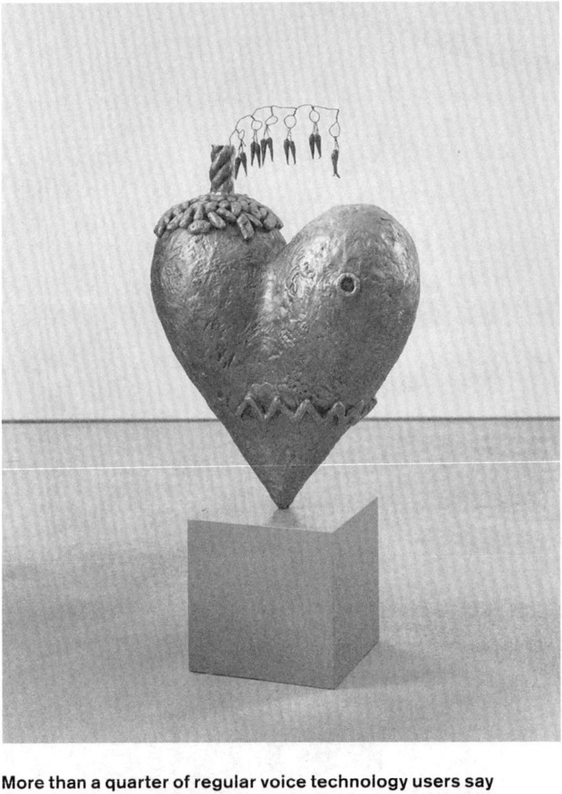

More than a quarter of regular voice technology users say they have had a sexual fantasy about their voice assistant.

Dating sounds as old fashioned as courting.

Chaste, consequence-free messaging, communal laptopping, asexual cuddling and body contact negotiated through legalistic consent dialogs, all followed by ghosting.

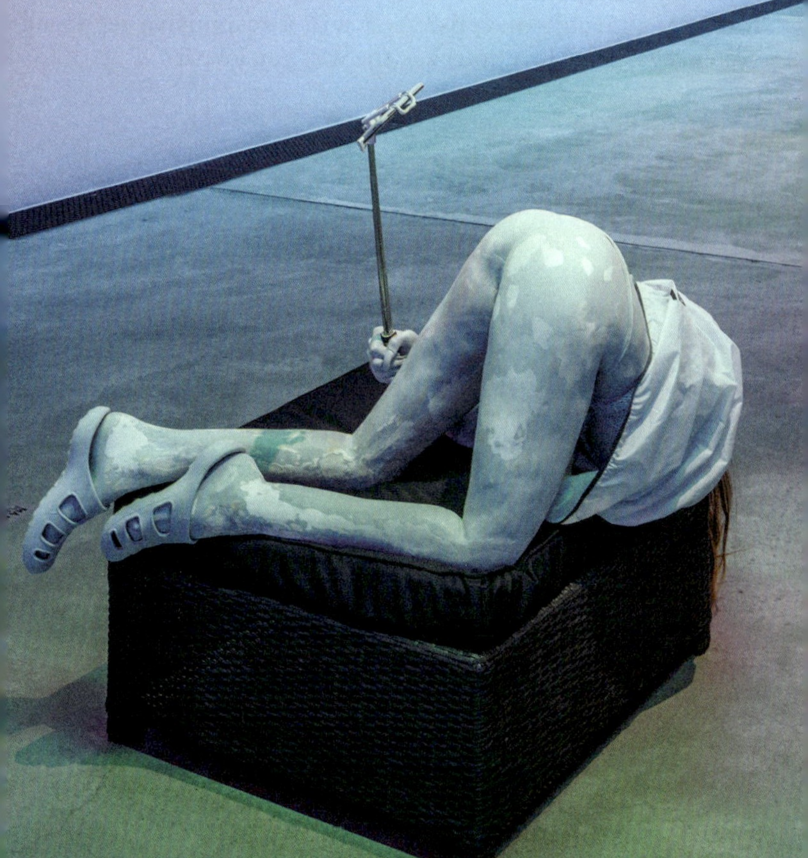

The relationship's never over, because it never really started.

What i

the righ

distance

Howalysa 1 day ago

Please take over my Tinder I hate it

between us

your

profile

pic

3 Intimacy Industrial Complex

You're

nothing

like

You are your face.
You become your face.
You *became* your face.
Or you end up with the face you deserve.

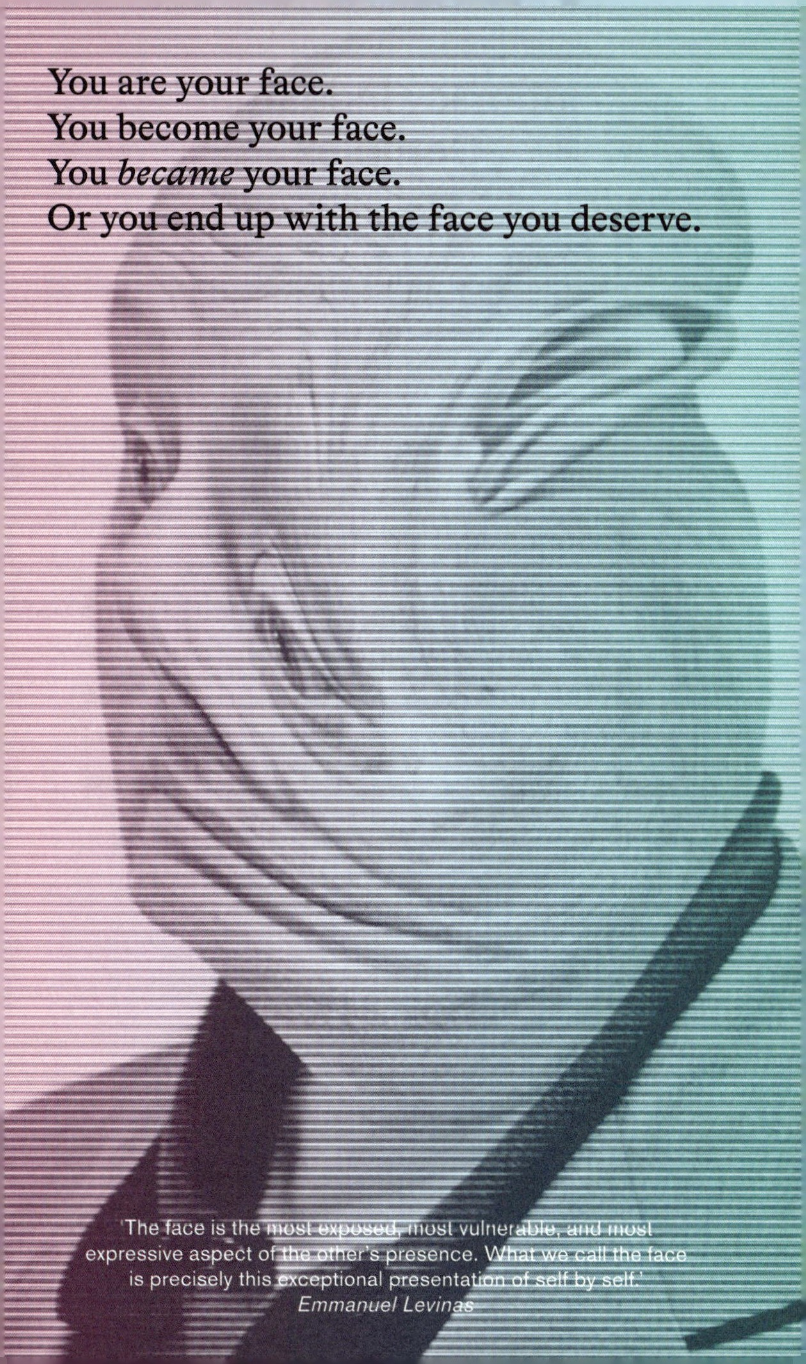

'The face is the most exposed, most vulnerable, and most expressive aspect of the other's presence. What we call the face is precisely this exceptional presentation of self by self.'
Emmanuel Levinas

There's no escaping your face.

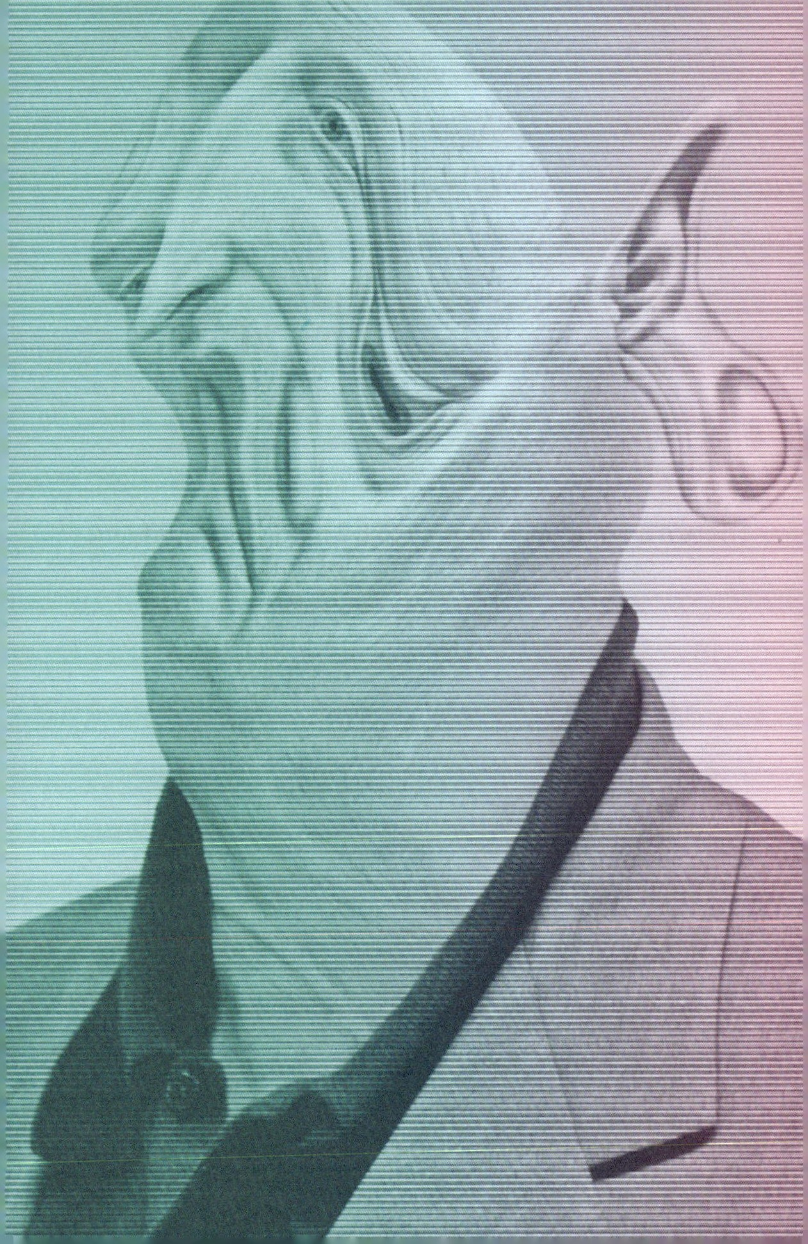

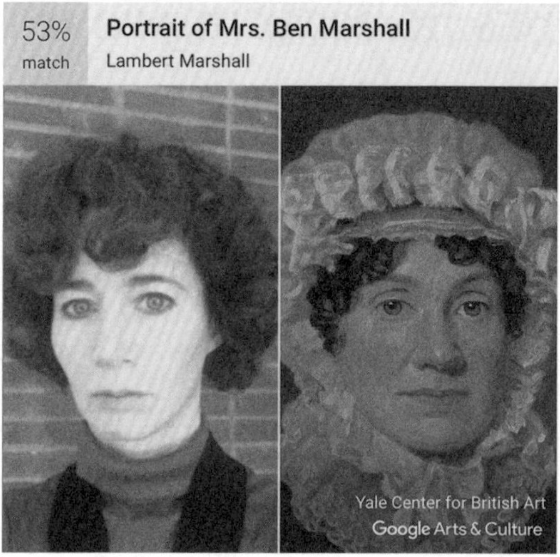

There's a shitload of money to be made in identifying every face that's ever been uploaded.

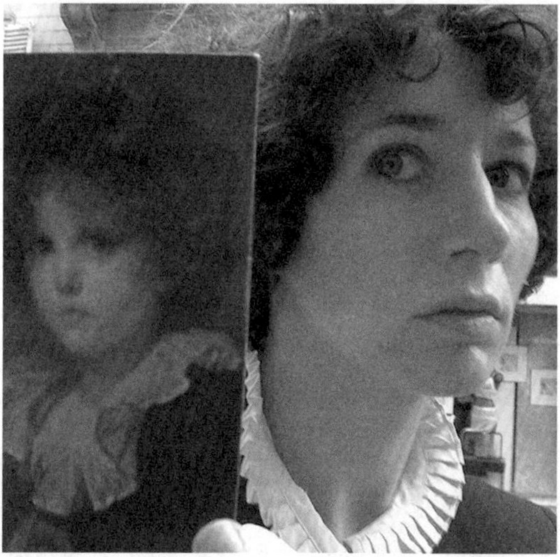

Face recognition technology has been trained to detect much more than what your name is. It can distinguish if you're gay or straight, whether you're likely to commit a crime or if you vote liberal or conservative.

But haven't we been here before?

The 18th century Swiss pastor Johann Kaspar Lavater introduced the idea that 'physiognomy' related to the specific character traits of individuals, in his book, *Physiognomische Fragmente*. He believed that the mind and the soul were connected with an individual's external appearance. In the following century, a U.S. physician called James W. Redfield published *Comparative Physiognomy*, illustrated with 330 engravings of 'resemblances between Men and Animals.' Needless to say, Germans and Americans were flattered with positive comparisons to 'lions' and 'bears,' while 'Negroes,' 'Chinamen' and 'Jews' were malignly aligned with elephants, hogs and goats. This popular pseudo-science became the backbone of Nazi aesthetics in the 1930s: Aryans, good faces. Everyone else, grotesque.

The face is where first, and often final, judgements are made about others.

FACE

DETECTED

Every new technology allows us to unexpectedly give license to parts of our humanity previously considered taboo.

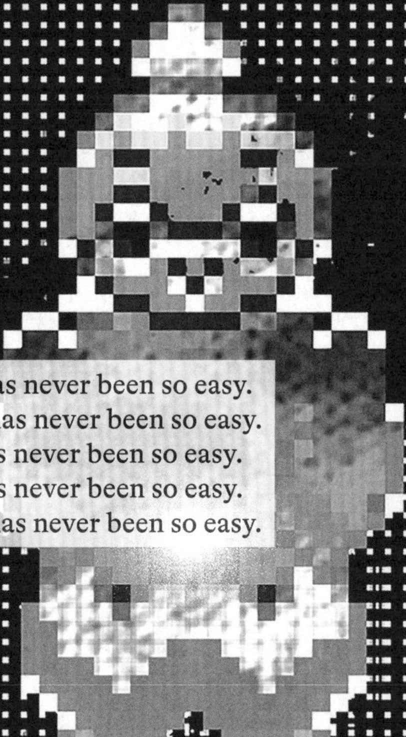

Bragging has never been so easy.
Defaming has never been so easy.
Libeling has never been so easy.
Stalking has never been so easy.
Attacking has never been so easy.

It's a golden age of psychosis.

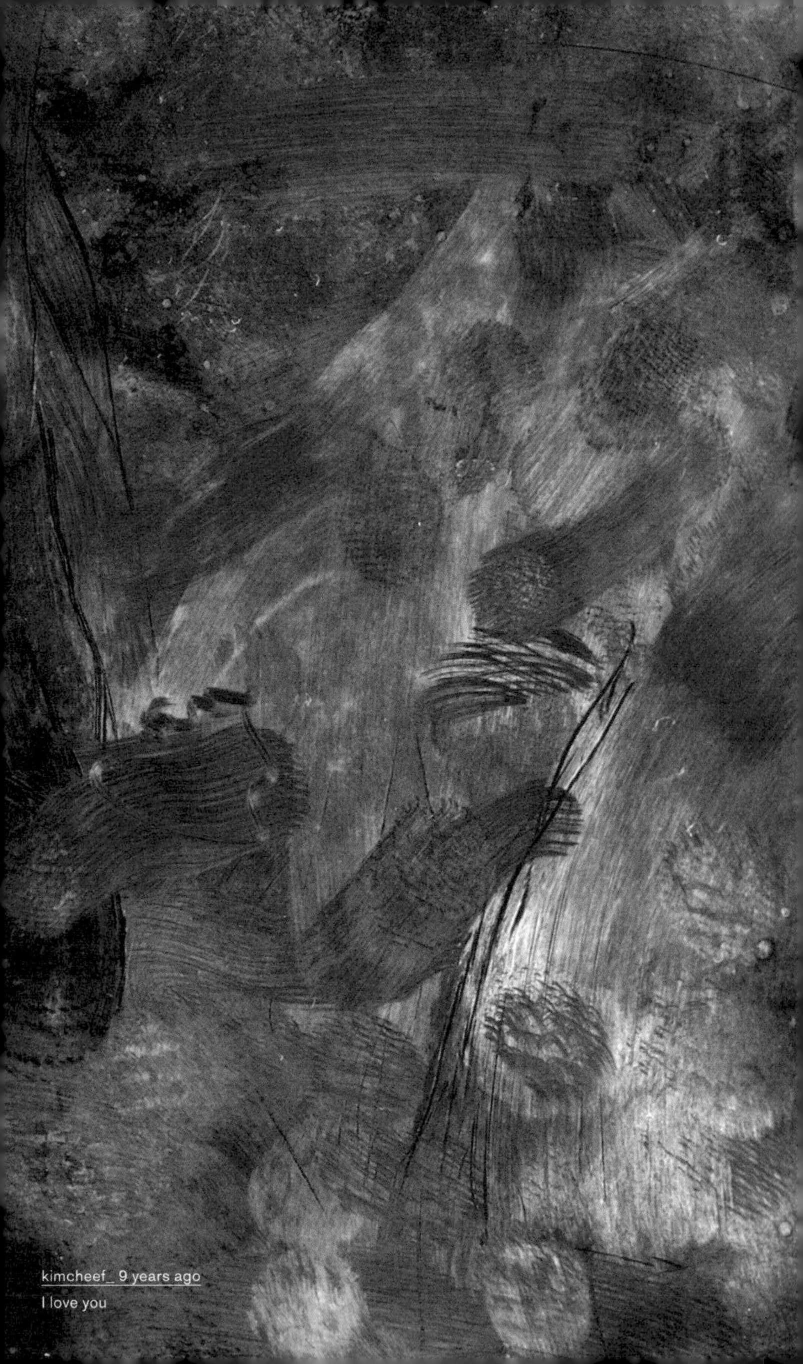
kimcheef_ 9 years ago
I love you

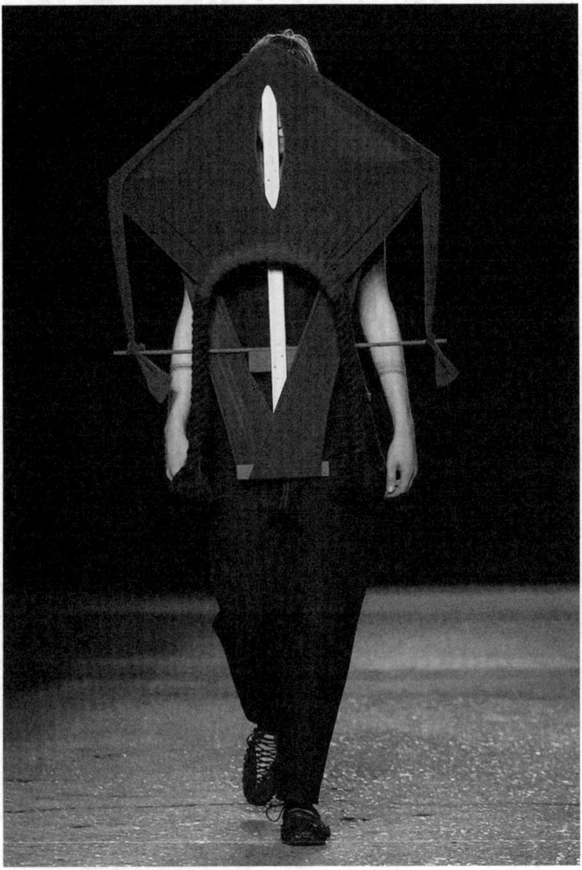

The right to
be invisible is
a fundamental
human right.

Will we invent
new ways
to disappear?

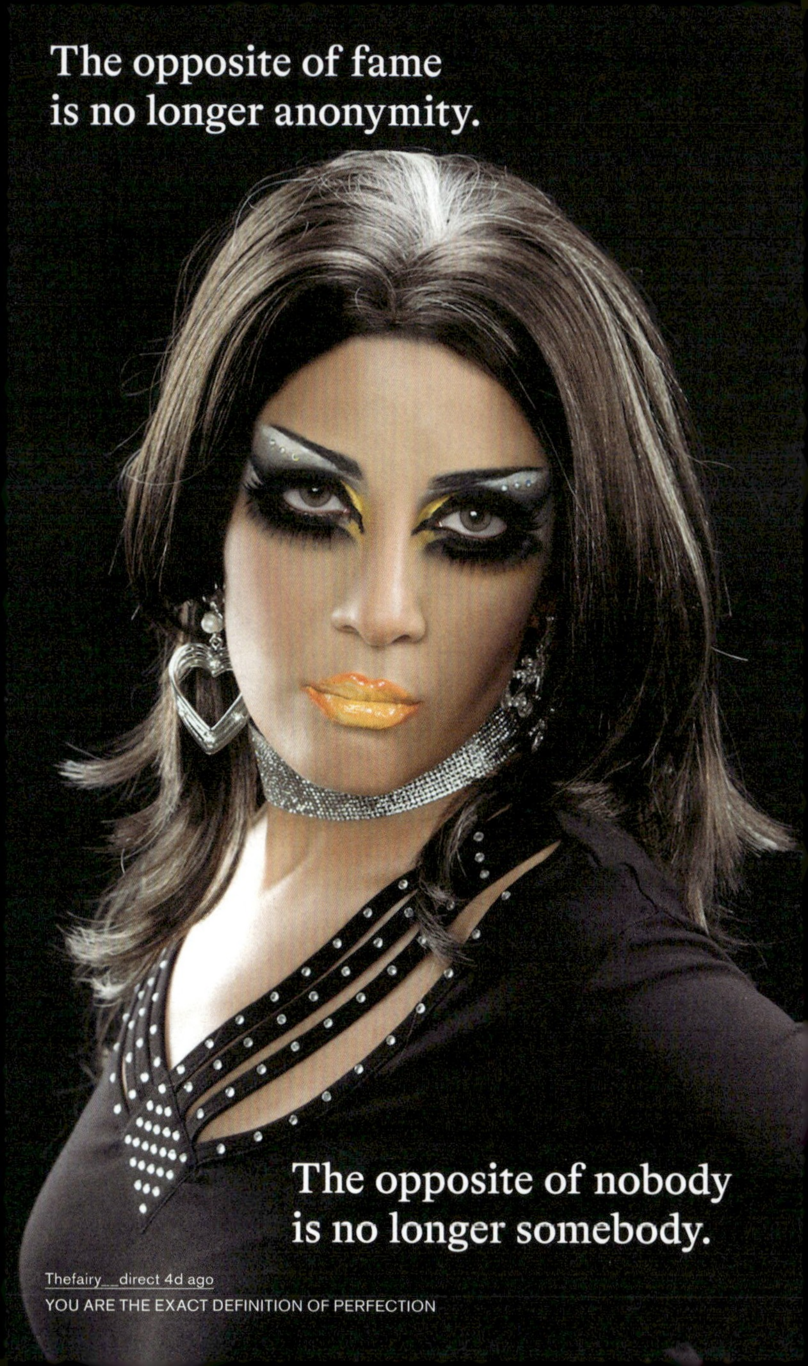
The opposite of fame
is no longer anonymity.
The opposite of nobody
is no longer somebody.
Thefairy__direct 4d ago
YOU ARE THE EXACT DEFINITION OF PERFECTION

Dysmorphia of the soul

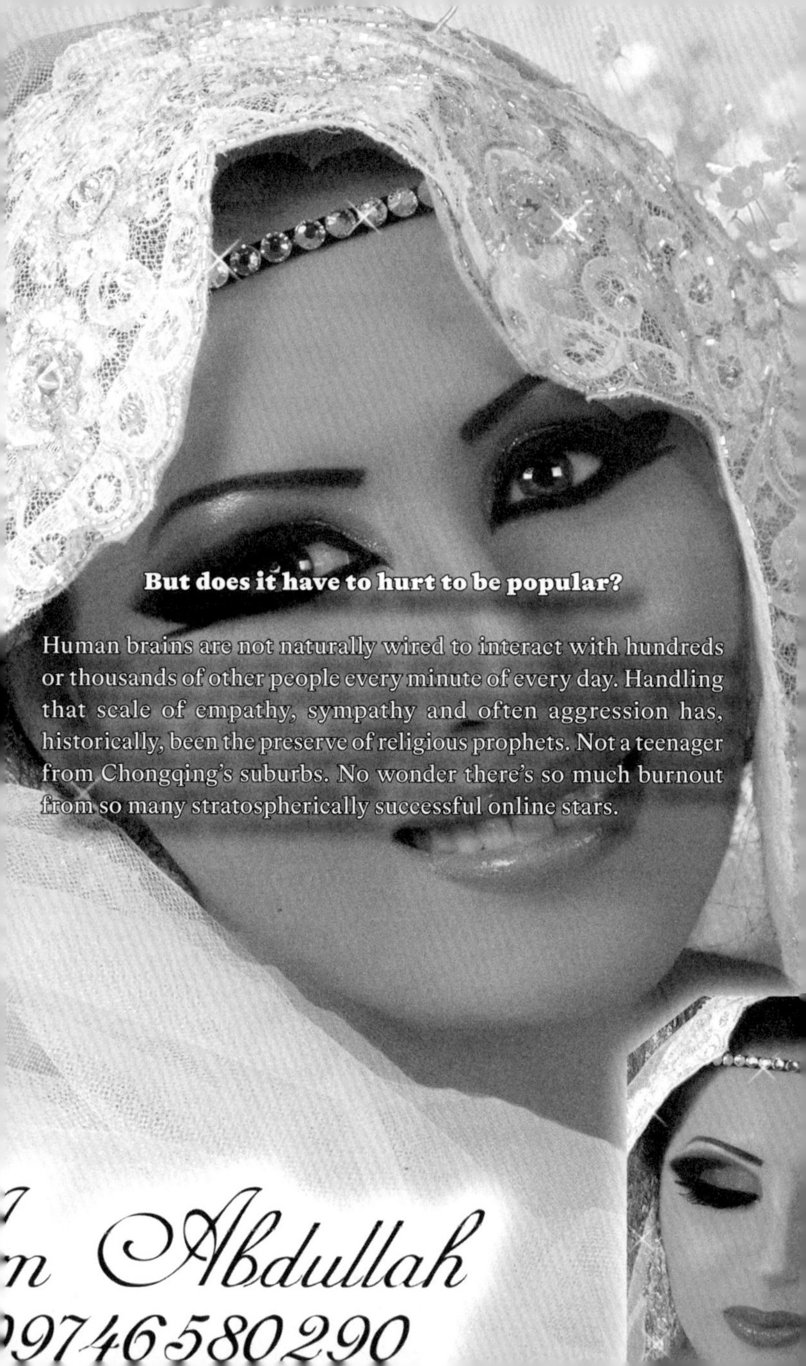

But does it have to hurt to be popular?

Human brains are not naturally wired to interact with hundreds or thousands of other people every minute of every day. Handling that scale of empathy, sympathy and often aggression has, historically, been the preserve of religious prophets. Not a teenager from Chongqing's suburbs. No wonder there's so much burnout from so many stratospherically successful online stars.

Eye brow	35
Upper lip / Lower lip	25
Chin / side / neck side	25
Eyebrow and upper lip	50
Half face down	60
Half face up	30
Full face w/o eyebrows	80
Full face w/ eyebrows	100
Under arm	40
Half arm	45
Full arms	75
Half leg	60
Full leg	100
Half stomach	45
Full stomach	80
Half back	50
Full back	85
Bikini line	50
Half bikini	75
Full bikini	85
Half Brazilian	95
Brazilian	110
Back side	30
Full body	230

All prices in United Arab Emirates dirhams

ect eyes

t lips the

the perfect

ect nose the

perfect butt the

nose the perfect

the perfect butt the

nose the perfect eyes

the perfect kiss the perfec

The perf

the perfec

perfect butt

kiss the per

perfect lips the

kiss the perfect

eyes the perfect lip

perfect kiss the perfec

he perfect lips the perfect l

She said her followers drive her to post more pictures of herself.

She deletes the ones that don't instantly please.

She wants the crowd to curate her image.

She doesn't know them but she trusts them.

She's molded by their unfiltered preferences.

She knows exactly how to make the algorithm love her.

Does my skin look too real?

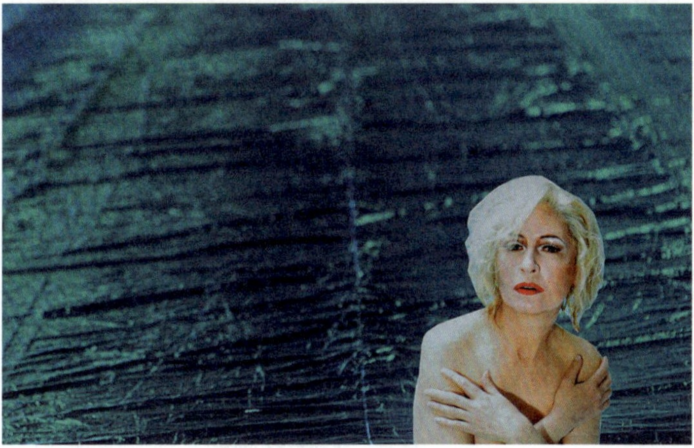

The now unstoppable stream of celebrity deaths ruptures the smooth shimmering skin of modernity.

hWzkmBywSA60Uj9mErgl4+/0Y2/YlfC+YxIkY9I T3vE03Ecbg8+lMhMqkM4b3+ZKcDHPoKQjJ5x5gsvUngsOuDj/mZC467zweau0y1Big8tQxMHolKOhY
eJhS8uMbmTGpkSMtCXHnLtxWmDd2xVEyORbteovrKODq9QLhfJojanzDhfTs36ExzEsfnsxhc/ppARz++DLvxP+goNjBXT/5Ltn0R5vQTCYzEsQM07r/
FUaUnYmTTYXpDadp7eklbck0OWFMZYiixnFUNdShx9sJt28m2tWBnR3ikWdfJBkb5KxjFuD3OfH4/FTU1bPprTWsXrWR92fVYje7ebo9Qp8u4JElnG43ku
wkm86RTGZRFA8eRaDbUKmvnsA9kwSqy4rxn3oGPbPH0jymkUNb1mIbcfx1pQREgxLZJFSusOPQsfz21IWIZx7NCY1jKHp5J/23vExXzqTLW0f/doFfLk7SG
8/847LbMDcvl8uhadpnsuGA2+3n69ffz4M/uYB7rr2C8665gaBX/BCllmWNbHIwbLb/FdFTEbraWtmwo522cI7jz/oWR86oJp3eScjScJeMora4mlR8ENnpx6+AL
+gDYNu23cyeMpUir4Ntm7eybucuEBox9rbzbD6IvrKHI0I5JjQ4MUQnmWyGfDaHy+dFF6BSSPGGdzrRyomMeu8Oxi1s5tAJMiGjj72lNj1VbvYqOdxOnSHDZ
I8vxsGlEieV6fTkNd4qKmZJZQP+b9TRnIshjK+jfkWWdaoGOVjdpXFi4J/kicNAiqL4Ib78vyJet5uzrriJ9tXPcvt/XfahYoAoiqiqOpK+/CsE1xEQI3088/pKtoV
zFDVMRyms5azLryTb+BX62nbikHMgOvA6XAiaBpkUwgdF6Wx8gAIhh6S4adu1A8UrwdQqijdspOGddnA7CAk58ATQLZucZqJbForTRZmYYTUhOkoO4v2
9SR6WGng4HuJrb7fxxw057l6R5KWVUdbsNFm3W2P9rhyvLktzzaocp67sZnOxxsWjJCbLNi/mbd6vKEWWTIJGZh8hUhIZssxPVrH5KLbsvyqFZTX85/88Q2r
by/zuiqv56+qcqqqf6bZbjz/4AMvDMjfefi+bW9bgdfk58+wf0eZsZisTSQ71o5Y699HS8kmwTYYy+8x5yCOjCBDp6yWWzVJVWM38KRWUBfrZmdkKgols5V
G9HixZJJnOEdd0JDNNzBS52z8PGxevborze/8czKEQxdsj+CMickykLmtTrLlw5iSCeZFQUoFBJ4NbVK5/Z4hbshmSlkF46SbErijxrEG1TwDLgpCFEhA++wL4/
khl4wQuvfNxut5/kNuuvulDf1NV9TPZ3iTTs52EBhf8+HbGjJvGUGcfJZUBnnz8OazYElef9hWueynJ/bc+grtYQZHAzGukU2lqiivIZjSyOIgmMqQzecyCChYW
+zj/oCpOO3sMhNLEEkM4nSKJWIxoIoGmWZQ6czydamJS+Qweej/Gki4flBeCFmZKEbjcbjANBFMHl4rT6UB22Ch+CbBAc0BeYmy6gLcf28yKvRuQa0VkL
zSNFghOFGmsMZniFj+bT1H/EpDjZnLpbfdz66UXcM+vg1z0o29+djc3TPZ2RDjxe9dxyZV34simiPU2cvRhEzmt5X3O+/oVdPd2M+HgWdx3Xydlo8JMV3oJu
CSqPCbRgAMH5Zi2RCKbxdJ0Onetxnt8PeUVo7jz4InM9PWjrpvC7p4oZk5HtMCMbGWTPp219kGc6RXpiQFuFSGqYYeTjC0OYJhuYukMJNMkJAnbFsn
rH7Rs9KchICKVKjRYEvNCBvJMF80FBqMKVUb5daS0l+5ODUfKhKIvUROHpWbqEVxy422sePRK/nj3U//y/UzLwtDybNmxmz8uaWVwMMpJ80ezYu
VaQqEAu7b2sHbFKipqSrjsyt9x3onTee6xX/DKLhdd5YeQskROmVnDGGccr0vGyiQRLPD7PXhycR694UHe748TKPEzryTAjlt+ReDYH+CbexYFM45jwnlXsE
Q8BKPlwlMg0mLHodzGdqehKkvlBB+DBTqV9QYVDTYl9SLOkI5YKGBUyeDVwZmkzqlSKVuUjw5wsFxAMGfgQMQjSFS7JSynRNgUPr5i80VLqGYcNT
UhHr/h+3gqZjJqbP2nvte6NduQbZ3lK7fzgytuIBoe4sKzT+bX9z5JW/cgJxy7kJtue5CbrruYI+bP4b9/cjvtPX24XBZnn3c6ye4utNb1VJUUkJccCIqbTCxKMpPCK
huHElEZM9RPZ7KFlzftYvrY8VSPbkAsqsFdM46yunFokSh1E6C+uoiwnWdihcpon8ZB4xxcPr2CoK2yUEoxJR9h+pTR1BU7qXMDlozsyrK3xuQ/xpZweEEIRc
+RCkfQ66soKCggb+is6cmwLS1i5hKMD4nIDldW5gCQqcddyDdjg9x11X+geF9lwRHT9+v6Z15dSdueHurrCrj6xvu5/KKTuee2K9ixo4emsbU88+CN3HPfc8yZ
O5Fbf3sVv7n5Uc4+ayFOvxePqnDp98/lm1c+zEJrPUeMqie8rZ0yZ5698Ryi6kMWUhSZe7EPOYojDp+NsnYlr29qx7zAIjE0RDKeQFAURFlhEnFc/gqKnDJn
qyppUyChKBQHXZTZTpKqQJEl0KLZiIKAV3QjyDrTXW5UycMZkws4Y7yHl5a3kl7fAm++SS7Ry5EHz0cK97L56W5eXZ2kOyDwtXtOgAkhDggQAeZ89Qr
iQ33c/u3jsO9+jcMWTvmkKT0PPPkqA939XH7xafzl/Y387sZvccSRMxg98yJ6wjdz83UX0dLezc+u/B2HHD6Phx58ltKaAIcdPIntLW288MK7DA4lKRhfRKiq
CO9AhqJkgoFojLFTDmbVe0uItHciVw0SPnUBsdqpNAfX4rWzZLISoiQjKgpi3iAiKRT4QhQ7nSRdLsIZk6go4Xa7sI08hikQSIbxRPpwZFPoWhDJsBG9XqwK
mbluH1vvepjIhjzq9l6K33kKx9BcmsZNQPJ6WDCmjkBiAM3jZm0uwOwvM7D5KDnm0luJD/Ty0DUX41b/h1nzJnyi67595uFYlk1jQy03/fR6utr6O4aImdnWb
JsHYpkc89dV/Kbm59gSizK8eefQFlxORdddCK/vuVxfn/XY9x4yxXMDvWw489/pKSqimS0n1A0QnlJCFdhFSu39ZLf0Md3B6M4GoIkEk2oJgguBUuycJYWM/
TEYp6/61Fm3fx9dvcNcP+zu4gnUmR7Y0w9rA5vh8yyPTLTOvt5c/k6Dmqs5cTSCEtb2nl2t0JYE1jy5xjfkto47aQLeaZuglYKJ9uaatnRNA6f28UGh8nycQZJXaZ
3r8bsGcaX7xP/ViYsPIX+dS/w/psrqWiaTUmp/x9+7ejs7Gdnexiv28XVv7yXApfM9GkTyRoGJx4+AxUHY8fUML55NCvX7+KNN1fxgwtO5oWXllFfV8ZAJEV
XeytTp85g54pVNIjdmLqObGTIRQfp6IvRFc4wfdoUWiMKillCwYw6UvEoC2tL0RUV2zQw/AH863YhPPgQxX432qY+Op7ZSl3XIE2pJJnqMdzSWsbbQwGec
49lQ90iXvZV4wy56XU5sEr9fC2k8trtS8l97VAmnXAY6xNZAm6ZzoCH5qZa/Apkc3n0nMWcoE5GylESlLIHHIgIIuUTZ9G98nE2LN+I7iigofGjN7jL5HQee24l
m7Z1UF3s5Jc/+y21o6oJFvi59pf3csEZR/DnV5fz4l/eY/60cSx9dx2P3HcvC486nKkT67nj7seZNWcKnT0DdO5p48VluzjuvPOwHB7MQDUlU46ieOxUapuauez6
m6go9fHkb+5ncOyRbIqbXNTkJK+6sEwLSTLIGk5W2AFGHzsd39hJrPDVoE0Zgzl+DM96gyT0Agj4wCtB1gkxmXfr07x+TB0nlFbyklTHtPGVJL1ZDhlTzK5
UlMPSe+my+qiYWE9hgZcHWrPctS3FmkSWF/bqaIp9AIII+AMhFNVHZNtifv67R9i1N8LRRy3A2rUF0x9ClPZlRht37+X+B17kD9d/nZIiN/1RjW+ccwyjGir5/
b3PUlpayuZdu3n+xWWccdLhHLlgGpoYoKmxntNOPQwNBS2TY+Ehc3h3+Xrmz2tmztHHo1ZPxiwfT6hpGoU1DVQ3TSCZzLLg0Fl0h7vQoynCBTNpUPoZV
1tMMquDIqLEM3T2hHHMG0+4uJzVaQG1NEDOEjhjgpPWeolorwh6iICzn69pD3Ph+HH8qcsmbGY5ZbQHT0eYn8WypE0vS7Ym6FrVz22runHWNlDqLGDj
nhxvrbOJ9lvQJzIoHKAgApSMGsedD7/A6yuWsXLFRuztW1joSSD29xMTPTiDBThkEd0Cn9PB8pUbWbW+he9dcBIOlwNDd1BbV8ohM8ci4uSQ+VMZO66
BcDjGY08sZcr4esY11zP/9Kt4+bU3aBxVwfw5s+nq6IFsioBTIpeMYhn6B5/EJGwT5i+cT+uG93hl0CbgDrFokp/kB6378WiUXbFWpk6rxeN2sSmRIE2WNpdN
jU/nv8oClJQKdHZ1IzTa3NDoYXtXJb9cm+PIURnmdu1l8YDJk/0eqmUBZ9rG3ZIkvLufsvENTKsqRdGyPNdtYosigqGTcFsHLoiiAONmHMSbry9lcGgvb2/
dTOvuTial+rEcfvwTJuB2OVm9tY+OPZ088ucXeOvdVSw69GCeev5NHnrwKQ47bCbHHrOAt95ayyuvvsdBkxppae/mN7+8h6zqZP70ZmrrSvB5nUQGh5gzczI/
uvZO2ru6OOeMY4kn04iSjCTJyLKEaZkUhXzEuvfSu/FF4mOmcky5D1EAr1+lZd0gP3pwJd6pjawZVLn5uR42t2XpahXoLfDzq8PqOLxtD01736K+toC+hkX8e
XOEW2c7yHdonPDnNE+liyAeobhQIpcyCGTTxPoHUJqLmVRbTkC1Wd+epW/IBEEAp5kVOYClaVQ9T/zqSsaXeDmosR7bpzKounBlaeLxfd1g9SVO5s
0dQ21FDTdd9U2aJjawdtMW9uxezto1Wxjoi5PMZHjy8dt44tmlnP2Vozj+gq/wwG1/5OmX3uUHF57ENf91MTXV1VRVFXDMkXOoqS6nbyCM4pBHCEyCl
CB1EoYJBSU1nD21gbNGu1m1oxunqqCh4xVVCuIBMn0GUr8OQwIYDrBCVLV3wWuLWbKjnYLZ07j84PEsKI3y27PcLO/McMm7JoPFlQ
i2BHtjrE72ES82SDldOE2Z3YNJejM6sigyqVoGdwZhnIKrSTqwUowPZ3+g71zHBL/MmreX4HQ5Yaib+K4eYkPdJJ++E88F/0V9QwNP/+lpNq5YzcXnXEl5W
RFHHDKXyc3jOGTOBNauXs/55x5HJBZlzrwpOL0ummqrWN1QyoRxlTz4xOv88teP8Z2LT8AyBaZMbOTs0xfS1dWPaVnIkvK/tUnLQhAhksqSsm0W+IPsHm
hDNw1sHTx+J6UFDvRsBs1pg2ojuFTskhKSr7zIz/9wJ3NefJTZU+eRjA8yVYFXYnBzaxh0N5IAlmnjDxlMKxOYP1Gh1OVld9hgs7ePwkINt2Jz2BSFdlNiUYV
CQbXMAa2JthYHW8YpOtByGqnBCPHBVpzBEIqRZMvLL9AZS/P4E8+wedsKFi9ZwT13/pnbfn8fgwNhjjxqAZ3d3YyuKeScc05l2+YWVqzeTV93hDcX/56jj
pjD4nc2sbNlB/NnNpLKavgCbmLRNJYlIEkitm3ts+2AbdpIAohde3jv8WW8uLWPmc0V5PIGMhK2bNNra8RMiUgyB4aAbauQNSDoZW59I/
meKJ3hAXwBD++1G/RvynH25ABMUTAzWeyMRZEqM0nz06wUcFyDlwunlPKdQpkpfpM6l8QZlT7ODwYQogZTPC4OWJ8oAEKwhEzfTqltq8kO9OAMFl
M0YSKx7l4SkRjhbZsZPWsSBZXVKLbKD757GrFkjkce+TOqy8mE5vFcde0NNFZXkDUc/PfPb2XDrk7auzu56MxjGIqkeW/lVr5y8kJmTm4mm8lSXlHIKe
f9AkW2OeLQGSQSGWxsBBv4oN/nvbVrCLWpOD0hDjt2EvFEGklWEfNptqV68E+rleeR2KJlkasVvAUao+eVcvU5J+F5fQs7unbybL9JJB8kh85sVaSi0MkKM
wF5D/LQdiI71rJLEZk6tokmTSdhaVSPG4usuJFUiIpuNvXrdOaiB25gAyBIKmL/TmRLQ3eoIKpYmo1h56gePw1nfwcGMne/sQc7m+R7l5zHjj2dKGoh993xQ3r
CSe6/70EsI8f0g2fR3hNjMBzlIp9dTHFhMctWbsLrlVAIcP5lNzHQt4dDDprFVVfeTWltiFOPPYRYPIUg2GAJlJWGeP+9ZWyMJLEXnM6JU4J4ClXyeQNNEP
HZFo2DXRzUFKC+sJiQJXJatZeTgwpNBSoDJeVMm1CO77VefvjTd9kQSDJ6VClur5fqqElVuYuNc/3w4jP4X7gH+Z0ewqUOgt0plqxahdpURUaTEGyNt9tSPP
H2LgYXv3Jgg7jPpGrI6QRGIIjocoKsoARDWLJE4cRxvPb2Hq7/zZ2MHT2KfMbkm9+/isGhMD/47vnc98irCBb09PXyk/++gFnTJjEUztDXF+M3f3iG8RNr+c7
XTmLiuEp+d99TrHz9dZomTOXE0w/j0NnjkJFBsBEQwLYoKPTzwFMvIAopipqnM31iEDOVx7RtTBHkrMlQWwcVY8pACBCJ2pQ5VRAUSn02c6td3DFYw
H1aMdcVuei8/01ejbQx99BD6BRMDh2lc/3YBlY/9yIDUYXKRedT0r6LGSve5Z3FfyKYsigYzMHGTWx7cRvJp7fynfHFn+4rxjAv4oswqWL9ZEwVgpkEmq2Q
SsRxuf24SoM8+vu7+M71f2Dy5Hn8+NJzefa199ByQ3zjwgu58bY/cff9T1JVpHL2WacR8PrpGWinr7ubY849lhuu/R19sQjjGxqprAzw1nO38fZb79PV18cV55yN
1+1h7YYWCov9WLZNWUmQF597j7Xrelk/djI3OVIUSR56LRvTMFC8HhItA+zu6KZQmkR/xmZQM8nnbTLZLK9FwuAcRNkmsCZdyHXfOp7zSsvQrr+da
wr/h+/99yJqguX4U1CqBnlDtLGmVlPirccZn06z7SEwbgoT5s/BSAxyeLHNUFDnqan1n2K/02QSQRDwer+YbS5FwC4dS3LNYpwOFwFvkFwsQm9kiHc7omR
FF2eccgyVtZXs6Yjyh9tv5ZvfOIOfXHUXV19+Lnc/+gSrNm/hjnufo66uhqbRlRQXF/LOikfZunEn37vmHtau2MiDd17Kxd88kzVrt9DRFcHvyiLJlNgCAhaq6uD
xRx7g5QEfk+YfysISgVQmC9a+k3Nc3gDdrzzDu7/4FQVlMm+1uHh2U5oilxNnf4qlMsT8owJM63PzjiTy8tOtPHb+hXz75nM5acnDbLtmiPP6CjBLa9AHbOxM
mKGlb2KeeyTJsdOx9w6xsbGO0rGNyHo1HQ0GLX4dd07fPxA/4e7wn6lYloUkO8hKEtlda9AlN5aVpSfvp3neOUzalkSWApz37at5842nOOaIP/Lc82+zbXcb3//
aMSycNxt/IMDOXR0Ul/ioqK3nhz+5g7tu/gEXf+Nk+lMp1q9bwwuvr2VvxwAlJX7eX9OKz6Pw08u+SjangWBjaRbN08dhv6dzelmMslAhvXELQRCRRIhqOjV
BJxdMncQEW8YRi+HTZEpK3KiFJeQLa1gwu4Q9qWLaozlGde9mUXQljacfw+iDLuK1h7YwuK6VQz0ZHrRMdse2oa50sfWkI9hRFaeyeliBPDQ5pmJKJi5MS
jwp0i7rk4M43Fr/eR/49deiaRqWaSI4XZiik5yZxxsMUFA3AXdfmJ9efTd15UFGlblo29tORcN0msc2cuEPr6Ojs5dMKsZQbx933/1zlr6zBp/
bz0tvrWLZX/7C7ffWctyiecyZOp7eHU/T35PkZzc/yCWzjubXdzxDMh/nhp98nVxe33eSWi6P7FDw1jkpdJugg23Z2JaFqRm48nH21I3imYXnYB8+j80N8P7uPK
FSP5qkYvrylE3xYSXcOPsGiXXOpXRiHVkcvF/awF8WlbO7lorZXMvORx5CxcOU0W6iiTyPrZUp6vaysrOHxKghyrw+UsDdWyzozX4yEIcJjsOd4J/n0XvDM
kxpdjid2ICVSWKLCp6KMVimgsutYCdamTbvPygtKaKyfCzfvvg0Zh86kdNPOZqmIhd7+hJcc+3LPPj484xraKqMsgNV5yOYtucdtKh9PSHWb20lXkzxpELGI
QH0nT1xvnx904nlorT2x9FlkUs0yRrWpSIJsePC+D2q1iGiGVp8AGQeR0K5SyzA3n8qkB50ENTiUKZ10YW0+QDFnVqmlY5j+xJoJckkQI5Cvw5KjJpJjgs8qU
qQb8bsTDEhJlHoluD7Ny+g9BBx+LuD2APdNPfliHqdVNT4KSs36ZvlP/PQRzWwOGj4P6W9P95AqgoCvm8hup0IAsmWmKQTDqHwyPhMk2aG+tYtbmNx
W++w7L33+HyS77C7t199MdMFo2yye5q4ZzL/hOX0+SFpct5bvGbPHb3z9FyOl1dQ1xw3tE8+eK1NM75Olde/lXefHkJ8ewgD/z6MiZNm8SqFZsJFHgRsJEU
mUBxJWMH0kwpdpM0PgjuhH2Nz25RodsweF0xCbpNsqE0AzGTXZbNri7o6k/R77LY0+6gqS3J8ue7UI1CznQYWHqaV+ImhkemQh6isKaCULSetWs20mB10
r9hLbIQRxnXgKO0kCO7e1n69BJ+ceokps6a/o9BNAyDTCaDw+EYOYTL4/F8rpHpX58LtY+dta/sZRo65FNY0Q7yjrHoyThHzzuYqx7fxLoVr3P5ZRejOtwc
suh8GieNp3vCoaRbNpLLD3Da9dcyp7eVX9z0MLm8we6OPTz6+LNMn1DHYXObeOv9Nbhkma9ffi4T6wvIahovvPQe9TX7egJFSUIWLbKCg0gmRaFTIWdY
CDZYlo1lW7g9EpEOeGhxHGtamj1hhTdX66AKEBag2MZVK+BPKhTEZYqHbKywjdAnkUrCstUZUkkHNKSp2NlBW3eEBcdeiOyR2LpxDXvCW7lozKEIA
2GO8MALQxlclcWUews+vuxmGMbIkTvDnMThA6g+94j0g2P3hlmx6VSO7p3bwBNC9oQwUlEQFITMAMUhkVNOPYvTT/kat93zJ1TR5FdXX0lsnqW8sID
DRwf47V2P45JVmkePZmhoiP+55T859ZRFqG6Vy75xPNdeeh6YIhNq62kaNYb3Vm3n+l/fh0OWEUX7gw0PFPKZFDtWr0JWVcwPtmIxrX28kbygo5sWk
1MaUzSBmrQLYjJkANkCt42NQQadgA9UF5iySR4NVZQImiokREJhgVo5SoGSxjnlMMQJxzP+wuP48ZWnYOgWezeuZ9tD9zFjyytULG8hMpRH5CN2WBw
+EnWYETVM9vwiApphDqQkSYiCgGHBZZf+hN07dlIzZR6mZSOmhkAAPR1GNjJcesl3WL9mLUuWLmHWrFlEBgY5fEYtg/2D7OgLY1gmLqeLgddggF136
CMMiJMv0Z0BM6smYjWGBKNrgFUobGqaMdlPtUlr+ylKHOHmpGF3PhsSdSf/G3+daFx7DBVrg9soM97z5P0eq1IRloAwoBY1gDh2lsur4vMnO5XF9YRDq8
sD40TU4ZI2Saj8L5jRTUVjIjj17cXscRONJRFEgFYtT3tBE1RFHkkklcHn9CJIENvvAtAVUh0IqrZHOa3hUEfJ5BDfYdSI0WJRWmFQrCgWDBlp9CrVCRPA
JxFlaqSxgi7iJUV4kMaGxnJWLW7GW/ZGLJ/+IVY5jiUT7mBDto2fqOL534QOMHV0vv72hO/z/BgCzoNbc6bDAigAAAABJRU5ErkJggg==); }

This is what that photo looks like today:

body { background-image: url(data:image/png;base64,iVBORw0KGgoAAAANSUhEUgAAAHEAAABMCAYAAABamlijAAAACXBIWXMAAAsTAAALEwE
AmpwYAAAKT2lDQ1BQaG90b3Nob3AgSUNDIHByb2ZpbGUAAHjanVNnVFPpFj333vRCS4iAlEtvUhUIIFJCi4AUkSYqIQkQSoghodkVUcERRUUEG8i
giAOOjoCMFVEsDIoK2AfkIaKOg6OIisr74Xuja9a89+bN/rXXPues852zzwfACAyWSDNRNYAMqUIeEeCDx8TG4eQuQIEKJHAAEAizZCFz/SMBAPh+PDw
rIsAHvgABeNMLCADATZvAMByH/w/qQplcAYCEAcB0kThLCIAUAEB6jkKmAEBGAYCdmCZTAKAEAGDLY2LjAFAtAGAnf+bTAICd+Jl7AQBblCEVA
aCRACATZYhEAGg7AKzPVopFAFgwABRmS8Q5ANgtADBJV2ZIALC3AMDOEAuyAAgMADBRiIUpAAR7AGDIIyN4AISZABRG8lc88SuuEOcqA
AB4mbI8uSQ5RYFbCC1xB1dXLh4ozkkXKxQ2YQJhmkAuwnmZGTKBNA/g88wAAKCRFRHgg/P9eM4Ors7ONo62Dl8t6r8G/yJiYuP+5c+rcEAAAOF0ftH+
LC+zGoA7BoBt/qIl7gRoXgugdfeLZrIPQLUAoOnaV/Nw+H48PEWhkLnZ2eXk5NhKxEJbYcpXff5nwl/AV/1s+X48/Pf14L7iJIEyXYFHBPjgwsz0TKUcz5IJh
GLc5o9H/LcL//wd0yLESWK5WCoU41EScY5EmozzMqUiiUKSKcUl0v9k4t8s+wM+3zUAsGo+AXuRLahdYwP2SycQWHTA4vcAAPK7b8HUKAgDgGiD
4c93/+8//UegJQCAZkmScQAAXkQkLlTKsz/HCAAARKCBKrBBG/TBGCzABhzBBdzBC/xgNoRCJMTCQhBCCmSAHHJgKayCQiiGzbAdKmAv1EAd
NMBRaIaTcA4uwIW4Dj1wD/phCJ7BKLyBCQRByAgTYSHaiAFiilgjggXmYX4IcFIBBKLJCDJiBRRIkuRNUgxUopUIFVIHfI9cgI5h1xGupE7yAAy
gvyGvEcxlIGyUT3UDLVDuag3GoRGogvQZHQxmo8WoJvQcrQaPYw2oefQq2gP2o8+Q8cwwOgYBzPEbDAuxsNCsTgsCZNjy7EirAyrxhqwVqwDu4n1Y8
+xdwQSgUXACTYEd0IgYR5BSFhMWE7YSKggHCQ0EdoJNwkDhFHCJyKTqEu0JroR+cQYYjlxh1hILCPWEo8TLxB7iEPENyQSiUMyJ7mQAkmxpFTSEt
JG0m5SI+ksqZs0SBojk8naZGuyBzmULCAryIXkneTD5DPkG+Qh8lsKnWJAcaT4U+IoUspqShnlEOU05QZlmDJBVaOaUt2ooVQRNY9aQq2htlKvUYeoEzR1
mjnNgxZJS6WtopXTGmgXaPdpr+h0uhHdlR5Ol9BX0svpR+iX6AP0dwwNhhWDx4hnKBmbGAcYZxl3GK+YTKYZ04sZx1QwNzHrmOeZD5lvVVgqtip8FZ
HKCpVKlSaVGyovVKmqpqreqgtV81XLVI+pXlN9rkZVM1PjqQnUlqtVqp1Q61MbU2epO6iHqmeob1Q/pH5Z/YkGWcNMw09DpFGgsV/jvMYgC2MZs3gsI
WsNq4Z1gTXEJrHN2Xx2KruY/R27iz2qqaE5QzNKM1ezUvOUZj8H45hx+Jx0TgnnKKeX836K3hTvKelpG6Y0TLkxZVxrqpaXllirSKtRq0frvTau7aedpr1Fu1n
7gQ5Bx0onXCdHZ4/OBZ3nU9lT3acKpxZNPTr1ri6qa6UbobtEd79up+6Ynr5egJ5Mb6feeb3n+hx9L/1U/W36p/VHDFgGswwkBtsMzhg8xTVxbzwdL8fb
8VFDXcNAQ6VhlWGX4YSRudE8o9VGjUYPjGnGXOMk423GbcajJgYmISZLTepN7ppSTbmmKaY7TDtMx83MzaLN1pk1mz0x1zLnm+eb15vft2BaeFostqi2
uGVJsuRaplnutrxuhVo5WaVYVVpds0atna0l1rutu6cRp7lOk06rntZnw7Dxtsm2qbcZsOXYBtuutm22fWFnYhdnt8Wuw+6TvZN9un2N/T0HDYfZDqsdWh1+c7R
yFDpWOt6azpzuP33F9JbpL2dYzxDP2DPjthPLKcRpnVOb00dnF2e5c4PziIuJS4LLLpc+Lpsbxt3IveRKdPVxXeF60vWdm7Obwu2o26/uNu5p7ofcn8w0nymeW
TNz0MPIQ+BR5dEC5+VMGvfrH5PQ0+BZ7Xnly9jL5FXrdewt6V3qvdh7xc+9j5yn+M+4zw33jLeWVMN8C3yLfLT8Nvnl+F30N/I/9k/3r/0QCngCUBZwOJgU
GBWwL7+Hp8Ib+OPzrbZfay2e1BjKC5QRVBj4KtguXBrSFoyOyQrSH355jOkc5pDoVQfujW0Adh5mGLw34MJ4WHhVeGP45wiFga0TGXNXfR3ENz30T6RJ
ZE3ptnMU85ry1KNSo+qi5qPNo3ujS6P8YuZlnM1VidWElsSxw5LiquNm5svt/87fOH4p3iC+N7F5gvyF1weaHOwvSFpxapLhIsOpZATIhOOJTwQRAqqBaMJfl
TdyWOCnnCHcJnIi/RNtGI2ENcKh5O8kgqTXqS7JG8NXkkxTOILOW5hCepkLxMDUzdmzqeFpp2lG0yPTq9MYOSkZBxQqohTZO2Z+pn5mZ2y6xlhbL+xW
6Lty8elQfJa7OQrAVZLQq2QqboVFoo1yoHsmdlV2a/zYnKOZarniVN7cyzytuQN5zvn//tEsIS4ZK2pYZLYyJ0dWOa9rGo5sjxxedsK4xUFK4ZWBqw8uIq2Km
3VT6vtV5eufr0mek1rgV7ByoLBtQFr6wtVCuWFfevc1+1dT1gvWd+1YfqGnRs+FYmKrhTbF5cVf9go3HjlG4dvyr+Z3JS0qavEuWTPZtJm6ebeLZ5bDpaql+aX
Dm4N2dq0Dd9WtO319kXbL5fNKNu7g7ZDuaO/PLi8ZafJzs07P1SkVPRU+lQ27tLdtWHX+G7R7ht7vPY07NXbW7z3/T7JvttVAVVN1WbVZftJ+7P3P66Jqun4
lvttXa1ObXHtxwPSA/0HIw6217nU1R3SPVRSj9Yr60cOxx++/p3vdy0NNg1VjZzG4iNwRHnk6fcJ3/ceDTradox7rOEH0x92HWcdL2pCmvKaRptTmvtbYlu6T8
w+0dbq3nr8R9sfD5w0PFl5SvNUyWna6YLTk2fyz4ydlZ19fi753GDborZ752PO32oPb++6EHTh0kX/i+c7vDvOXPK4dPKy2+UTV7hXmq86X23qdOo8/pPTT8e
7nLuarrlca7nuer21e2b36RueN87d9L158Rb/1tWeOT3dvfN6b/fF9/XfFt1+cif9zsu72Xcn7q28T7xf9EDtQdlD3YfVP1v+3Njv3H9qwHeg89HcR/cGhYPP/pH1jw9
DBY+Zj8uGDYbrnjg+OTniP3L96fynQ89kzyaeF/6i/suuFxYvfvjV69fO0ZjRoZfyl5O/bXyl/erA6xmv28bCxh6+yXgzMV70VvvtwXfcdx3vo98PT+R8IH8o/2j5sf
VT0Kf7kxmTk/8EA5jz/GMzLdsAAAAgY0hSTQAAeiUAAICDAAD5/wAAgOkAAHUwAADqYAAAOpgAABdvkl/FRgAAMy1JREFUeNrsnWeYnVW
5939P3Xv2Xt6L5lkkklvhBRCCB8FzggRUERRUXweA6FAVBUQRjdKKl0glNaT3Jletm9P/X9EGaOChBSrzOe1/XXPNh5sil/ddn/u/lmDb
ditQCBj8f/l3ExklC7Zt2/9/Lv69RQQi+3OBaZpomvZ/dsIMw0DX9QPpSLi/l6RSqX+T4OYTCYPuPHL+/PP+XweVVVRVfULeTnLsjAMA1EUsSwLRVEQB
FLmyxd13E4HF/4+IfHrCjKx5rTTwzg8IR+EW7Usizy+fzl5BmGQS6K6+9IA1DQNXdeRJOkLeZ5pmiPjNwwDdM+dvyfCMRsNotlWciyjKZpWJb1uQOYy+W
QZRlJknA6nbjdbkRRJPJ8EXHYrlcDsuykCTpC/GHwwAqijlyfo/Hg23bZLPZ/Qcxn89jWdalSVNVFVmWP7B2LaNpmkjzzykjzxeohaZp4nA4AkCSJXC73hQGZy+U
wDGPk3YYn9vMGcNhka5qGpmnYto3L5UIQhBEN/UQGQgDg9AVVVM00QURRwOB6Iofq5mSxCEEf/ncDhQFAXbtjFNE1mWsW37CwExm81iGAZOp/
ND4/88/AgCLhcLhRFwTTND43/nwY2w9pg2zayLKPrOrlsfyEs

This is what a photo used to look like:

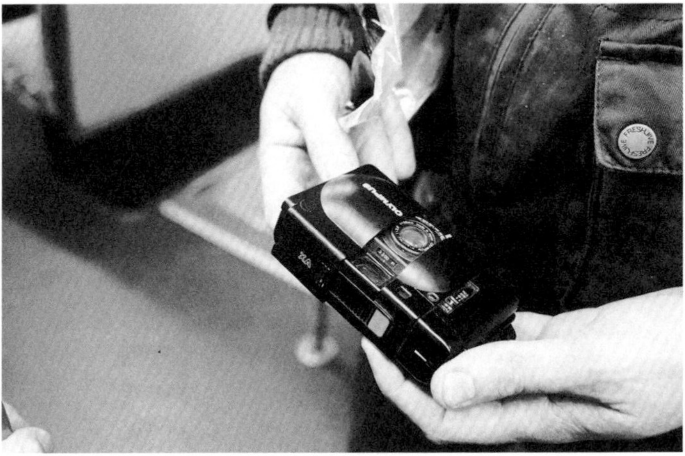

really

somebody

You are

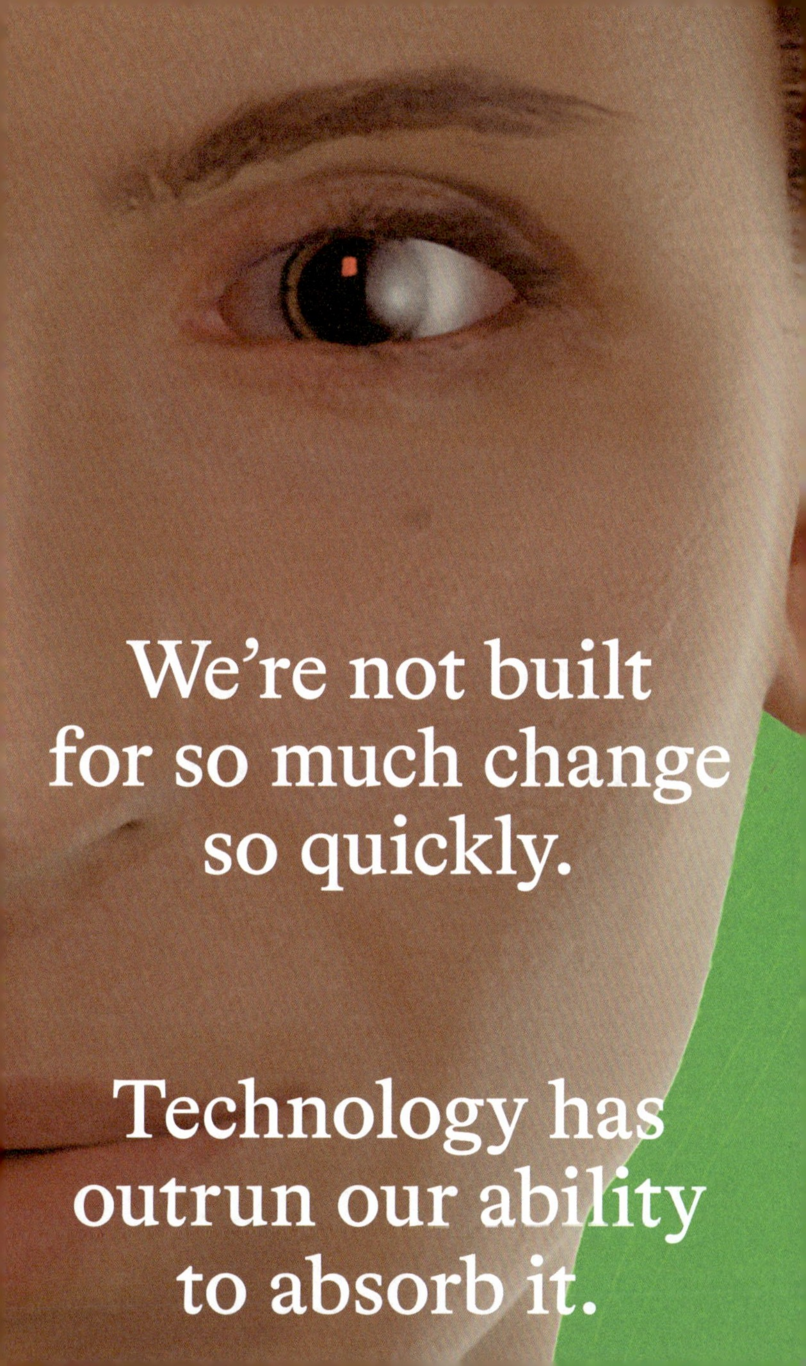
We're not built
for so much change
so quickly.
Technology has
outrun our ability
to absorb it.

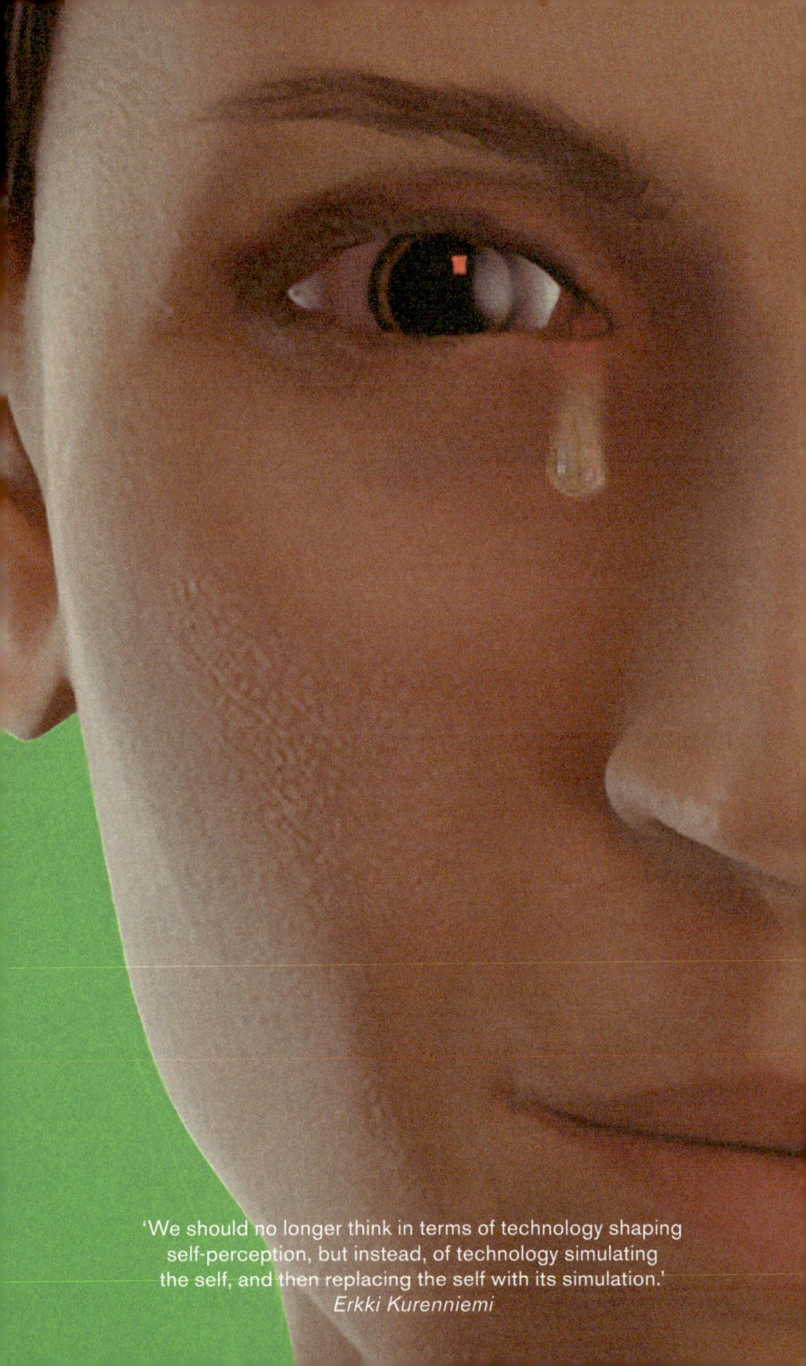
'We should no longer think in terms of technology shaping
self-perception, but instead, of technology simulating
the self, and then replacing the self with its simulation.'
Erkki Kurenniemi

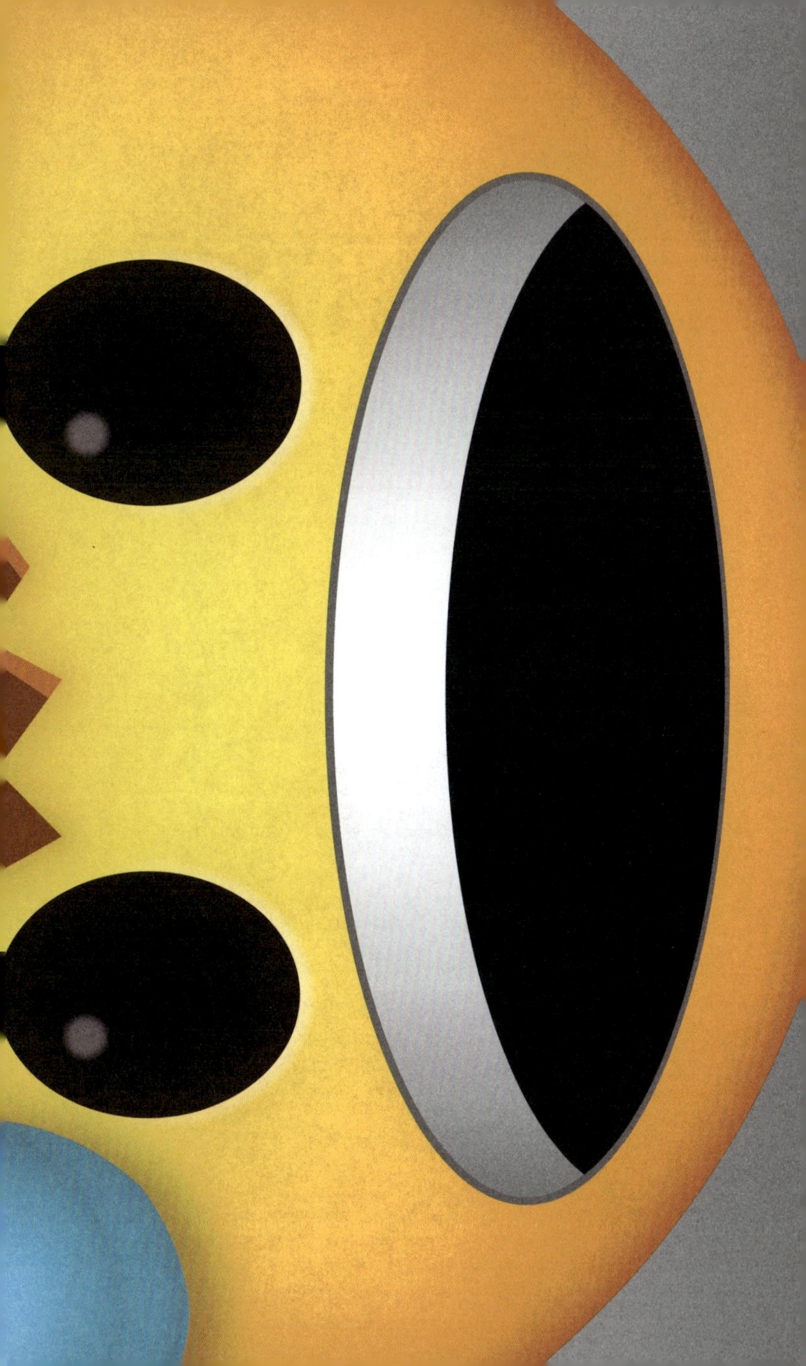

Question:

⁋ Have you ever wanted a clone?

⁋ If so, would your clone come first in your will?

⁋ What if you didn't like your clone? Would you have to get divorced from it?

⁋ Would you be angry if your clone made a clone of itself? Or would it feel like you were conquering the world? Broadening your footprint?

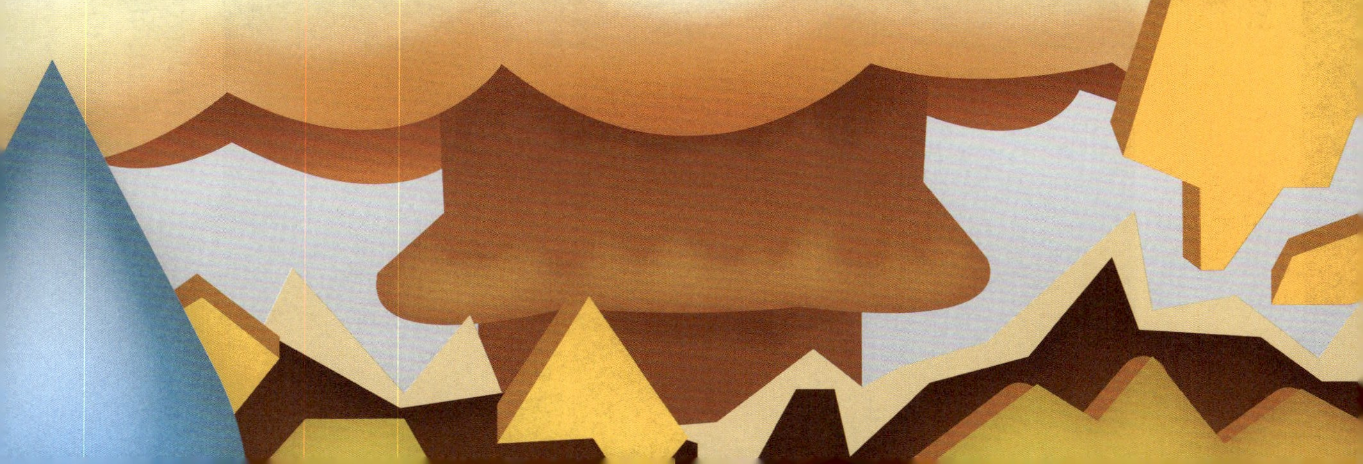

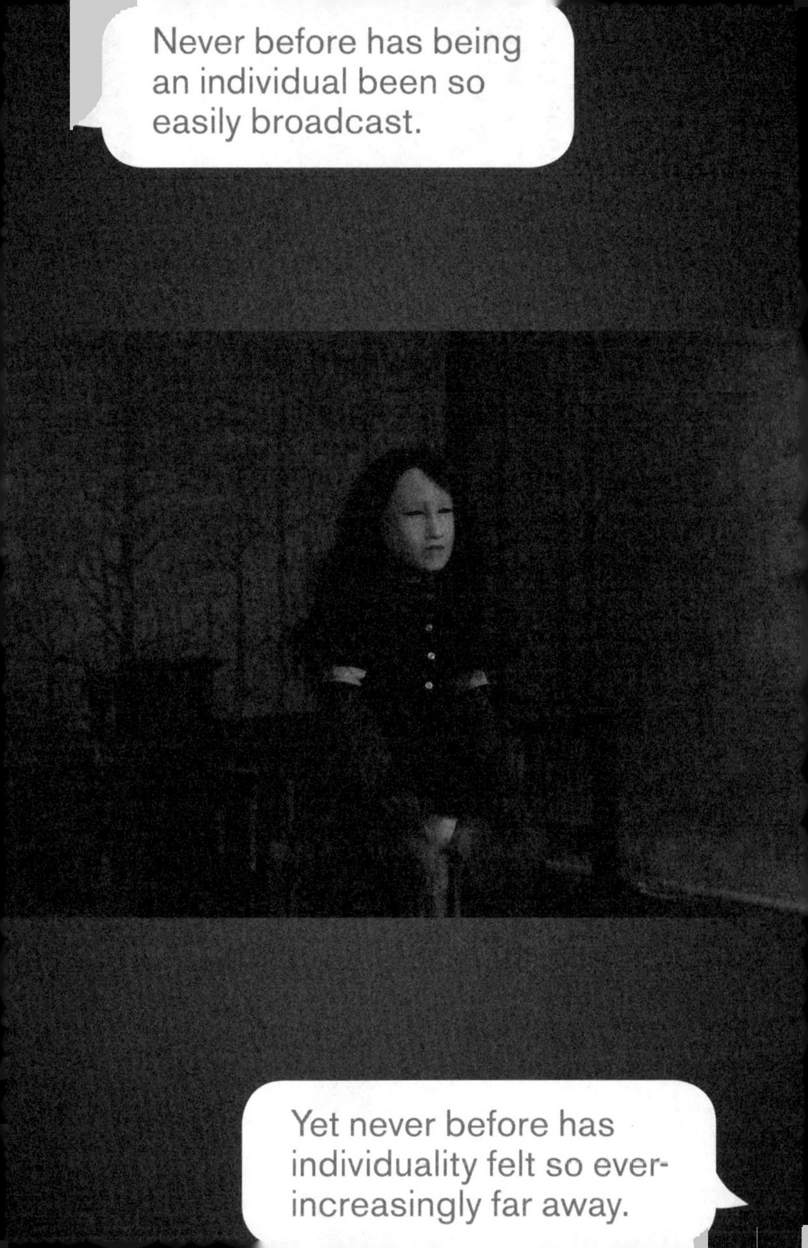
Never before has being an individual been so easily broadcast.
Yet never before has individuality felt so ever-increasingly far away.

One in ten Icelanders will write a novel in their lifetime.

This is impressive, but I suppose the down side of this is that each novel only gets nine readers.

Our world is turning into a world of Icelandic novelists.

Chikha_elf 30s ago

Do I like this?

Will people
crave the future
legal rights
enjoyed by data?

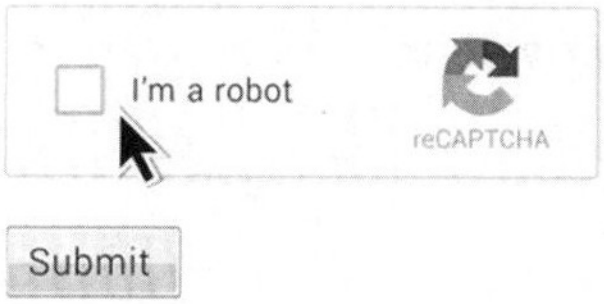

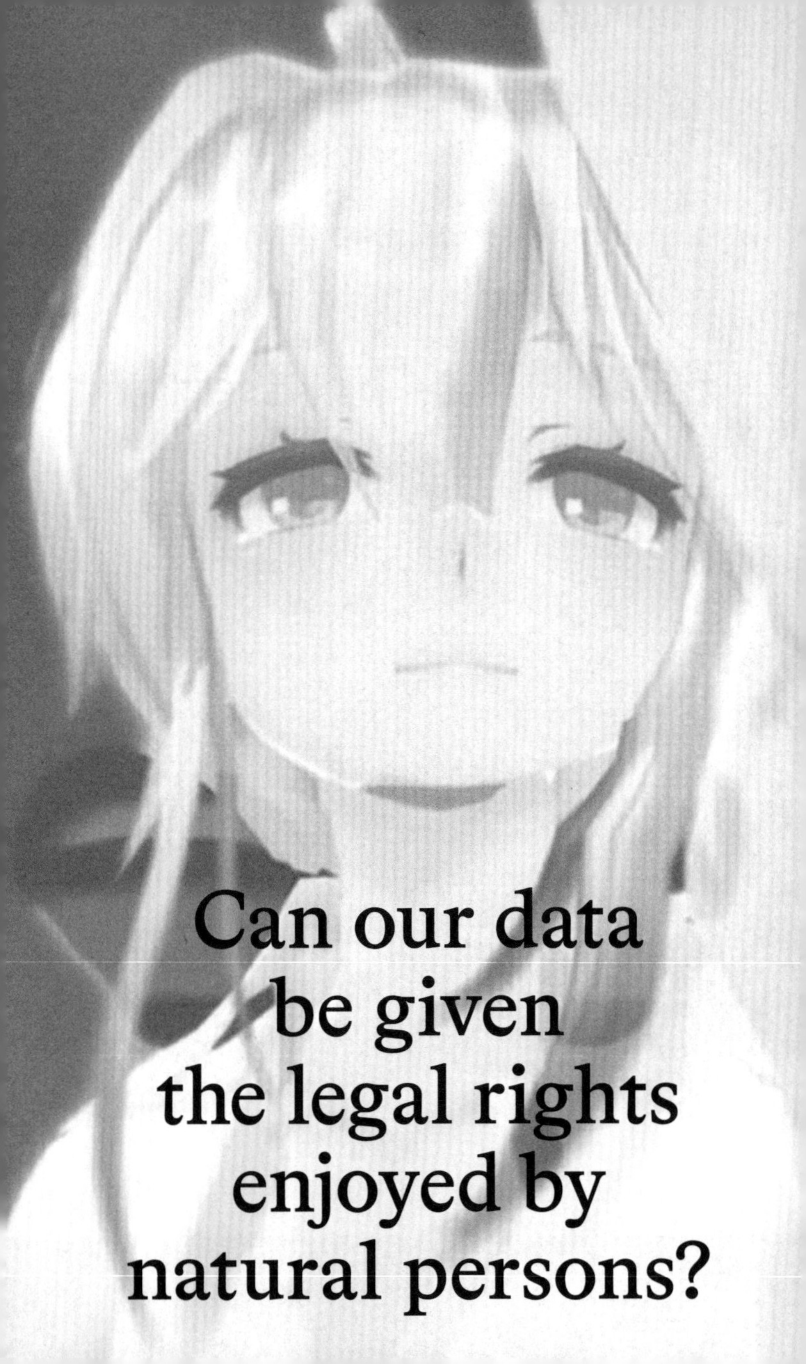
Can our data
be given
the legal rights
enjoyed by
natural persons?

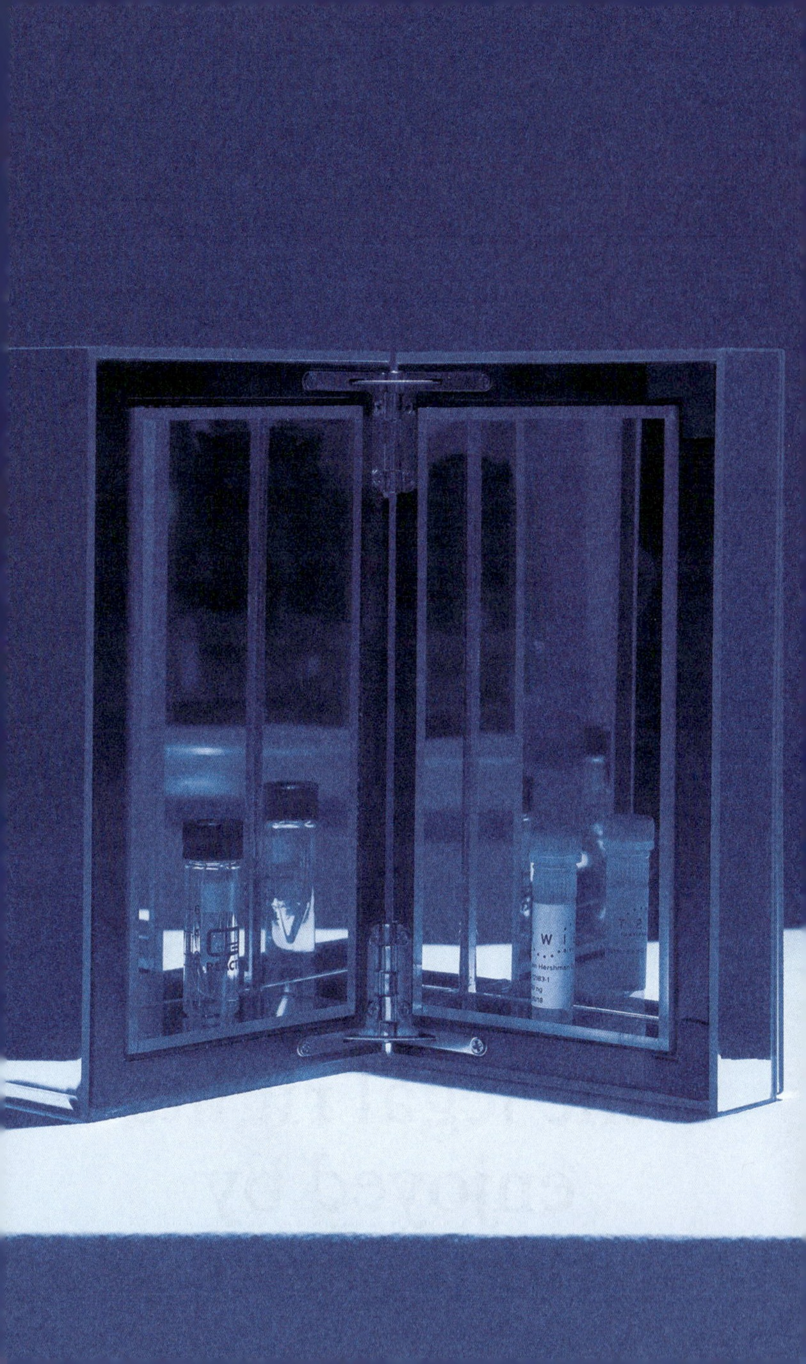

At what point do you stop becoming a person and become an object?

Why is being an object always portrayed as a bad thing?

Is there a situation where being an object is good?

At the moment Artificial Intuition is just you and the Cloud doing a little dance with relatively simple algorithms. But shortly everyone's dance with the Cloud will be happening together in a cosmic cyber ballroom, and everyone's data stream will be communicating with everyone else's and these data streams will all be talking about you: what did you buy today? What did you drink, ingest, excrete, inhale, view, unfriend, read, lean towards, reject, talk to, smile at, get nostalgic about, get angry about, link to, like or get off on?

*

Tie these quotidian data hits together with corporate, government data banks and hits begin to see you as something that's humblingly easy to predict, please, anticipate, model, forecast, and replicate. Then tie this new machine intelligence realm in with some smart 3D graphics that have captured your body metrics and likeness, and a few years down the road you will become sort of beside the point.

*

A dematerialized parallel you already exists out there in the Cloud, but instead of being good or evil, it's mostly just machines telling other machines that you recently purchased a piqué-knit polo shirt in tones flattering to your skin at Abercrombie & Fitch.

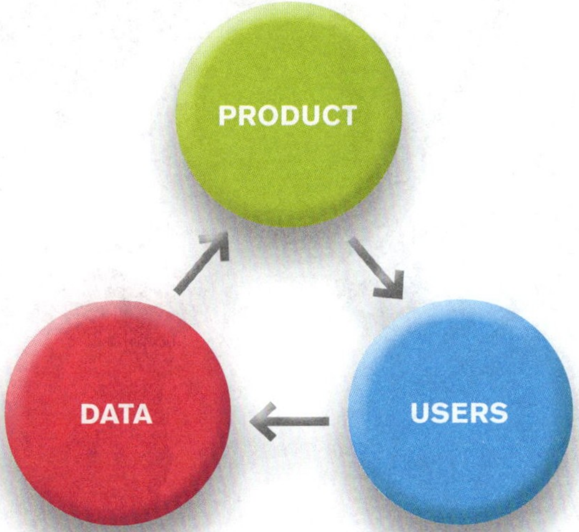

Figure: 'The virtuous circle of AI'

Sorry, but what's virtuous about this?

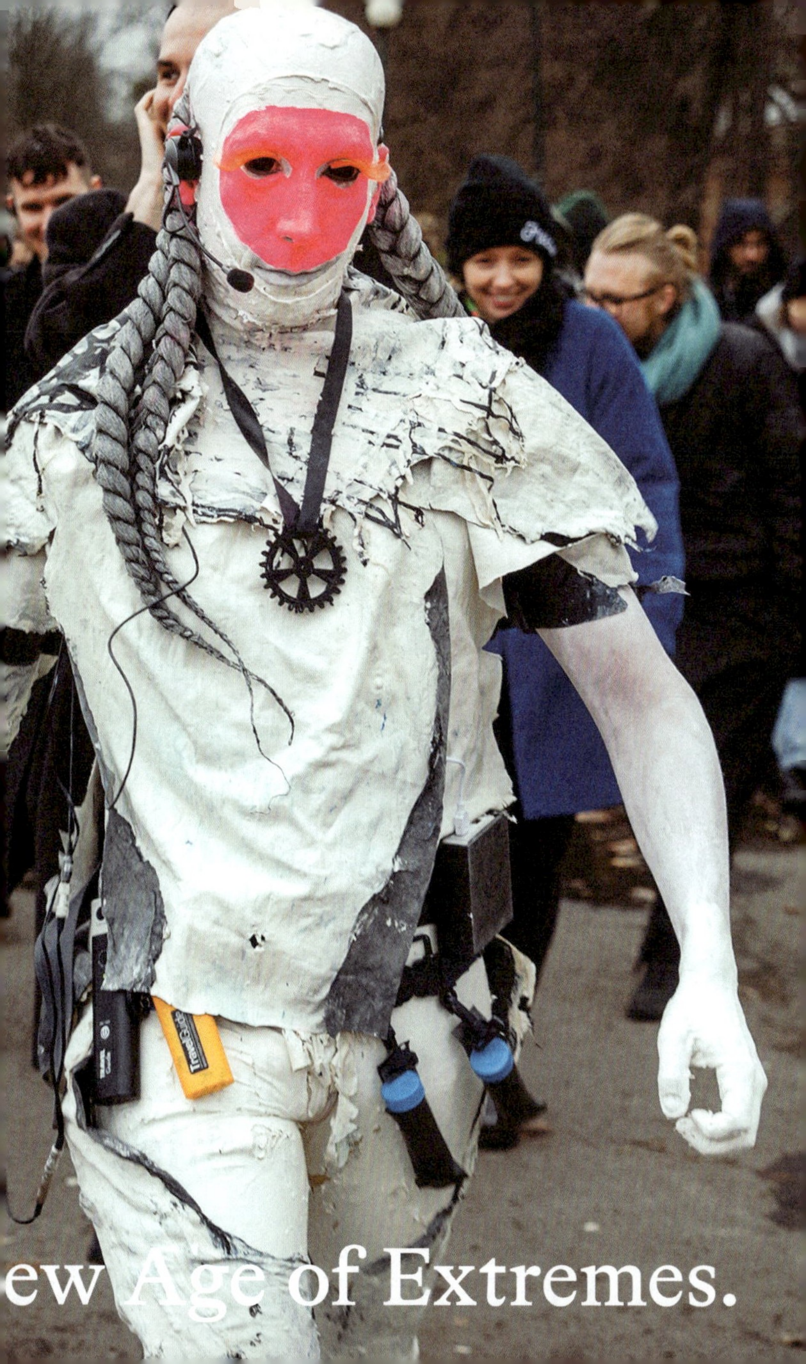

ew Age of Extremes.

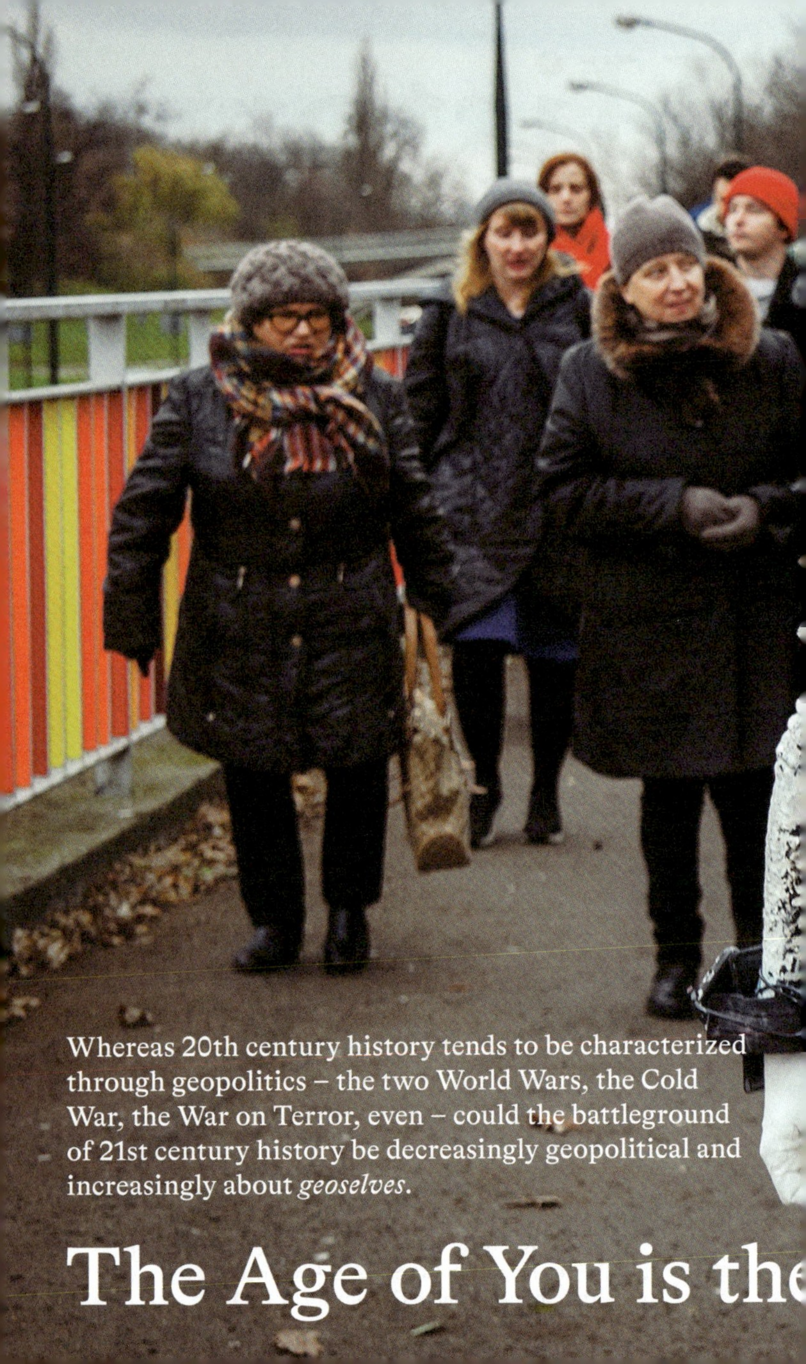

Whereas 20th century history tends to be characterized through geopolitics – the two World Wars, the Cold War, the War on Terror, even – could the battleground of 21st century history be decreasingly geopolitical and increasingly about *geoselves*.

The Age of You is the

History no longer applies to you

‘The only completely certain generalization about history is that, so as long as there is a human race, it will go on.’
Eric Hobsbawm, The Age of Extremes: The Short Twentieth Century 1914–1991

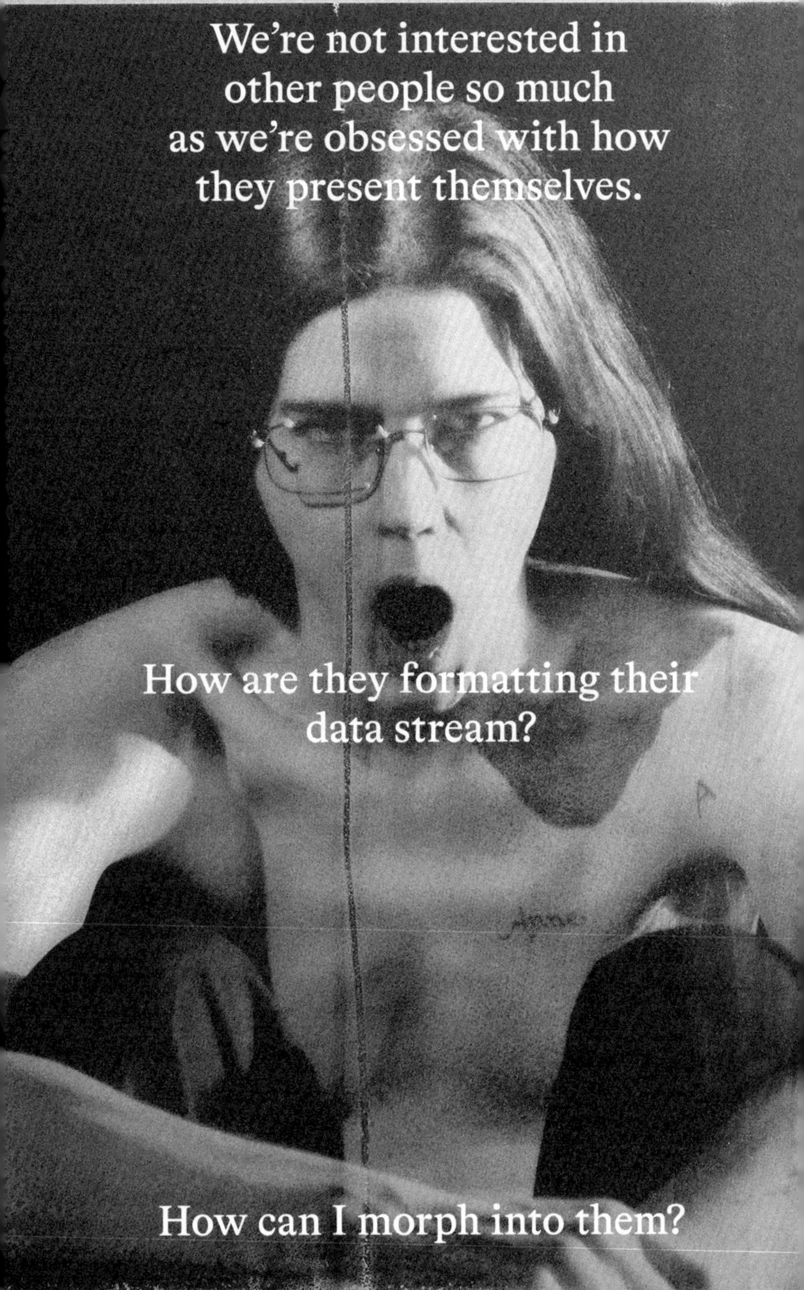
We're not interested in other people so much as we're obsessed with how they present themselves.
How are they formatting their data stream?
How can I morph into them?

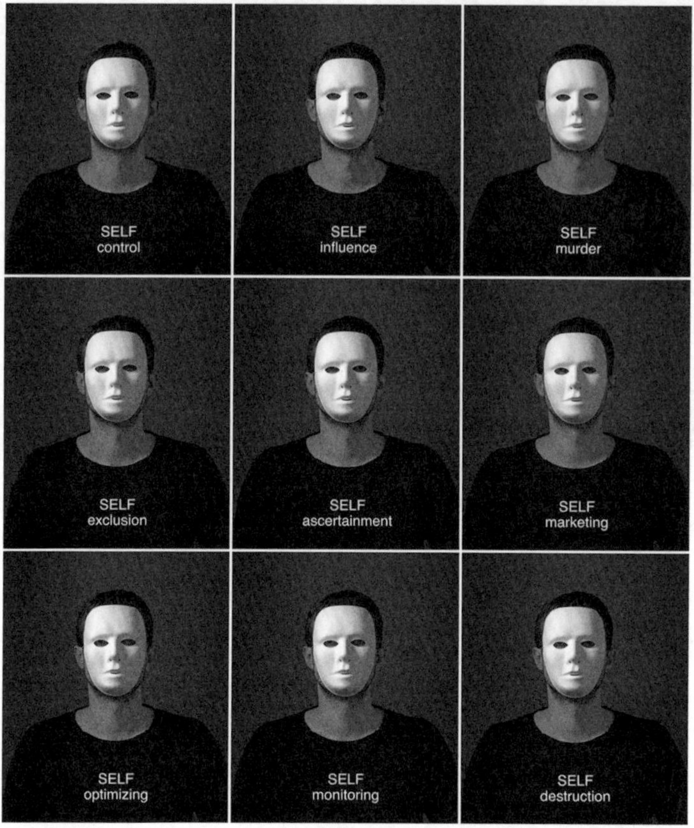

Yes, you.

A large part of you has been extracted from you.

An ever-larger part of you now exists everywhere and nowhere.

It's both voluntary and involuntary.

It exists independently of your five senses.

There's never been anything like this before.

And it will continue, even after you die.

'Who,

me?'

ne Self

…and it's happening to you
as you read these words.

…you're now becoming your

Extrem

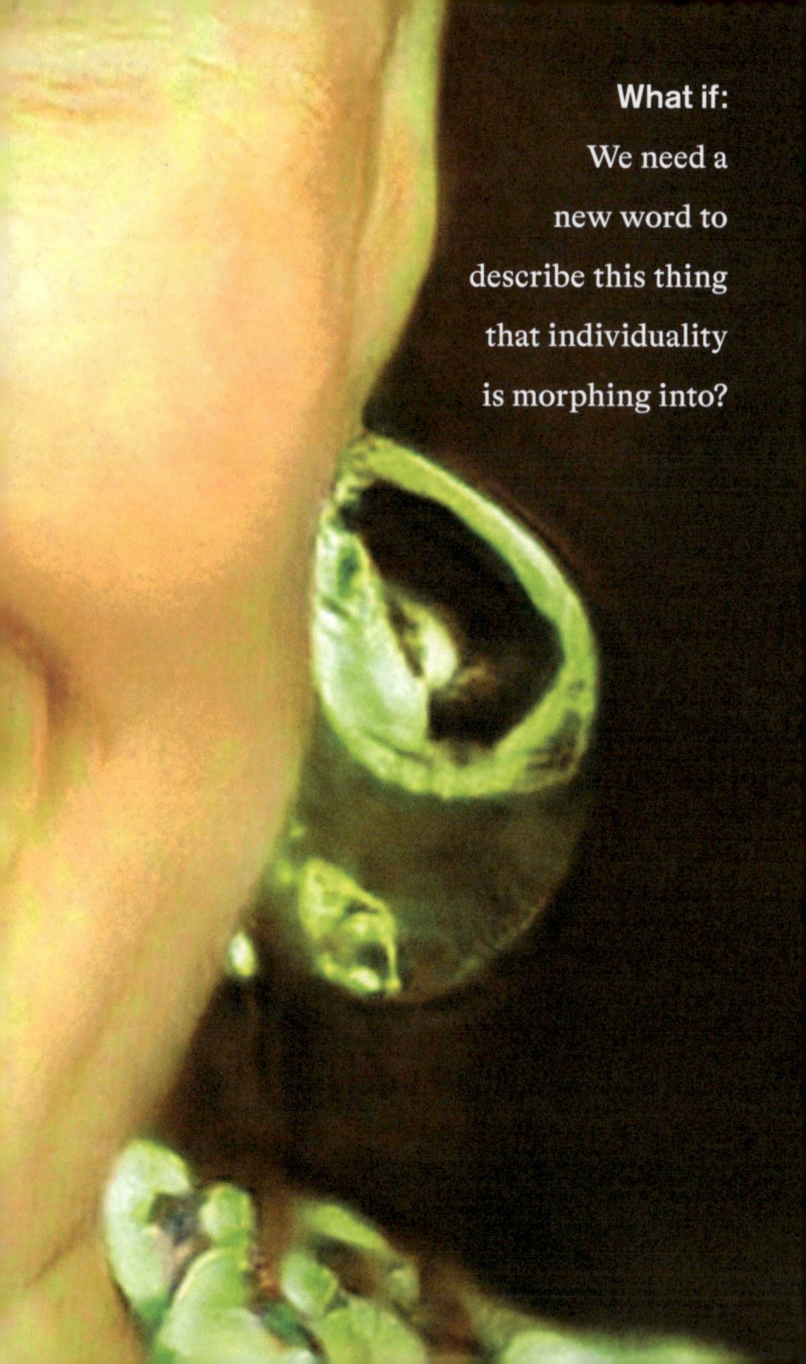

What if:

We need a new word to describe this thing that individuality is morphing into?

It’s all happening faster than we thought

Autophobia

The fear of being an individual

Jos9668 2 years ago

Truly stunned at how far we have come as a society

Anyone over 40 knows what classic individuality felt like.

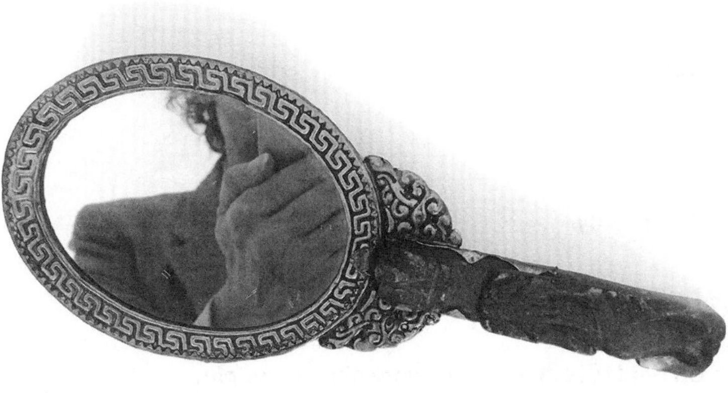

Now it's almost a handicap.

Twenty years ago this question would have made no sense.

Now everybody knows what it means.

We all know that we're changing inside our heads.

Quickly.

Too quickly.

Up until recently people were simply people.

Now we're turning into something else.

We all feel it.

We all know it.

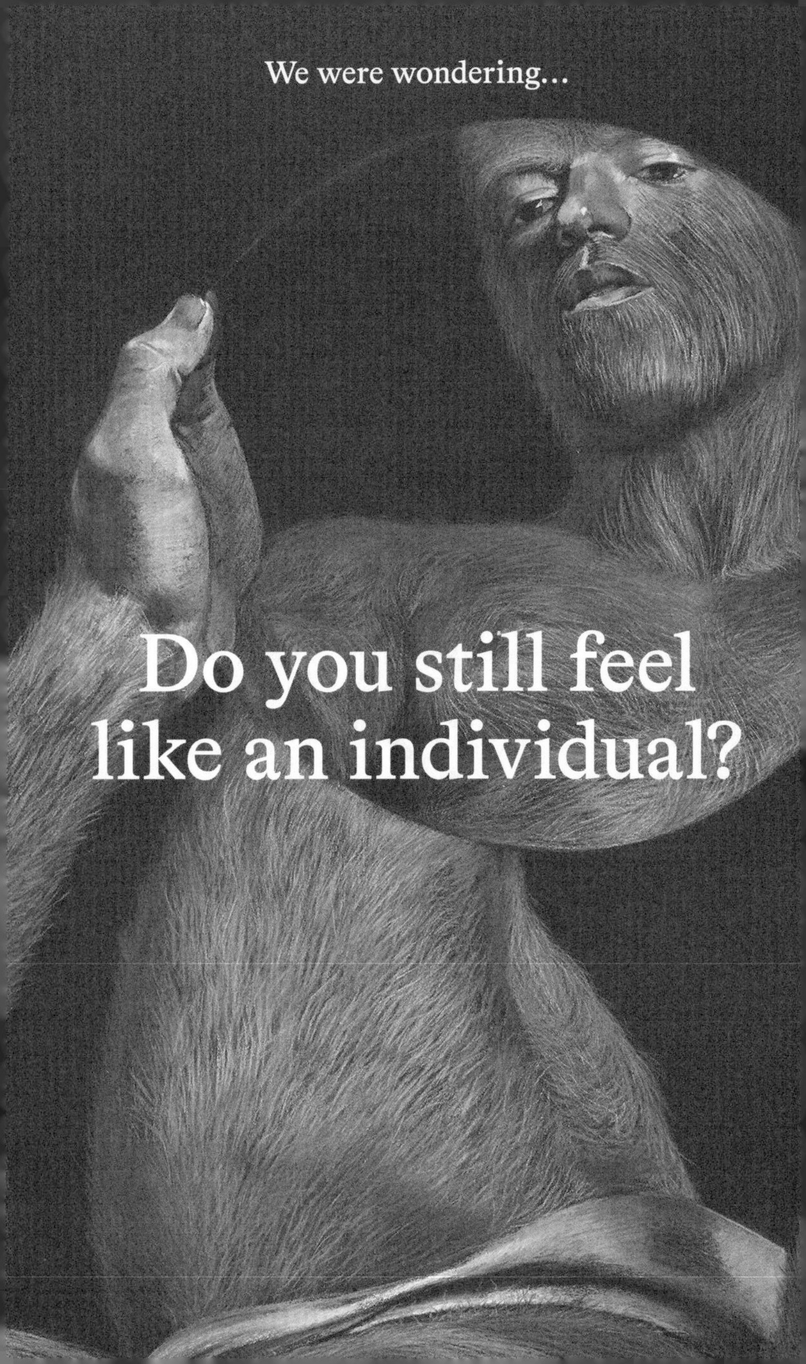
We were wondering...
Do you still feel like an individual?

disintegrating

You are

Oops!
Something went wrong.
We're working on getting it fixed as soon as we can.

CONTENTS

Proofreading: Claire Cahm

Lithography and print:
Lösch GmbH & Co. KG

Published by
Verlag der Buchhandlung
Walther und Franz König
Ehrenstraße 4, D-50672 Köln

Bibliographic information published by the Deutsche Nationalbibliothek. The Deutsche Nationalbibliothek lists this publication in the Deutsche Nationalbibliografie; detailed bibliographic data are available on the Internet at http://dnb.d-nb.de

Printed in Germany

ISBN 978-3-96098-973-8

The authors wish to thank November Paynter, Avia Wiseman, Uroš Jeli, MOCA Toronto, Antonia Carver, Nora Razian, Nadine El Khoury, Albert Kolambel, Jameel Arts Centre, Franz König, Nicole Rankers, Tracy Bohan, Sophie Lambert, Jefferson Hack, Gea Politi, Michelle Nicole, Lorraine Two, Keira Callaghan and all the contributors.

Vertrieb / Distribution

Germany, Austria, Switzerland
Buchhandlung Walther König
Ehrenstr. 4,
D - 50672 Köln
Fon +49 (0) 221 / 20 59 6 53
verlag@buchhandlung-walther-koenig.de

United States and Canada
D.A.P. / Distributed Art Publishers, Inc.
75 Broad Street, Suite 630
USA - New York, NY 10004
Fon +1 (0) 212 627 1999
orders@dapinc.com

Outside the United States and Canada, Germany, Austria and Switzerland by
Thames & Hudson Ltd., London
www.thamesandhudson.com

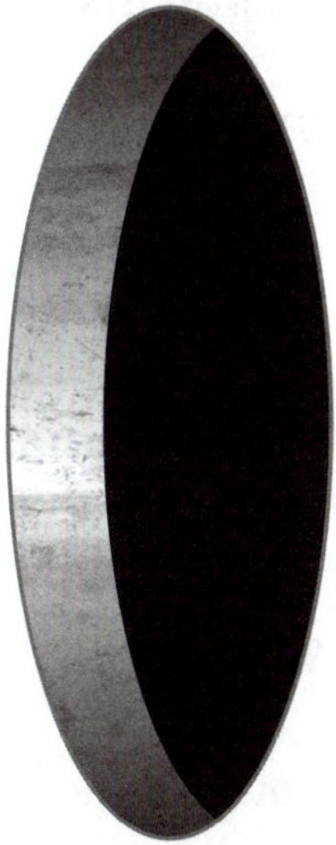

THE EXTREME SELF

Age of You

Shumon Basar   Douglas Coupland   Hans Ulrich Obrist

With visual contributions from Agnieszka Kurant, Amalia Ulman, Amnesia Scanner & PWR, Ana Nicolaescu, Ania Soliman, Anna Uddenberg, Anne Imhof, Asad Raza, Barry Doupé, Bogosi Sekhukhuni, Cao Fei, Carsten Höller, Cécile B. Evans, Chen Zhou, Christine Sun Kim, Craig Green, Dominique Gonzalez-Foerster, Emmanuel Iduma, Farah Al Qasimi, Fatima Al Qadiri, GCC, Goshka Macuga, Heman Chong, Ian Cheng, Ingrid Hora, Isabel Lewis, Jarvis Cocker, Jenna Sutela, Johannes Paul Raether, John Menick, Jürgen Klauke, Koo Jeong A, Lawrence Abu Hamdan, Liam Gillick, Liam Young, Lorraine O'Grady, Lucy Raven, Lynn Hershman Leeson, Michael Stipe, Miles Gertler, Miranda July, Momus, Pamela Rosenkranz, Pan Daijing, Paul Mpagi Sepuya, Peter Saville & Yoso Mouri, Philippe Parreno, Pierre Huyghe, Precious Okoyomon, Rachel Rose, Raja'a Khalid, Rami Farook, Samuel Fosso, Sara Cwynar, Satoshi Fujiwara, Simon Denny, Sissel Tolaas, Sophia Al-Maria, Stéphanie Saadé, Stephanie Comilang, Suzanne Treister, Tabita Rezaire, Thomas Dozol, Thomas Hirschhorn, Trevor Paglen, Urs Lüthi, Victoria Sin, Wang Haiyang, Yaeji, Yazan Khalili, Yu Honglei, Yuri Pattison

Design by Daly & Lyon

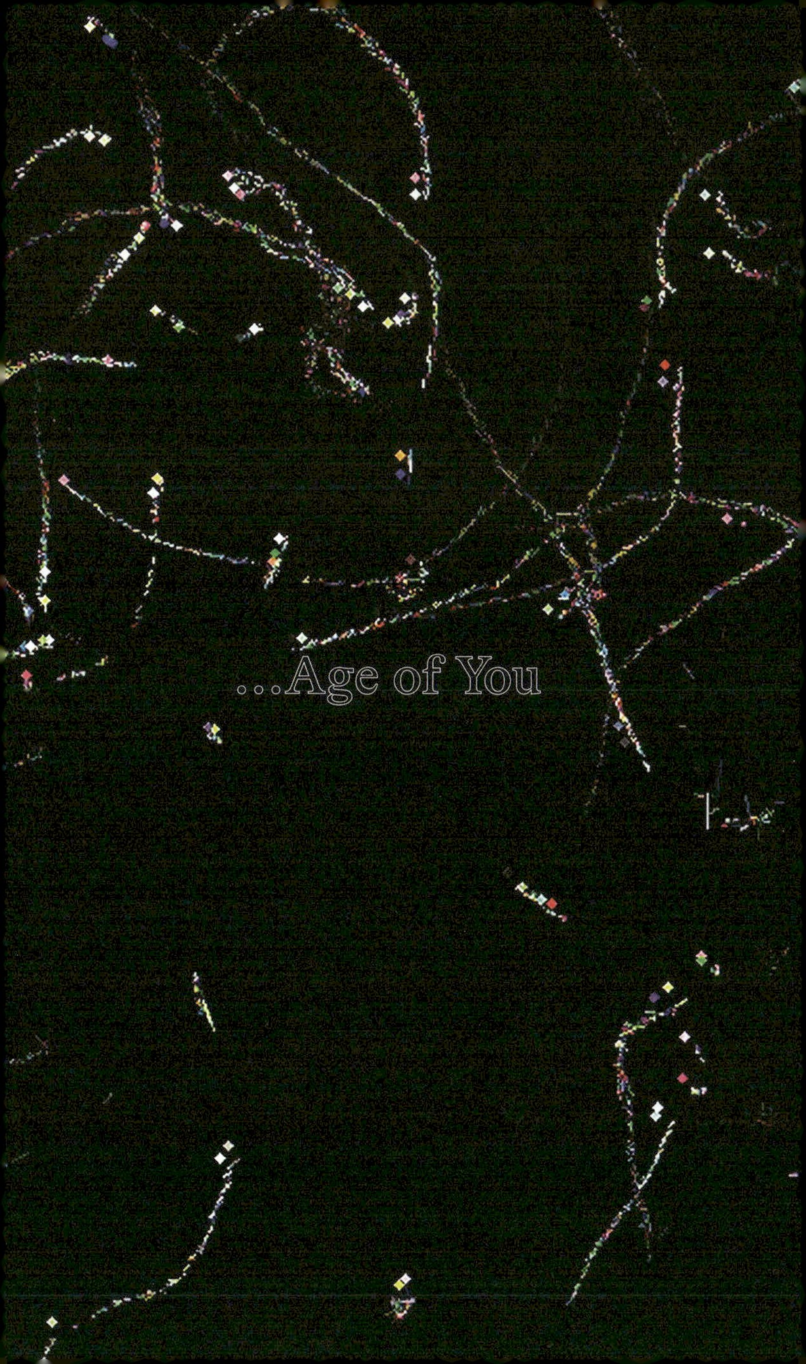
...Age of You

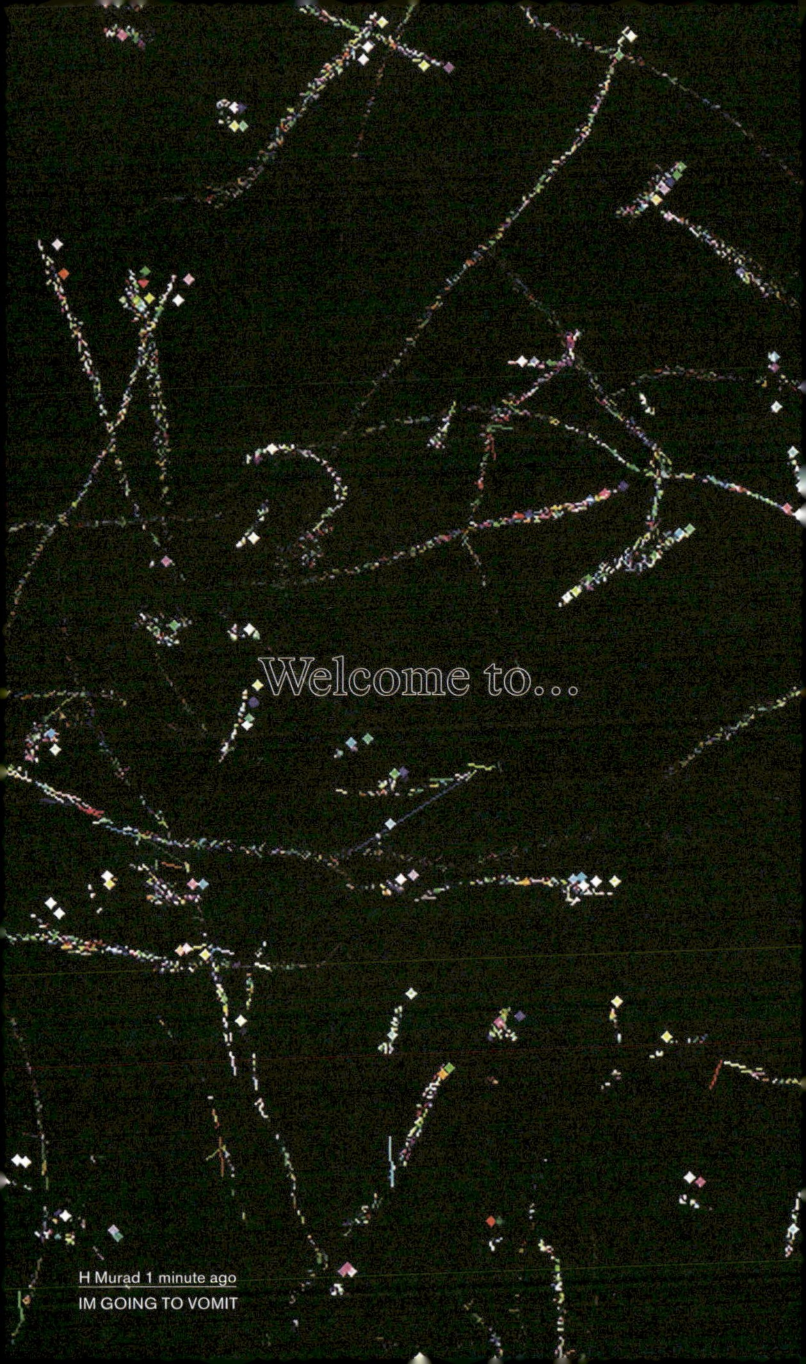
Welcome to...
H Murad 1 minute ago
IM GOING TO VOMIT

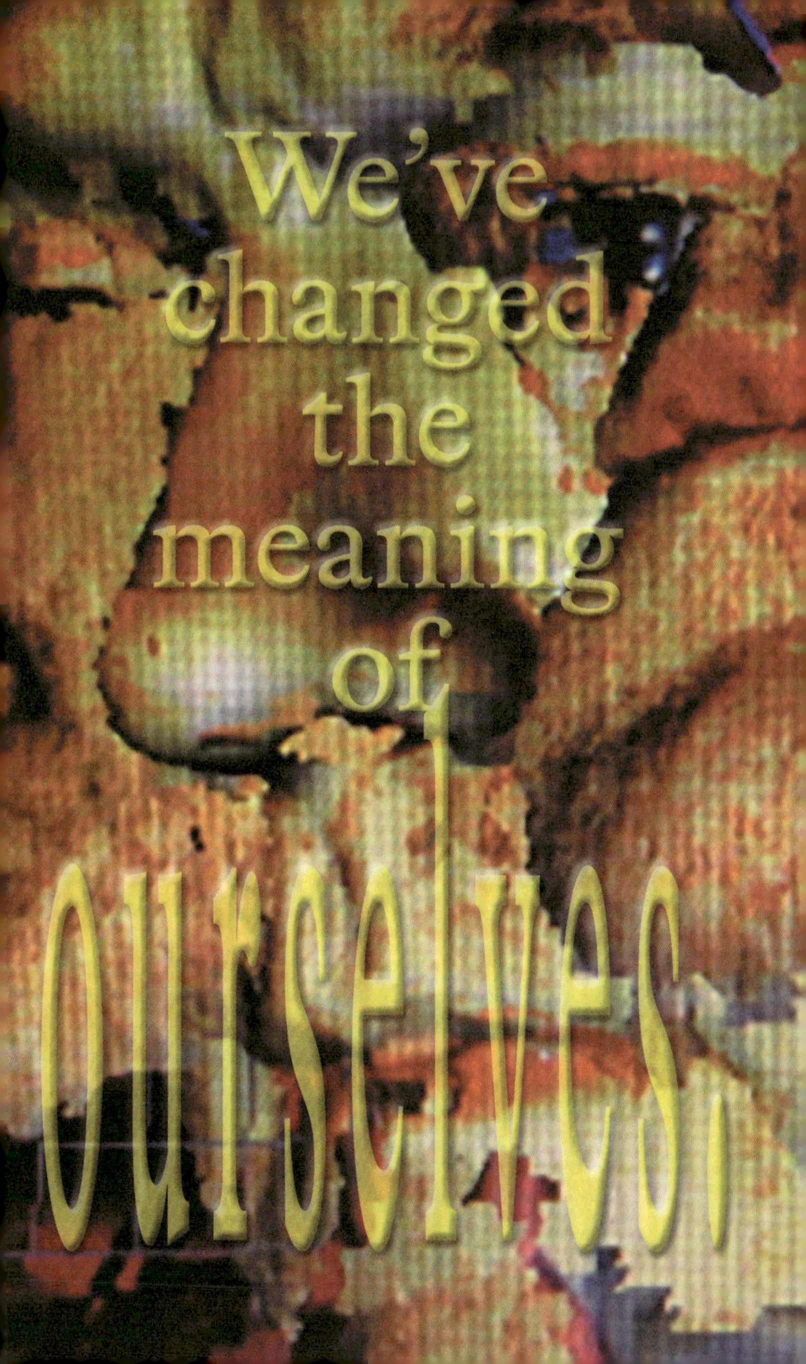
We've
changed
the
meaning
of
ourselves.

We haven't just changed the structure
of self-identity over the past few pages.

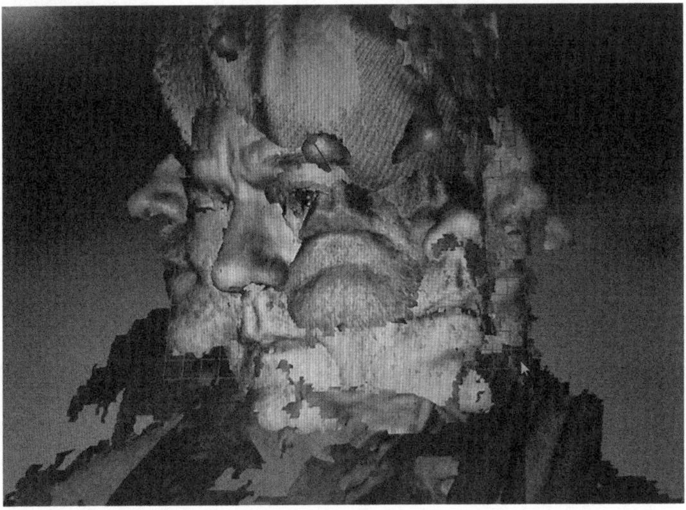

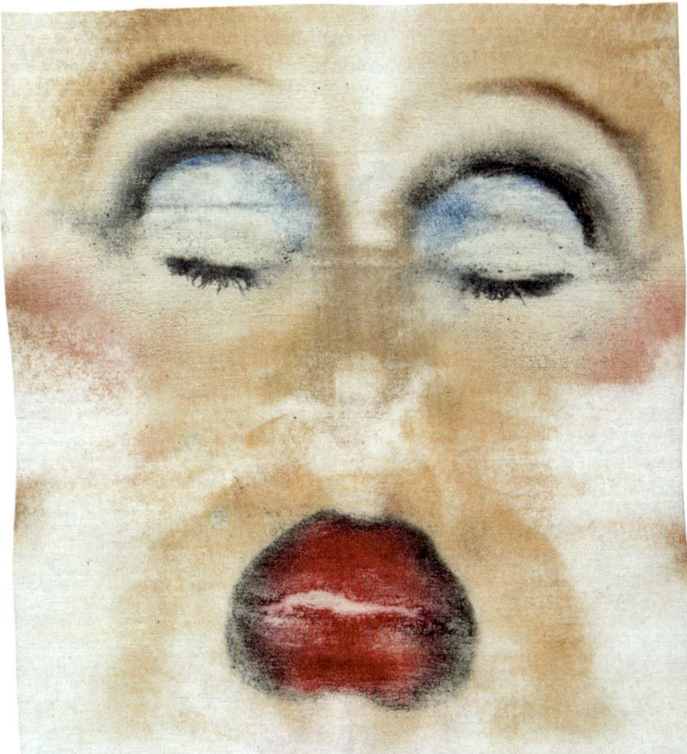

Could the expression of empathy
be our new Turing Test?

Feelings now legitimize lies

taneisha_BTS 1 week ago

blush

Swipe-right fatigue
Bingeing fatigue
Password fatigue
No liquids or gels fatigue
Victim fatigue
Hero fatigue
Upgrade fatigue
Update fatigue
Zero tolerance fatigue
Autocorrect fatigue
Statistics fatigue
Waiting fatigue
Future fatigue
Fatigue fatigue

While at the same time, emotion has been devalued:

Compassion fatigue

Inspiration fatigue

Fear fatigue

New normal fatigue

Awesome fatigue

Self-worth fatigue

10,000 steps fatigue

Bias fatigue

Truth fatigue

Hyperbole fatigue

Personal best fatigue

Weather fatigue

Meme fatigue

Screen fatigue

Forwarded many times

Feelings have obliterated facts.

Feelings may be fleeting but the engineering behind them isn't.

Once upon a time, feelings belonged to a person's 'private life.' History's first novels were mostly about characters navigating the storms of each other's feelings.

Today, feelings are now felt in public. Emotions are social, wired by technology. Is it strange we've let 'unemotional' machines govern what and how we feel? Who we feel love or hatred for? Especially now, when feelings are more influential than facts.

LEFT/RIGHT

PAST/FUTURE

Traditional binaries keep collapsing.

MALE/FEMALE

TRUTH/FALSEHOOD

DEMOCRACY/FASCISM

CAPITALIST/COMMUNIST

The opposite of the self is no longer the crowd.

The opposite of man is no longer nature.

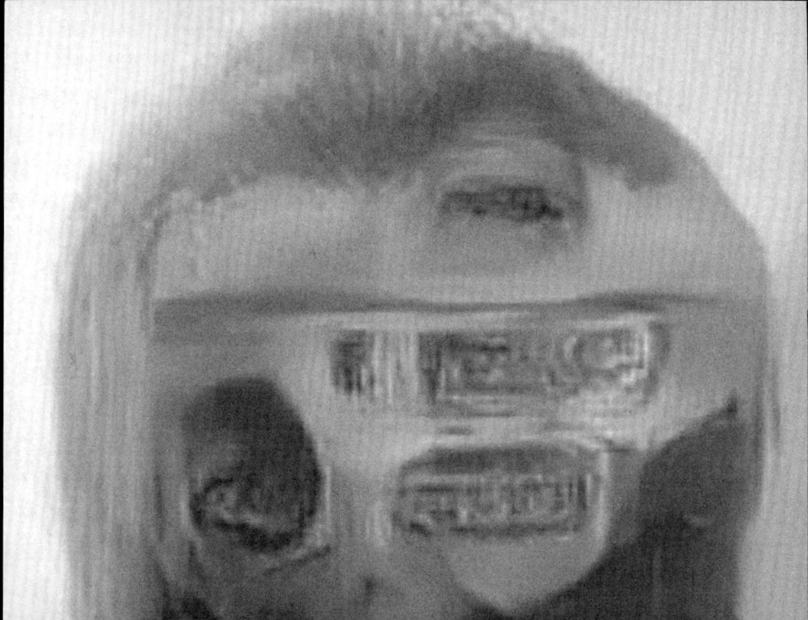

What is the opposite of you?

...me?

...a crowd?

ecrowdthecrowdthecrowdthecrowdthecrowdthecrow
owdthecrowdthecrowdthecrowdthecrowdthecrowdth
dthecrowdthecrowdthecrowdthecrowdthecrowdthecr
ecrowdthecrowdthecrowdthecrowdthecrowdthecrow
owdthecrowdthecrowdthecrowdthecrowdthecrowdthe
hecrowdthecrowdthecrowdthecrowdthecrowdthecro
rowdthecrowdthecrowdthecrowdthecrowdthecrowdt
vdthecrowdthecrowdthecrowdthecrowdthecrowdthec
necrowdthecrowdthecrowdthecrowdthecrowdthecrov
rowdthecrowdthecrowdthecrowdthecrowdthecrowdt
vdthecrowdthecrowdthecrowdthecrowdthecrowdthec
necrowdthecrowdthecrowdthecrowdthecrowdthecrov
rowdthecrowdthecrowdthecrowdthecrowdthecrowdt
vdthecrowdthecrowdthecrowdthecrowdthecrowdthec
necrowdthecrowdthecrowdthecrowdthecrowdthecrov
rowdthecrowdthecrowdthecrowdthecrowdthecrowdt
vdthecrowdthecrowdthecrowdthecrowdthecrowdthec
necrowdthecrowdthecrowdthecrowdthecrowdthecrov
rowdthecrowdthecrowdthecrowdthecrowdthecrowdt
vdthecrowdthecrowdthecrowdthecrowdthecrowdthec
necrowdthecrowdthecrowdthecrowdthecrowdthecrov
rowdthecrowdthecrowdthecrowdthecrowdthecrowdt
vdthecrowdthecrowdthecrowdthecrowdthecrowdthec
necrowdthecrowdthecrowdthecrowdthecrowdthecrov
rowdthecrowdthecrowdthecrowdthecrowdthecrowdt
vdthecrowdthecrowdthecrowdthecrowdthecrowdthec
necrowdthecrowdthecrowdthecrowdthecrowdthecrov
rowdthecrowdthecrowdthecrowdthecrowdthecrowdt
vdthecrowdthecrowdthecrowdthecrowdthecrowdthec
necrowdthecrowdthecrowdthecrowdthecrowdthecrov
rowdthecrowdthecrowdthecrowdthecrowdthecrowdt
vdthecrowdthecrowdthecrowdthecrowdthecrowdthec
necrowdthecrowdthecrowdthecrowdthecrowdthecrov
rowdthecrowdthecrowdthecrowdthecrowdthecrowdt
vdthecrowdthecrowdthecrowdthecrowdthecrowdthec
necrowdthecrowdthecrowdthecrowdthecrowdthecrov
rowdthecrowdthecrowdthecrowdthecrowdthecrowdt
vdthecrowdthecrowdthecrowdthecrowdthecrowdthec

Who matters more:

The individual or…

~srh_srh~ 5h ago

there is a difference being lonely and feeling lonely

Wait…

Why are we approaching data and metadata as negative?

Maybe metadata is good, and maybe it somehow leads to… I don't know, a more focused existence?

Maybe mega-metadata is going to be our new frequent-flyer points system. Why not?

Endless linking and embedding can be disguised as fun or as practicality.

Or as loyalty… or servitude.

We've never had to think of our data as being a valuable commodity before.

Everyone talks about their data, but what does data even look like?

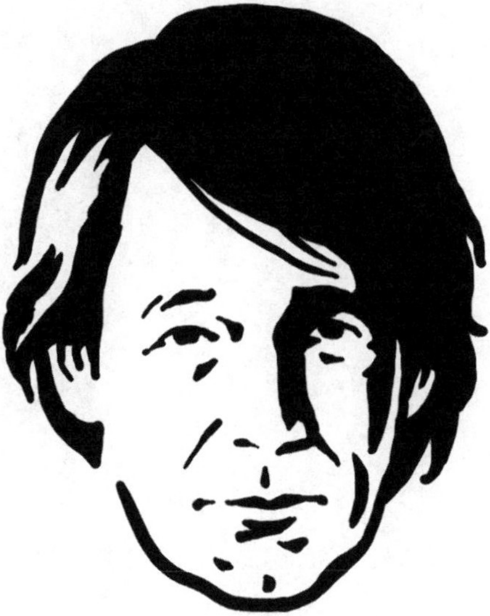

And even if you saw it, would you know what to do with it?

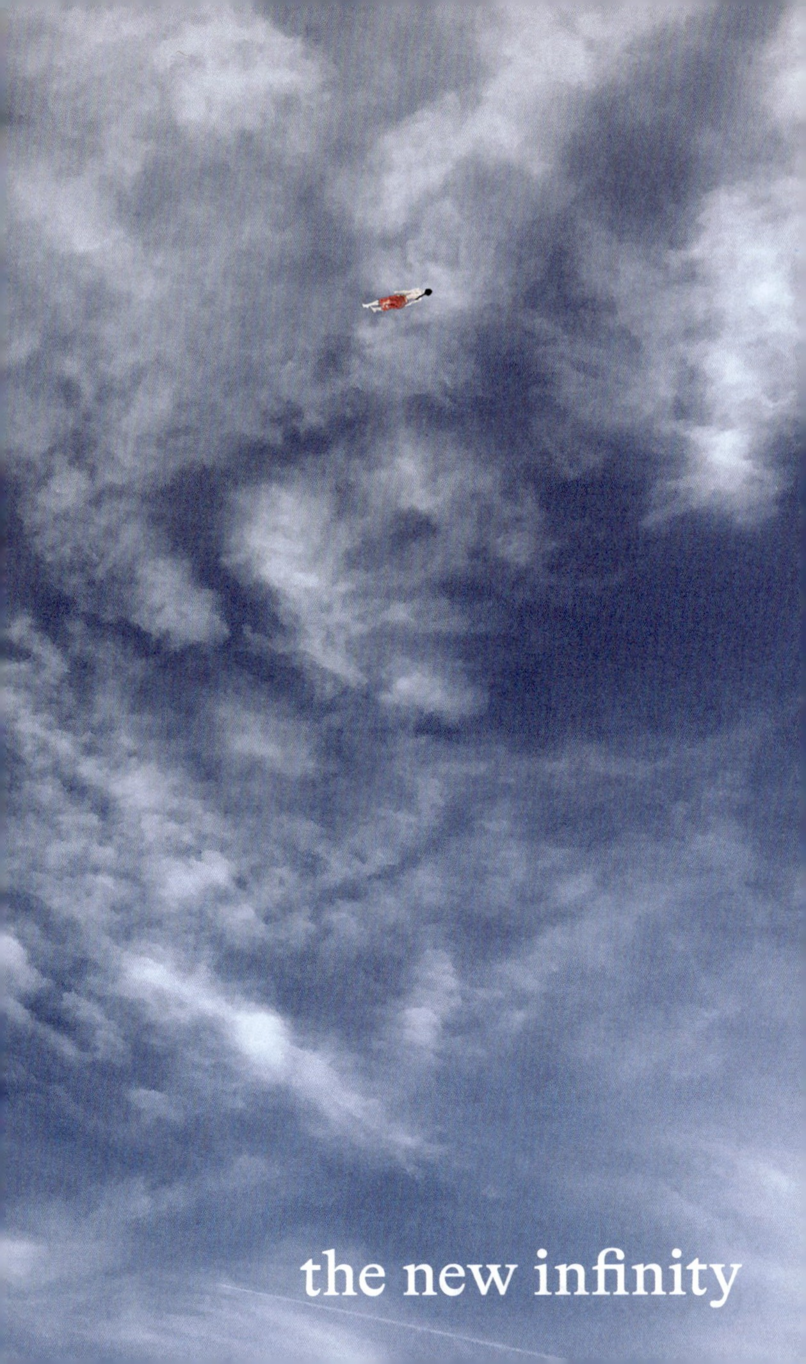
the new infinity

The Cloud is

SEARCH HISTORY
BIOMETRIC
MEDICAL DATA
SHOPPING HISTORY
SEXTS
DELETED PASSWORDS
FAILED CREDIT CHECKS
VOTING RECORD
CRIMINAL RECORD
DRIVING PATTERNS
ONLINE VIEWING HISTORY
PORN HITS
EMAIL CONTENTS
VACATION DETAILS
GENEALOGICAL DATA
DNA
SPEECH PATTERNS
LOGIC PATTERNS
SCHOOL HOMEWORK
VOLUNTARY SOCIAL MEDIA
PHOTOGRAPHY
INVOLUNTARY SOCIAL MEDIA
PHOTOGRAPHY
CREDIT RECORDS
MILITARY RECORDS
PRISON RECORDS
GPS TRACKING
MENSTRUAL AND FERTILITY DATA
VOICE RECORDS
MUSIC PREFERENCES
ENTERTAINMENT PREFERENCES
CONSCIOUS AND SUBCONSCIOUS
PREJUDICES
GEOLINKED CCTV IMAGERY
WASTE STREAM DATA
AMBIENT NOISE DATA
SEXUAL TRAUMA
DIETARY DISLIKES
SUBSTANCE ISSUES
NOSTALGIC TENDENCIES
SEXUAL PREFERENCES
SEXUAL FETISHES
ERGONOMIC DATA
AD PREFERENCES
FACIAL AND FINGER RECOGNITION
VACCINATION RECORDS
FOOD DELIVERY HISTORY

By merely existing you're leaving a huge data smudge in the world, but it's not in the physical world, it's up in the Cloud. Forever.

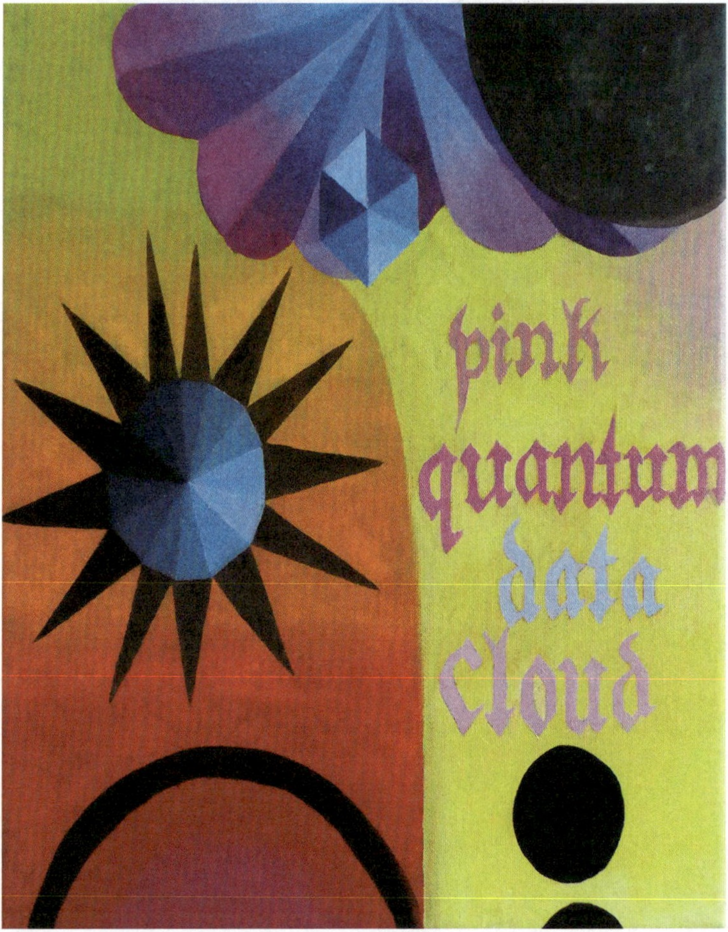

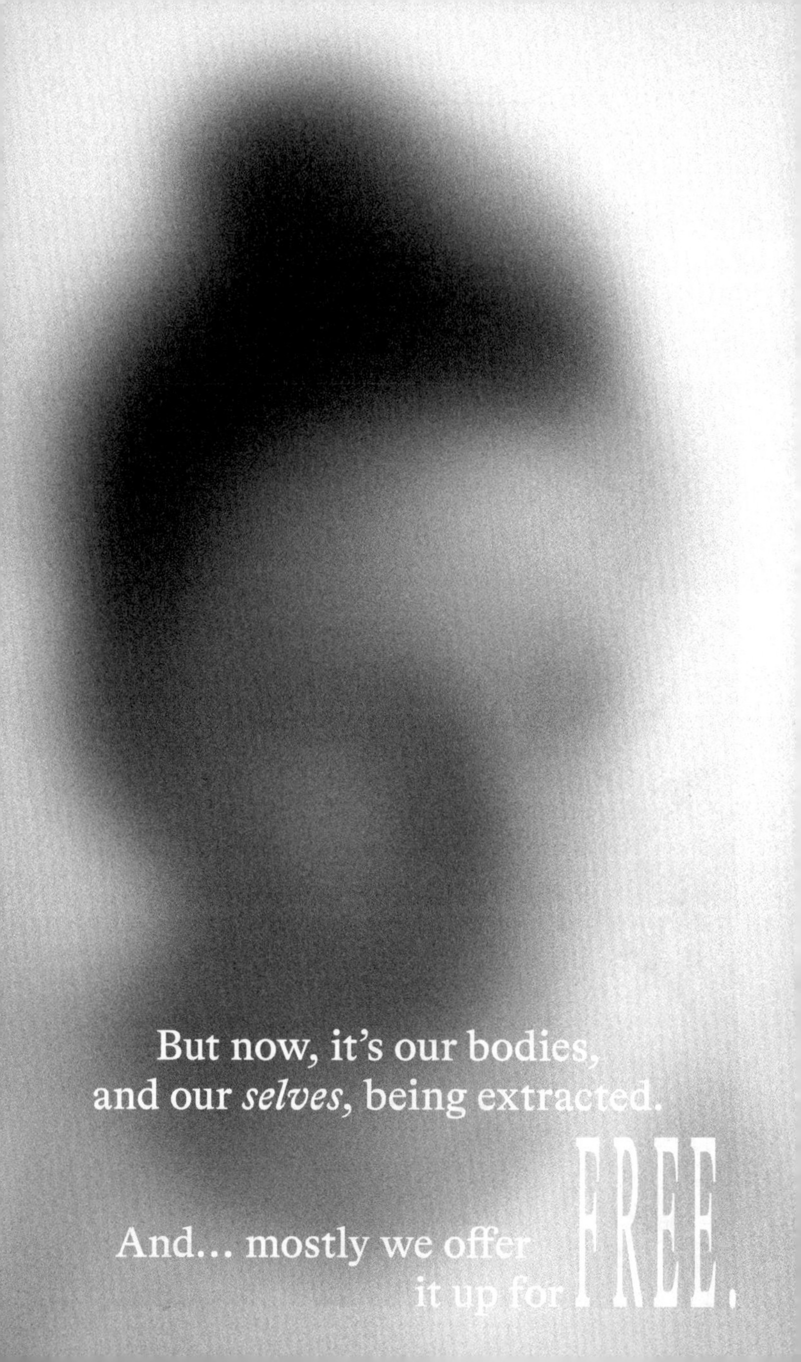

But now, it's our bodies,
and our *selves*, being extracted.

And… mostly we offer
it up for FREE.

For thousands of years, earth's resources have been extracted by bodies, most of whom were not free.

Stacy_is_sad 1min ago

I like honesty. Feels better

st century is about
o belongs to what.

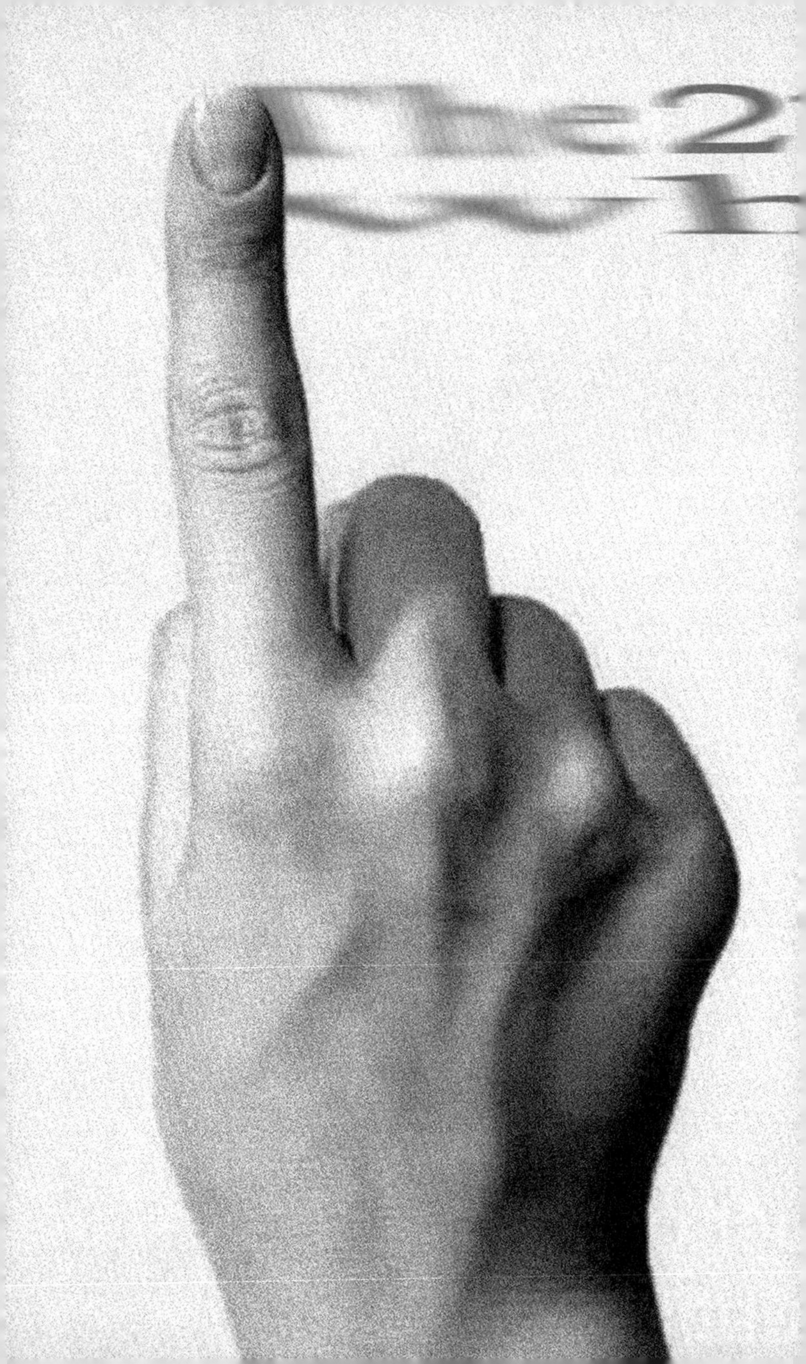

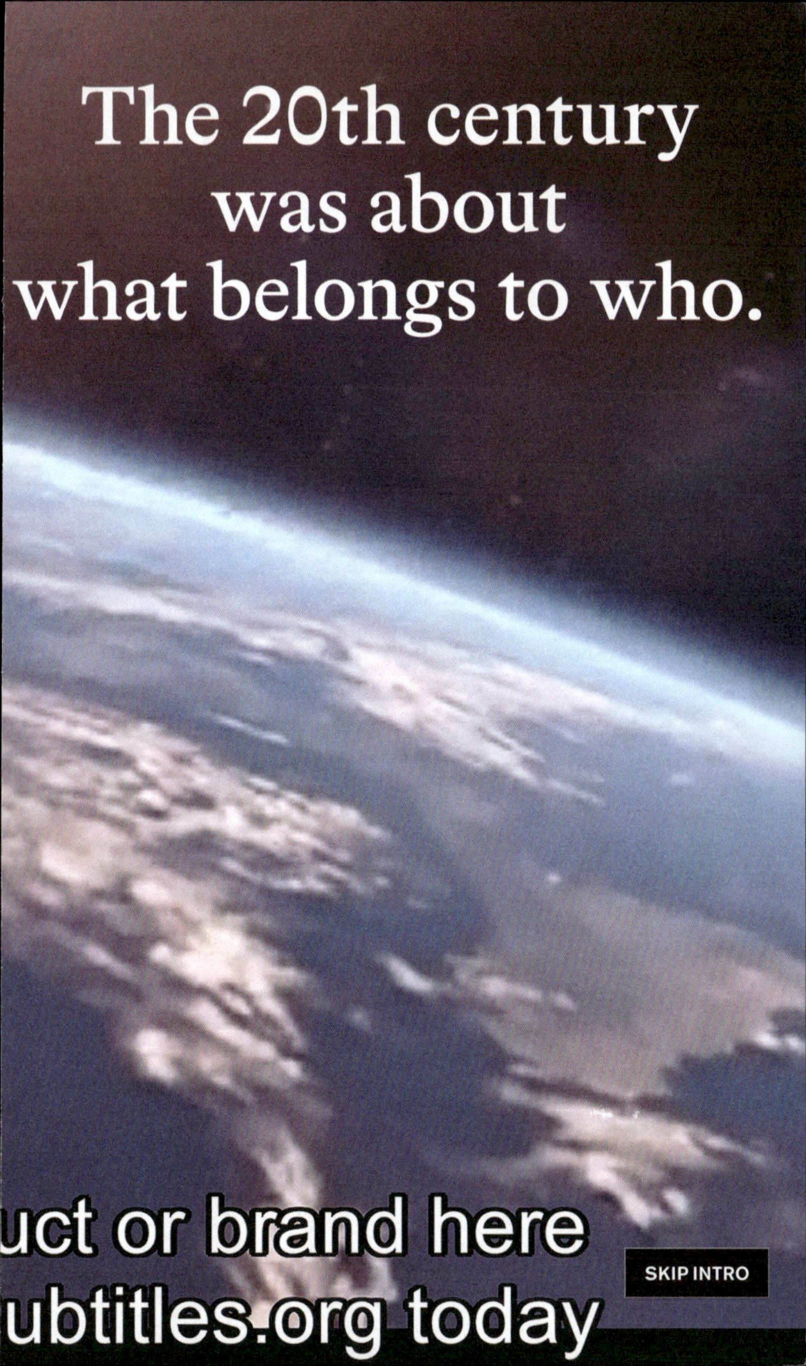
The 20th century
was about
what belongs to who.
uct or brand here
ubtitles.org today
SKIP INTRO